RESEARCH IN OCCUPATIONAL STRESS AND WELL-BEING

Series Editors: Pamela L. Perrewé, Peter D. Harms and Chu-Hsiang (Daisy) Chang

STRESS AND WELL-BEING AT THE STRATEGIC LEVEL

Editors:

Chu-Hsiang (Daisy) Chang – Michigan State University, USA

Peter D. Harms – Department of Management, University of Alabama, USA

RESEARCH IN OCCUPATIONAL STRESS AND
WELL-BEING VOLUME 21

STRESS AND WELL-BEING AT THE STRATEGIC LEVEL

EDITED BY

PETER D. HARMS
University of Alabama, USA

AND

CHU-HSIANG (DAISY) CHANG
Michigan State University, USA

United Kingdom – North America – Japan –
India – Malaysia – China

Emerald Publishing Limited
Emerald Publishing, Floor 5, Northspring, 21-23 Wellington Street, Leeds LS1 4DL.

First edition 2024

British Library Cataloguing in Publication Data
A catalogue record for this book is available from the British Library

ISBN: 978-1-83797-359-0 (Print)
ISBN: 978-1-83797-358-3 (Online)
ISBN: 978-1-83797-360-6 (Epub)

ISSN: 1479-3555 (Series)

INVESTOR IN PEOPLE

OVERVIEW

Volume 21 of *Research in Occupational Stress and Well-being* is focused on promoting theory and research in the increasingly important area of occupational stress, health, and well-being. In the past few years, as the world has dealt with the ongoing consequences of a global pandemic, the critical role played by institutions in the well-being of their employees and citizens has become increasingly clear. To that end, we felt the need to shine a spotlight on an oft-overlooked area of research concerning how organizations can both promote and inhibit well-being. To that end, we solicited a series of chapters investigating how organizational policies and decisions could impact stress and well-being (whether intentionally or not), how best to assess stress and well-being in organizations, how individuals in the upper echelons of companies shaped the emotional tone of their organizations and the experiences of their followers, and how the experiences and obligations of strategic leaders shape their own lives.

Although research on stress and well-being is well-established in the organizational literature when it comes to the study of individuals, this is generally not the case for scholars who investigate macro-level phenomena. Consequently, we were thrilled to be able to assemble an eclectic and talented group of authors who have broken new ground when it comes to understanding how, when, and why psychological phenomena such as stress and well-being can play a role in organizational functioning and success.

In our chapter by Bass, Milosevic, and DeArmond, the authors change the level of analysis for stress and well-being and utilize conservation of resource theory and dynamic capabilities to examine how firms experience and adapt to stress events. Our second chapter by Irwin and Willis expands on this by examining how strategic decisions impact members of firms, both leaders and employees, and stress and well-being can, in turn, impact strategic decisions. In the third chapter, Cobb and Brummel further delve into the issue of strategic decision-making by expanding on how policy decisions by corporate leaders can impact the stress and well-being of their employees by promoting or hindering their ability to establish health boundaries and balance between their work and nonwork lives. The next chapters both dig deeper into how stress, well-being, and emotions impact the decision-makers themselves. First, in the fourth chapter, Wright, Silard, and Bourgoin shed light on the nature of loneliness in the CEO position and how the various aspects of the job can contribute to feelings of isolation even among the highly successful. Next, in the fifth chapter, Hyde and Borgholthaus investigate how CEO affect intensity can influence strategic decision-making with regard to risk and also firm performance. Finally, in the last two chapters, we have examples of innovative methods for assessing and understanding stress, well-being, and emotions at the organizational level. In the sixth chapter, Lindgren, Wang,

Upadhyay, and Kobayashi use sentiment analysis to assess the emotional tone of organizations in order to enable a deeper understanding of corporate values and priorities. And finally, in the seventh chapter, Welbourne reviews 20 years of research concerning the assessment and promotion of energy in the workplace and how it can drive firm-level performance and sustainability.

Our goal for this issue was to provide avenues for expanding the study of stress and well-being beyond the individual. We are thrilled with our author teams and how they managed to introduce and integrate such a diverse and interesting set of ideas, both in terms of advancing theory and methods. We believe that this volume provides critical insights into the cutting-edge research going on in our field and we are grateful to the author teams and the staff at Emerald who helped to put it all together in this volume of *Research in Occupational Stress and Well-being*.

Peter D. Harms and Chu-Hsiang (Daisy) Chang

CONTENTS

ABOUT THE CONTRIBUTORS

A. Erin Bass, Ph.D., University of Nebraska-Lincoln, is an Associate Professor of Management at the University of Nebraska Omaha. Her research centers on stakeholder management, corporate social responsibility, and resource and capability development and deployment in firms. She is particularly interested in these concepts in the context of the energy industry. Her work has been published in the *Academy of Management Review, Journal of International Business Studies*, among others.

Cameron J. Borgholthaus is an Assistant Professor of Management at Southern Illinois University Edwardsville. He received his Ph.D. with an emphasis in Strategic Management from the University of Nebraska-Lincoln. His research focuses on strategic leadership and corporate governance, placing particular emphasis on CEO personality, the dyadic relationship between a firm's CEO and its board of directors, and the effects of TMT/board diversity.

Alaric Bourgoin is an Associate Professor and Co-director of the Top Executives and Strategic Management Hub at HEC Montreal. His research focuses on management consulting, professional service firms, complex transformations, and strategic dialogue. He has published in leading management journals such as the *Academy of Management Journal, Organization Studies,* and *Human Relations*.

Bradley J. Brummel, Ph.D., studies leader development in the context of professional ethics, with a focus on personal narratives, and with the goal of meaningful and safe workplaces. He received his Doctorate in Industrial–Organizational Psychology from the University of Illinois at Urbana-Champaign in 2008 and will be a Professor of Industrial–Organizational Psychology at the University of Houston in Fall 2023. He is currently the President of the Society of Psychologists in Leadership.

Haley R. Cobb, Ph.D., studies work–nonwork boundary management and other topics related to worker well-being and occupational health psychology. She received her Doctorate in Industrial–Organizational Psychology from Saint Louis University in Spring 2023 and will be an Assistant Professor of Industrial–Organizational Psychology at Louisiana State University in Fall 2023.

Sarah DeArmond, Ph.D., Colorado State University, is a Professor of Management and Human Resources at the University of Wisconsin Oshkosh. She has authored numerous articles in journals such as *Academy of Management Learning and Education* and *Journal of Personnel Psychology*. She has also presented her research at several conferences, including the Academy of Management and the

Society for Industrial and Organizational Psychology. She has received several awards for her outstanding contributions to teaching and research.

Steven J. Hyde is an Assistant Professor of Management in the College of Business and Economics at Boise State University. Steven received his Ph.D. in management from the University of Texas at San Antonio. His research lies at the intersection of corporate strategy, artificial intelligence, and psychology. You can find his work in the *Journal of Applied Psychology*, *Journal of Economics Behavior and Organization*, and *Equality Diversity and Inclusion*. Steven teaches *Strategic Tools and Business Policy and Strategy*.

Kris Irwin is an Assistant Professor in the Strome College of Business at Old Dominion University. She holds a Ph.D. in Management from the Culverhouse College of Business at the University of Alabama, an MBA from the Fuqua School of Business at Duke University, and a Bachelor of Science from the School of Engineering at Vanderbilt University. Her research interests include mergers and acquisitions, strategic human capital, and small-to-medium-sized enterprises/startups. Her research has been published in journals such as the *Journal of Business Research*, *Journal of Management & Organization*, and *Journal of Small Business Strategy*.

Vladimer B. Kobayashi is an Associate Professor at the University of the Philippines Mindanao (UP Mindanao), where he teaches Applied Mathematics and Computer Science. He was a former Department Chair and University Registrar of UP Mindanao. He is also a Certified Data Analytics Professional in the country. He was twice awarded a fellowship by the European Commission, one for Master's and another for Ph.D. His research has been presented at various international meetings, conferences, and symposia. He has published numerous papers primarily on the application of text mining in organizations, the application of data analytics to fecal source pollution identification, telehealth, and applications of artificial intelligence in environmental studies. He is involved in several data analytics projects that aim to address some of the world's problems.

Chapman J. Lindgren is a Ph.D. student of Industrial–Organizational Psychology in the Department of Psychology at Baruch College & the Graduate Center, CUNY, New York, NY. He received a Bachelor's degree in Psychology and minored in Health Policy and Management at the University of Georgia. His current research interests include crisis leadership, computational modeling, and novel methodologies with a primary focus on developing and promoting inclusive selection and assessment tools.

Ivana Milosevic, Ph.D., University of Nebraska-Lincoln, is an Assistant Professor of Management at the College of Charleston. Her research interests include microfoundations of corporate social responsibility and reliability as well as the process of firm growth. Her work has been published in *Journal of Management* and *Business & Society*, among others.

Anthony Silard is an Associate Professor of Leadership and the Director of the Center for Sustainable Leadership at Luiss Business School in Rome and the Distinguished Visiting Professor of Leadership at Tecnológico de Monterrey. He has published in leading academic journals such as the *Journal of Management, Human Relations, Journal of Organizational Behavior* and a featured author and columnist for *Psychology Today, The Huffington Post, Fast Company, The Financial Times*, among others.

Siddharth K. Upadhyay is a Ph.D. candidate in the Department of Global Leadership and Management, College of Business at Florida International University. He holds a Bachelor of Engineering degree in Information Technology from Gujarat Technological University, India, and a Master of Business Administration from Florida International University, Miami, Florida. Before pursuing Doctoral studies, he had a combined experience of three years in the corporate sector. His current research interests include diversity, equity and inclusion (DEI), selection and recruitment, and machine learning methods, with a primary focus on disability inclusion and political ideology. His previous works have been published in peer-reviewed business journals and have published award-winning case studies related to DEI.

Wei Wang is an Associate Professor of Psychology at the CUNY Graduate Center, where he directs the Computational Psychology Laboratory. His research primarily focuses on quantitative methods and computational modeling (e.g., machine learning, applied psychometrics, text analysis, network analysis, etc.), and their broad applications in various psychological, managerial, and educational areas.

Theresa M. Welbourne, Ph.D., is the Will and Maggie Brooke Professor in Entrepreneurship and Executive Director, Alabama Entrepreneurship Institute, Culverhouse College of Business at The University of Alabama. She works with students, faculty, staff, and business leaders to help drive both new venture development and ongoing growth within established firms. She also runs programming at The EDGE, which is Tuscaloosa's incubator and accelerator. Her expertise is in the areas of entrepreneurship, human capital management and strategic leadership in high growth, entrepreneurial, and high change organizations. She is the Founder, President, and CEO of eePulse, Inc., a human capital technology and consulting firm. Her research and work have been featured in popular publications such as *Inc. Magazine, Wall Street Journal, The Financial Times, Business Week, New York Times*, and *Entrepreneur Magazine*, and she is well published in numerous academic journals and books as well as business books. She also runs two large-scale research studies, one focused on high-growth companies and initial public offerings, and another that is focused on employee resource groups and how they drive innovation and firm-level growth. She was awarded the 2012 Academy of Management Distinguished Executive Award (for contributions to research, teaching, and practice), in 2017, she was named a Society of Industrial and Organizational Psychology Fellow, and in 2022, she made the Business Alabama list of the top 22 in 22 Women in Tech. She also holds an appointment as an Affiliated Senior Research Scientist with the Center for Effective Organizations, Marshall School of Business, University of Southern California.

Chris H. Willis is a Ph.D. candidate in the Strome College of Business at Old Dominion University. He holds a Master's degree in International Management from Thunderbird with concentrations in International Development and Cross-culture Negotiations and Mediation, an MBA from Virginia Tech with a Global Business Concentration and a BS in Technology from Appalachian State University. His research interests include the ways in which individual-level factors impact firm governance building upon the human capital and strategic decision-making literatures. His primary research area explores the influence of micro-level factors on firm performance outcomes. He has published in *Asia-Pacific Journal of Management* and was instrumental in the successful application for, and co-PI, of the 2020 E. M. Kauffman Knowledge Challenge ($400,000) Grant, which provides financial support for his research activities.

Sarah Wright is an Associate Professor of Organisational Behaviour at the University of Canterbury in New Zealand. At the heart of her research and teaching is a focus on human relationships within groups and organizations, with a particular focus on workplace loneliness and relationship quality. She has published in leading academic journals such as *Human Relations, Leadership Quarterly, Journal of Business Ethics,* and the *Academy of Management Learning & Education.*

FIRM STRESS, ADAPTIVE RESPONSES, AND UNPREDICTABLE, RESOURCE-DEPLETING EXTERNAL SHOCKS: LEVERAGING CONSERVATION OF RESOURCES THEORY AND DYNAMIC CAPABILITIES

A. Erin Bass, Ivana Milosevic and Sarah DeArmond

ABSTRACT

A growing body of literature suggests that unpredictable, resource-depleting shocks – ranging from natural disasters to public health crises and beyond – require the firm to respond adaptively. However, how firms do so remains largely undertheorized. To contribute to this line of literature, the authors borrow from the conservation of resources (COR) theory of stress and the dynamic capabilities perspective to introduce the concept of firm stress – a state of reduced and irregular readiness firms enter into following unpredictable, resource-depleting shocks. Our theoretical model illustrates that firms must punctuate the stress state to adapt by first deploying a retrenchment response, thereby conserving resources and allowing the firm to consider how to best redeploy its dynamic capabilities to adapt. Subsequently, the firm can redeploy its capabilities and adaptively respond in one of three ways: exiting (reconfiguring resources for alternative use), persevering (reconfiguring resources for better use), or innovating (developing new resources). Overall, the authors offer a process model of firm stress and adaptive responses

Stress and Well-Being at the Strategic Level
Research in Occupational Stress and Well-Being, Volume 21, 1–16
Copyright © 2024 by Emerald Publishing Limited
All rights of reproduction in any form reserved
ISSN: 1479-3555/doi:10.1108/S1479-355520230000021001

following an unpredictable, resource-depleting shock that paves the way for future research on stress in the strategy literature.

Keywords: Adaptive response; conservation of resources theory of stress; dynamic capabilities; evolutionary fitness; external shocks; firm stress; resource reconfiguration

INTRODUCTION

The ability to respond to external shocks is critical for contemporary firms (Brown & Eisenhardt, 1997; Moeen et al., 2020; Rindova & Courtney, 2020). Shepherd et al. (2000, p. 394) argues that external shocks comprise significant changes to the external environment "that alter the overall degree of novelty at a point in time," requiring the firm to adjust its activities fundamentally (Kammerlander et al., 2018; Rindova & Courtney, 2020). This is particularly evident today as many firms, regardless of size and innovative potential, grapple with how to appropriately respond to external shocks. These shocks can range from the nationalization of energy and other strategic industries, changes in climate leading to deadly wildfires and severe storms, to public health crises including contagious viruses, and beyond (Aunphattanasilp, 2018; Oh & Oetzel, 2022).

However, it is important to note that not all external shocks are created equal. For example, technological shocks, although disruptive and unpredictable, often create new growth opportunities for firms as well as introduce new platforms necessary for subsequent innovation. Other external shocks are negative due to being unpredictable and resource-depleting. For example, in its rapid global spread and considerable impact, COVID-19 most closely exemplifies an external shock that is high-impact, resource-depleting – and difficult to predict, thereby delaying an adaptive response (Uhl-Bien & Arena, 2018). These external shocks limit a firm's ability to reconfigure resources in a timely manner (because they are unpredictable) or acquire new external resources (because they are resource-depleting). Consequently, unpredictable, resource-depleting external shocks like COVID-19 introduce sudden and unexpected newness that is difficult to predict a priori, significantly disrupting the firm's ability to adaptively respond and risking its survival. Here, we focus on these unpredictable, resource-depleting shocks and theorize how firms can adaptively respond.

Previous literature has suggested that these external shocks are particularly challenging because they require the firm to make sense of the unexpected newness and adapt and respond to it while maintaining operations (Simsek et al., 2005; Thomas & Douglas, 2022; Uhl-Bien et al., 2007). As such, the literature has pointed to the importance of acquiring new resources for facilitating an adaptive response to the shock that enables the firm to overcome it (Kammerlander et al., 2018; Uhl-Bien & Arena, 2018). In this view, the initial condition of the firm and its resource base can impact how the firm subsequently responds. That is, if a firm has a strong innovative capability, it may be leveraged to create new resources necessary for the adaptive response (Berglund et al., 2020; Milosevic et al., 2022). However, if the firm focuses on efficiency and exploitation before the shock, it may leverage its current resources to achieve higher efficiencies for the adaptive response (Benner & Tushman, 2003). Thus, differences in the firm's initial condition and subsequent adaptive responses remain undertheorized (Eggers & Park, 2018; Thomas & Douglas, 2022).

The purpose of this chapter is to theoretically explore what happens to the firm as it experiences an external shock that is unpredictable and resource-depleting and how it creates an adaptive response based on its initial condition prior to the shock. To do so, we borrow insights from the dynamic capability view of the firm (Barreto, 2010; Helfat et al., 2007; Teece et al., 1997) and the COR theory of stress (Hobfoll, 1989; Lazarus & Folkman, 1984; LePine et al., 2004). More specifically, with its emphasis on evolutionary fitness, defined as "how well a dynamic capability enables an organization to make a living by creating, extending or modifying its resource base" (Helfat et al., 2007, p. 7), the dynamic capability view provides an appropriate framework to theorize the dynamics of adaptive responses to external shocks. Additionally, the COR theory of stress provides the terminology necessary to consider the firm's experience following an external shock and the mechanisms through which it forms an adaptive response.

We offer three contributions to the extant literature. First, we introduce *firm stress* as a concept that describes a state of reduced and irregular readiness experienced following a resource-depleting external shock. Borrowing from the stress literature, we theorize that firms experience considerable stress when an external event requires significant resources to respond to and confront it (Harms et al., 2017; Lazarus & Folkman, 1984). This triggers a state of reduced readiness that may strain the firm's current operations and aggravate existing resource constraints that, if not reconfigured, may ultimately threaten the firm's survival.

We further theorize that in aggravating existing resource constraints, a stress state may manifest in two forms: too much efficiency and too much innovation, each requiring a different response. More specifically, when the firm has an extreme focus on efficiency, it reaffirms existing patterns and mires within feedback loops of past routines when confronted with external shock. This is further amplified in resource-poor firms (firms that are so focused on efficiency that new resources are rarely acquired or needed to maintain operations) (Boisot & McKelvey, 2010; Uhl-Bien, 2021; Wenzel et al., 2020). Conversely, when the firm has an extreme focus on innovation, it is mired in vicious cycles of innovative reactions, which can produce counterproductive activities, further stifling an adaptive response to an external shock (Es-Sajjade et al., 2021; Uhl-Bien & Arena, 2018).

Finally, utilizing insights from the dynamic capability view of the firm and COR theory of stress, we theorize how a firm may deploy an adaptive response. More specifically, we suggest that when the firm enters a stress state, its first adaptive response should be retrenchment, regardless of the initial condition. Retrenchment conserves the firm's resources, preventing further depletion of resources through fruitless pursuits. Subsequently, depending on whether there is a stronger (weaker) capability for efficiency or innovation, the firm must consider three adaptive responses to punctuate the stress state: exiting, persevering, or innovating (Wenzel et al., 2020). Our overarching contribution is a process model of firm stress and adaptive responses following an external shock. We discuss relevant literature next.

THEORETICAL CONTEXT
Dynamic Capabilities and External Shocks

As the dynamism and volatility of external environments increased, interest in how firms respond to a "new normal" has taken center stage (Barreto, 2010; Davis et al., 2009; Teece et al., 1997; Uhl-Bien et al., 2007). The resource-based view and its focus on firms' valuable, unique, and difficult-to-imitate resources (Barney, 1991), combined with insights regarding how firms leverage those resources to create value (Teece et al., 1997), has become increasingly important. Dynamic capabilities emerged from the resource-based view of the firm, driven by the realization that a firm's inability to respond quickly to environmental changes and achieve evolutionary fitness may have grave consequences (Davis et al., 2009; Makkonen et al., 2014). To this end, dynamic capabilities, defined as "the capacity of an organization to purposefully create, extend and modify its resource base" (Helfat et al., 2007, p. 4), are a differentiator between firms that can successfully respond to environmental changes and those that cannot.

In contrast to ordinary capabilities that focus on maintaining the status quo, dynamic capabilities enable the firm to respond to external shocks through the creation of new activities and new processes (Barreto, 2010; Makkonen et al., 2014). More specifically, dynamic capabilities induce change needed to achieve fit by disrupting routines through individual interactions, processes, and structures (Felin et al., 2012; Salvato & Vassolo, 2018; Zahra et al., 2006). Despite these insights, the nuances of dynamic capabilities and how firms deploy them to create adaptive responses to major external shocks remain underexplored.

Yet, this is important to consider because external shocks comprise

> unanticipated and disruptive changes in a firm's external environment (Meyer et al., 1990) [that] may be mild or severe, and may affect specific organizations (Brege & Brandes, 1993), industrial segments (Sheppard & Chowdhury, 2005), or entire economies (Singh & Yip, 2000). (Chakrabarti, 2015, p. 354, citations in original text)

Many external shocks are difficult to predict a priori because they are derived from unpredictable, unprecedented, and exogenous events, which can substantially affect the firm's operations and position in the competitive environment (Chakrabarti, 2015). When external shocks are both unpredictable and resource-depleting, they require a drastic firm response (Romanelli & Tushman, 1994), such as revising its core business by developing new resources and capabilities not just to adapt but, in some cases, to survive (Chakrabarti, 2015; Volberda, 1996).

One way firms can respond to such disruptions is via a system-level process that leverages or develops new capabilities. The key assumption underpinning this literature is that firms maintain a tension between efficiency and innovation and deploy that tension to facilitate an adaptive response (Sarkees & Hulland, 2009; Shepherd et al., 2000). Indeed, this focus on efficiency and innovation enabled 3M to leverage "surge capacity" and double global production of N95 masks in response to the COVID-19 pandemic (Gruley & Clough, 2020). For 3M, the ability to adapt included building capacity at the system level as well as adapting employee practices at the individual level (i.e., marking the floor with yellow tape to ensure a six-foot barrier and assembling emergency response teams ready to jump in whenever an external shock may occur – from tornadoes to hurricanes, wildfires, and pandemics) (Gruley & Clough, 2020).

However, the extant literature does not consider the process underpinning the adaptive response nor how the firm's initial condition may shape the nature of the response. Building on the framework put forth by Wenzel et al. (2020), we suggest that firms may take at least four adaptive responses: retrenchment, exiting, persevering, and innovating (Wenzel et al., 2020). We further enrich the framework using the COR theory of stress to examine which adaptive responses are most appropriate based on the firm's initial condition. We review the COR theory of stress next.

COR Theory of Stress

Stress research is wide-reaching, given its relevance to various academic disciplines, including management, psychology, public health, and medicine. This research is relevant to academics, practitioners, and the public, appearing in various outlets (i.e., journals, books, and conferences), making it complex to summarize (Ganster & Rosen, 2013; Griffin & Clarke, 2011). Even more complex are the many different conceptualizations of stress, which have included views that stress refers to stimuli in the external environment that impact individuals; stress is the reaction that people have to stimuli; and stress is a process that involves the interaction of the two (Ganster & Perrewé, 2011; Ganster & Rosen, 2013; Sonnentag & Frese, 2013). In the third conceptualization, environmental stimuli are referenced as stressors and the reactions to those stimuli as strain. For our purposes, we build from the third conceptualization of stress to theorize the state following an external shock (the stressor).

Numerous theories have helped to shape and propel stress research forward: the allostatic load model of stress (McEwen & Seeman, 1999; Seeman et al., 1997); the transactional model of stress, and the job demands–resources theory (Bakker & Demerouti, 2007; Demerouti et al., 2001). However, given its focus on resources as critical to responding to stress, we borrow predominately from the COR theory of stress (COR theory) to conceptualize firm stress (Hobfoll, 1989, 2001). COR theory is consistent with many assumptions of the job demands–resource theory, particularly the process of resource depletion stemming from increased demands and the role of acquiring resources to moderate the relationship between stressors and experienced strain (for a complete review of the model and its evolution, see Bakker & Demerouti, 2017). However, it also departs from the job demands resource theory in its focus on conserving and acquiring resources.

More specifically, COR theory suggests that resources are critical for functioning and, therefore, individuals are motivated and act to prevent resource loss (conservation) and/or gain resources (acquisition). According to this theory, the stress state results from the threat of resource loss or a deficiency of resources. Therefore, environmental stressors are not inherently problematic as long as the individual has sufficient resources to cope with them. However, external stressors can also deplete resources if there is repeated exposure or if the stressor is significant, as is the case of external shocks. Hobfoll (1989) suggested the idea of a loss spiral, indicating that those with inadequate resources before the external stressor (initial condition) are at the most risk of losing even more resources and experiencing difficulty in responding to the stress. In other words, if an individual or an entity has an initial condition of already-depleted resources or has insufficient resources, it may be particularly ill-equipped to deal with the stressor or any additional stressors. Likewise, those with an initial condition of more resources are better positioned to acquire additional resources and deal with the stressor or additional stressors (Hobfoll, 2001). Given the central role of resources in this model, we use it as a building block for understanding firm stress, a concept we introduce next.

FIRM STRESS AND THE PROCESS OF ADAPTIVE RESPONSES

Introducing Firm Stress

Building from COR theory, we introduce *firm stress* and define it as the state of reduced readiness the firm enters following an unpredictable, resource-depleting external shock. More specifically, these shocks bring about sudden and unexpected newness that the firm cannot immediately comprehend. In this context, operations are strained (i.e., disrupted supply chains), yet the potential to change operations is also limited because of the unpredictable and reduced ability to resource the change (Barrot & Sauvagnat, 2016; Rindova & Courtney, 2020). As such, the firm enters a state of reduced readiness – the stress state – characterized by the imbalance between its current capabilities and resource base and a suddenly shifting external environment that prevents the adaptive response.

We argue that firm stress may manifest differently based on the firm's initial condition: the condition it was in *before* the external shock (Marion & Uhl-Bien, 2001). Although often overlooked by extant studies in the strategy literature, the initial is critically important as it, no matter how slightly different, may significantly impact the adaptive response of the firm. This is in line with COR theory as it describes how stress is handled – dependent, in part, on the individual's cognitive, emotional, and social state before the experienced stressor or the individual's initial condition (Hobfoll, 1989). To this end, we argue that based on the firm's initial condition, the stress state following the shock may manifest in one of two forms: reduced readiness due to innovation loops or reduced readiness due to efficiency loops.

In the stress state marked by innovation loops, the firm experiences a state of chaotic interactions in which capabilities are used and developed for an "expanding and diverging process of discovery" (Cheng & Van de Ven, 1996, p. 593). More specifically, when the initial condition is one of strong innovative capabilities, the external shock may trigger the overuse of those capabilities in search of new solutions. This can increase variety beyond an optimal level and launch the firm into a chaotic state marked by ongoing and unproductive innovation loops. This extreme innovation may risk the firm's rapid depletion of resources and spiral failure traps (Andriopoulos & Lewis, 2010; Es-Sajjade et al., 2021). The stress literature has described this process as ongoing efforts to adapt to stressors through variations in stress hormones. However, if repeatedly engaged in – as in the case of a firm trying to redeploy its innovative capabilities continually – these efforts may result in significant adverse outcomes and even failure (Perrewé & Ganster, 2011; Seeman et al., 1997).

Conversely, in the stress state marked by efficiency loops, the shock may trigger the overreliance on past practices, launching the firm into regimented order marked by ongoing and unproductive efficiency loops. New or unpredictable information created by the external shock is filtered out of the firm or ignored, and past practices are continually repeated (Boisot & McKelvey, 2010). This creates rigidity within the status quo – or the competence trap (Leonard-Barton, 1992). When this occurs, the firm is mired in its past routines, unable to make sense of the new novelty in the external environment (Milosevic et al., 2018). Stress research suggests that when biological systems are mired in the stress state without opportunities for change and an influx of novel resources, continuing to engage in the same activities over time will exhaust all the resources, resulting in adverse outcomes (Harms et al., 2017; Hobfoll, 1989; Lazarus & Folkman, 1984).

In sum, we argue that unpredictable, resource-depleting shocks act as a potent stressor that induces strain on the firm and aggravates its initial condition. To withstand and overcome the stress from the shock, the firm must form an adaptive response – redeploying its capabilities in an idiosyncratically appropriate manner, thereby achieving evolutionary fitness (Riviere et al., 2018). Below, we utilize insights from the COR theory of stress and the dynamic capability perspective to theorize how firms achieve one of four adaptive responses from Wenzel et al. (2020): retrenchment, exiting, persevering, and innovating using a phased approach.

Punctuating the Stress State: A Phased Approach to Adaptive Responses

COR theory suggests that, when experiencing stress, individuals seek to "protect their current resources (conservation) and acquire new resources (acquisition)" (Halbesleben et al., 2014, p. 1335). We offer that firms should partially mirror this process. More specifically, we offer a phased approach to adaptive response, consisting of first conserving current resources (retrenchment) and subsequently acquiring new resources to generate an appropriate response. Thus, resource conservation, at least initially, is prioritized over resource acquisition, enabling the firm to purposefully reconfigure – acquire, develop, and recombine – its resource base (i.e., leverage dynamic capabilities) to facilitate value-adding adaptation given the firm's initial condition (Eisenhardt & Martin, 2000; Helfat et al., 2007; Schilke et al., 2018). We provide a graphical depiction of firm stress and adaptive responses following an unpredictable, resource-depleting external shock in Fig. 1 and a summary of the four adaptive responses in Table 1.

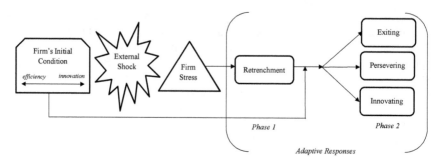

Fig. 1.   Firm Stress and Adaptive Responses Following an External Shock.

Table 1.   Adaptive Responses to External Shocks and Firm Stress.

	Adaptive Response	Dynamic Capabilities Deployed	Initial Condition	Time Horizon of Effectiveness
Phase 1	Retrenchment	Conserving the resource base	Both	Short term
Phase 2	Exiting	Terminating or reconfiguring/ developing the resource base for alternative markets	Both: more likely utilized in the efficiency-focused initial condition	Long term
	Persevering	Reconfiguring resource base for higher efficiency	Efficiency-focused	Medium to long term
	Innovating	Developing a new resource base through innovative capabilities	Innovation-focused	Long term

Phase 1: Retrenchment

Retrenchment describes an adaptive response in which the firm focuses on resource conservation through "reductions in costs, assets, products, product lines, and overhead" (Pearce & Robbins, 1993, p. 614). When the firm enters the stress state following an unpredictable, resource-depleting shock (see Fig. 1), it needs to focus recovery on avoiding or refraining from activities that further tax the firm (e.g., if the external shock significantly affects the firm's supply chain, slowing down or even stopping production may be appropriate). In doing so, the firm limits the impact of the stressor and conserves its resource base. By conserving its resource base, it focuses on stabilizing the firm's activities and using what is directly required or needed to survive the unpredictable, resource-depleting external shock. Thus, in the retrenchment adaptive response, the firm is not yet focused on evolutionary fitness but on preventing the further drain of resources before it can determine how to reconfigure its resource base to create value given the changing external environment. See Table 1 for a summary of this adaptive response.

To this end, we argue that retrenchment may be an effective adaptive response in the short term. We follow this theorizing and suggest that retrenchment is the immediate adaptive response of all firms as they enter the stress state following an unpredictable, resource-depleting external shock. In line with COR theory, which suggests that protecting resources is the immediate response to a stressor (Hobfoll, 1989), when firms experience stress, they also seek to protect resources and minimize operations and activities immediately. Though effective in the short term, retrenchment is less likely to be effective in the long term, given that it may erode the firm's ability to move out of the stress state. Retrenchment and the continued COR means the firm is not using, but instead protecting, its resource base and may be unable to compete in the changing environment with this adaptive response alone. In this way, retrenchment creates an unpredictable future for this firm. Once the firm has conserved its resources via retrenchment, it must reconfigure its resource base to achieve evolutionary fitness in the new, changed, environment. We expand on these three adaptive responses below and how the firm's initial condition impacts which of these three adaptive responses may be deployed.

Phase 2: Adaptive Responses Following Retrenchment

Although retrenchment enables the firm to sustain within the stress state, it does not allow it to exit the stress state, thereby, in the long run, risking the firm's survival. To achieve evolutionary fitness, the firm must move beyond the retrenchment response. Indeed, because of changes in the external environment, the firm's existing activities and operations must also change to adjust to its "new normal." COR theory suggests that individuals conserve resources in response to a stressor but must also develop new resources to move forward. Similarly, we argue that post-retrenchment, the firm must develop or reconfigure resources that will allow it to move out of the stress state and toward success in the "new normal." We offer that the firm has at least three adaptive responses it can deploy to achieve evolutionary fitness, the most appropriate of which is a function of its initial condition: existing, persevering, and innovating (Wenzel et al., 2020).

The firm's initial condition describes its resource and capabilities before experiencing the external shock (see Fig. 1), which can range from an initial condition focused on efficiency to one focused on innovation. Firms with an initial condition focused on innovation may already possess routines and processes necessary to develop or acquire new resources. In these contexts, the retrenchment allows the firm to reconsider its innovative capabilities and redeploy them purposefully, thereby avoiding counterproductive innovation loops (i.e., creating innovative yet inappropriate or useless responses, Es-Sajjade et al., 2021; Milosevic et al., 2022). In contrast, those with an initial condition focused on efficiency may have rarely acquired or developed additional resources and, therefore, more likely lack routines and processes to do so. Indeed, in their seminal piece, Eisenhardt and Martin (2000, p. 1106) argued that in the absence of external dynamism, firms develop routines that rely extensively on existing knowledge and linear execution to produce predictable outcomes. In these contexts, retrenchment enables the firm to reconsider its current routines and avoid counterproductive efficiency loops (Uhl-Bien et al., 2007).

As such, we theorize that failure to consider the initial condition puts the firm at greater risk of losing the existing resources and less likely able to generate an appropriate adaptive response (Hobfoll, 1989). Following the COR theory, we theorize that depending on the initial condition, the firm may most appropriately deploy its idiosyncratic dynamic capabilities for the following adaptive responses: exiting, persevering, and innovating.

Exiting. Following retrenchment, some firms may exit the industry (see Fig. 1). Exiting describes an adaptive response in which the firm discontinues its operations (Argyres et al., 2015). Like retrenchment, this response may be most appropriate when the firm's initial condition is either one of extreme efficiency or extreme innovation – thereby preventing the firm from most appropriately redeploying its capabilities. In this context, retrenchment enables the firm to "see" that achieving evolutionary fitness may not be possible, and thus exiting the industry/market is the most appropriate response. Exiting may entail reconfiguring the resources to be leveraged in alternative markets (Cozzolino et al., 2018), the creation of new markets (Thomas & Douglas, 2022), or complete discontinuation of operations (Dai et al., 2017). Indeed, in their study of multinational enterprises in war-afflicted countries, Dai et al. (2017, p. 1478) suggest that "the best way to cope with a crisis may be to exit." A summary of this adaptive response is provided in Table 1.

Persevering. As an alternative to exiting, the firm may seek to deploy an adaptive response that moves the firm forward following the unpredictable, resource-depleting external shock. A firm with an initial condition focused on efficiency may reconfigure its resources to refocus on its core business. In this instance, retrenchment enables the firm to reconsider its routines purposefully, evaluate past practices and inefficiencies that sneaked in during times of stability, and reinvest in its core, thereby preserving to move forward in the "new normal" (see Fig. 1). Persevering is an adaptive response in which the firm sustains its resources by reversing to the initial status quo (Wenzel et al., 2020). This response does not indicate that the firm ignores the unpredictable, resource-depleting external shock or fails to recognize the changes in the external environment. Rather, the firm senses the new changes in the environment (Teece et al., 1997) and overcomes these changes to be able to continue its business activities "better" in its "new normal" (De Carolis et al., 2009). See Table 1 for a summary of this adaptive response.

Innovating. When the firm's initial condition focuses on innovation, it may achieve evolutionary fitness by purposefully developing new resources through its pre-stressor innovative capabilities. Innovating is an adaptive response in which the firm realizes strategic renewal, replacing or refurbishing existing operations by emphasizing the firm's "processes, its ability to capitalize on opportunities, and its use of internal and external partners (Schmitt et al., 2018)" (Riviere & Bass, 2019, p. 2, citation in original) following an external shock (Wenzel et al., 2020). Similar to persevering, this adaptive response follows retrenchment in an attempt to move the firm forward (see Fig. 1). However, an innovating adaptive response departs from preserving because it requires the firm to purposefully, yet mindfully, destabilize its operations to find new ways of operating following an unpredictable, resource-depleting external shock. In this way, the firm uses the changing external environment to identify "new ways of doing" in its "new normal." See Table 1 for a summary of this adaptive response.

In sum, when faced with an unpredictable, resource-depleting external shock, firms have a variety of adaptive responses at their disposal. However, the appropriateness of each adaptive response is a function of the initial condition, or the firm's resources and capabilities before the firm experienced the shock. Furthermore, we argue that the adaptive responses are phased: firms must enter retrenchment as an initial adaptive response to prevent the further drain of resources following an external shock before purposefully redeploying its capabilities in pursuit of one of the three adaptive responses and avoiding counterproductive innovative or efficiency loops. As such, our model introduces firm stress as a macro-level concept using tenets of dynamic capabilities and COR theory. In doing so, our model elucidates the stress state that firms enter following an unpredictable, resource-depleting external shock and how the firm might deploy an adaptive response to move forward. We reflect on our model and its implications in the following section.

CONCLUDING REMARKS AND FUTURE DIRECTIONS

The past decade has been marked by an unprecedented level of unpredictable, resource-depleting shocks, ranging from natural disasters such as the wildfires that have plagued the west coast of North America to public health crises ranging from the Ebola outbreak to COVID-19, and beyond. These external shocks fundamentally shift the external environment, requiring firms to respond and adapt to the "new normal." Indeed, a firm that once had synergistic evolutionary fitness might struggle to maintain operations following an external shock (Bass & Milosevic, 2018). Although there is a growing body of literature on the challenge created by external shocks, how firms adaptively respond to them remains undertheorized.

Our model of firm stress and adaptive responses following unpredictable, resource-depleting external shocks attempts to address this issue by theorizing the firm's stress state – and how it recovers from this state – when faced with a significant shift in the external environment. By integrating insights from dynamic capabilities and COR theory, we suggest that the firm enters a stress state of reduced and irregular readiness following an unpredictable, resource-depleting external shock. When this occurs, we argue that firms must engage in retrenchment – a first adaptive response – to conserve resources and create space for subsequent purposeful action. However, we caution that a retrenchment adaptive response, though effective in the short term, may be ineffective in the long term as the firm must achieve evolutionary fitness. Indeed, retrenchment is a necessary yet insufficient adaptive response. It enables the firm to reconsider its focus (innovative vs. efficiency) and redeploy its capabilities most appropriately to generate one of the three responses: exiting, persevering, and innovating.

To this end, our model provides the first step in understanding firm stress and adaptive responses following an external shock and makes several contributions to the literature. First, we introduce a new concept to the literature – firm stress – and define it as a state of reduced and irregular readiness experienced following an unpredictable, resource-depleting external shock. By leveraging insights from the COR Theory of Stress, we theorize the dynamics of the stress at the firm level and identify how firms can differentially leverage their dynamic capabilities not just to navigate and exit the stress state but, more importantly, achieve success in the "new normal."

Second, we amplify the importance of the firm's initial condition when considering how it might deploy an adaptive response following the stress state. Firms with routines developed based on past knowledge and focus on efficient deployment of such routines (efficiency capabilities) risk entering efficiency loops in the stress state and, thereby, the inability to adapt. Conversely, firms with extensive innovative capabilities may risk entering innovative loops in the stress state, continually generating responses that, although innovative, are counterproductive (Milosevic et al., 2022).

As such, we argue that the most appropriate immediate adaptive response is retrenchment, where the firm can reconsider its initial condition and purposefully consider how to move forward. However, retrenchment does not facilitate evolutionary fitness; it presents a necessary yet insufficient adaptive response. The firm must use retrenchment to consider how to deploy its capabilities based on its initial condition and work forward one of the three adaptive responses. In doing so, it is positioned to meaningfully innovate its business model and thrive in hostile environments after unpredictable, resource-depleting shocks.

Third, we leverage dynamic capabilities and COR theory insights to theorize how a firm deploys an adaptive response following a stress state. We provide a process model that depicts what happens to the firm immediately following an external shock and how it can move forward to achieve evolutionary fitness in a changing external environment. We build from insights on how firms respond to crises (Wenzel et al., 2020) to describe how firms recover from a stress state. We suggest that when the firm enters a stress state, its first adaptive response is retrenchment, conserving its resources. Subsequently, depending on its initial condition, the firm enters into at least one of three adaptive responses: exiting, persevering, or innovating (Wenzel et al., 2020). Our overarching contribution is a process model of firm stress following an unpredictable, resource-depleting external shock.

Our contributions provide the first step in future research in this area. First, our definition of firm stress considers the firm's state after an unpredictable, resource-depleting external shock, which, following the stress literature, might most closely resemble an acute stressor. However, a firm might also experience chronic stressors. In the micro literature, acute stressors are stimuli that do not occur often, are of short duration, and are unlikely to recur (American Psychological Association APA Working Group on Stress and Health Disparities, 2017; Day & Livingstone, 2001). Examples might be witnessing a shooting at work or experiencing a plant closing. However, chronic stressors persist over time and are something that individuals experience daily (Carayon, 1995). Examples include role stressors (e.g., role ambiguity, role conflict), interpersonal conflict, and heavy workload. Future research might consider the different chronic stressors firms might experience – such as supply chain shortages or rising costs due to inflation. What are the chronic stressors that firms experience, and how does the presence of a chronic stressor alter the proposed model?

Additionally, we followed research on firm responses to crisis, identifying retrenchment, exiting, persevering, and innovating. Although these four responses seem to capture the bulk of how firms respond to external shocks, additional adaptive responses could be considered. Are there instances where a firm might accelerate its operations following an external shock? What effect do these additional adaptive responses have on the firm's resource base?

Finally, we included a simple conceptualization of the firm's initial condition as one focused on efficiency or innovation. Indeed, efficiency and innovation are often viewed as opposing demands on organizations because "internal battles for resources often tip the scales in favor of an emphasis on efficiency or innovation, but rarely both" (Sarkees & Hulland, 2009, p. 45). Thus, we focus only on efficiency and innovation when describing the firm's initial condition, but future research could consider other capabilities and/or resource demands of the firm. Considering other capabilities and/or resource demands of the firm could enrich our understanding of the firm's initial condition to inform better how the firm responds to stress – whether acute as described in our model or chronic – as future research could investigate.

Our theoretical exercise of elevating the general concept of stress to the firm level broadens our understanding of what happens to a firm as it experiences a disruption in the external environment. Given the rich literature on strategy for external shocks, understanding the firm's condition before and immediately following the external shock broadens our consideration of how firms respond and recover. We put forth a process model that describes the stress state endured by the firm following the unpredictable, resource-depleting external shock and four adaptive responses that firms can deploy as they recover from the stress state and move forward in a changing external environment. We hope this effort opens a new understanding of this phenomenon and spurs important research on how firms experience and respond to stress in a continuous effort to achieve evolutionary fitness.

REFERENCES

American Psychological Association APA Working Group on Stress and Health Disparities. (2017). *Stress and health disparities: Contexts, mechanisms, and interventions among racial/ethnic minority and low-socioeconomic status populations.* http://www.apa.org/pi/health-disparities/resources/stress-report.aspx

Andriopoulos, C., & Lewis, M. W. (2010). Managing innovation paradoxes: Ambidexterity lessons from leading product design companies. *Long Range Planning, 43*(1), 104–122.

Argyres, N., Bigelow, L., & Nickerson, J. A. (2015). Dominant designs, innovation shocks, and the follower's dilemma. *Strategic Management Journal, 36*(2), 216–234.

Aunphattanasilp, C. (2018). From decentralization to re-nationalization: Energy policy networks and energy agenda setting in Thailand (1987–2017). *Energy Policy, 120*, 593–599.

Bakker, A. B., & Demerouti, E. (2007). The job demands–resources model: State of the art. *Journal of Managerial Psychology, 22*, 3.

Bakker, A. B., & Demerouti, E. (2017). Job demands resources theory: Taking stock and looking forward. *Journal of Occupational Health Psychology, 22*, 3.

Barney, J. (1991). Firm resources and sustained competitive advantage. *Journal of Management, 17*(1), 99–120. https://doi.org/10.1177/014920639101700108

Barreto, I. (2010). Dynamic capabilities: A review of past research and an agenda for the future. *Journal of Management, 36*(1), 256–280.

Barrot, J.-N., & Sauvagnat, J. (2016). Input specificity and the propagation of idiosyncratic shocks in production networks. *The Quarterly Journal of Economics, 131*(3), 1543–1592.

Bass, A. E., & Milosevic, I. (2018). In the wake of disaster: Resilient organizing and a new path for the future. In H. Krämer & M. Wenzel (Eds.), *How organizations manage the future: Theoretical perspectives and empirical insights* (pp. 193–214). Palgrave Macmillan.

Benner, M. J., & Tushman, M. L. (2003). Exploitation, exploration, and process management: The productivity dilemma revisited. *Academy of Management Review, 28*(2), 238–256.

Berglund, H., Bousfiha, M., & Mansoori, Y. (2020). Opportunities as artifacts and entrepreneurship as design. *Academy of Management Review, 45*(4), 825–846.

Boisot, M., & McKelvey, B. (2010). Integrating modernist and postmodernist perspectives on organizations: A complexity science bridge. *Academy of Management Review, 35*(3), 415–433.

Brege, S., & Brandes, O. (1993). The successful double turnaround of ASEA and ABB—Twenty lessons. *Strategic Change, 2*(4), 185–205.

Brown, S. L., & Eisenhardt, K. M. (1997). The art of continuous change: Linking complexity theory and time-paced evolution in relentlessly shifting organizations. *Administrative Science Quarterly, 42*(1), 1–34.

Carayon, P. (1995). Chronic effect of job control, supervisor social support, and work pressure on office worker stress. In S. L. Sauter & L. R. Murphy (Eds.), *Organizational risk factors for job stress* (pp. 357–370). American Psychological Association.

Chakrabarti, A. (2015). Organizational adaptation in an economic shock: The role of growth reconfiguration. *Strategic Management Journal, 36*(11), 1717–1738.

Cheng, Y.-T., & Van de Ven, A. H. (1996). Learning the innovation journey: Order out of chaos? *Organization Science, 7*(6), 593–614. http://10.0.5.7/orsc.7.6.593

Cozzolino, A., Verona, G., & Rothaermel, F. T. (2018). Unpacking the disruption process: New technology, business models, and incumbent adaptation. *Journal of Management Studies, 55*(7), 1166–1202.

Dai, L., Eden, L., & Beamish, P. W. (2017). Caught in the crossfire: Dimensions of vulnerability and foreign multinationals' exit from war-afflicted countries. *Strategic Management Journal, 38*(7), 1478–1498.

Davis, J. P., Eisenhardt, K. M., & Bingham, C. B. (2009). Optimal structure, market dynamism, and the strategy of simple rules. *Administrative Science Quarterly, 54*(3), 413–452.

Day, A. L., & Livingstone, H. A. (2001). Chronic and acute stressors among military personnel: Do coping styles buffer their negative impact on health? *Journal of Occupational Health Psychology, 6*, 4.

De Carolis, D. M., Yang, Y., Deeds, D. L., & Nelling, E. (2009). Weathering the storm: the benefit of resources to high-technology ventures navigating adverse events. *Strategic Entrepreneurship Journal, 3*(2), 147–160.

Demerouti, E., Bakker, A. B., Nachreiner, F., & Schaufeli, W. B. (2001). The job demands–resources model of burnout. *Journal of Applied Psychology, 86*(3), 499–512.

Eggers, J. P., & Park, K. F. (2018). Incumbent adaptation to technological change: The past, present, and future of research on heterogeneous incumbent response. *Academy of Management Annals, 12*(1), 357–389.

Eisenhardt, K. M., & Martin, J. A. (2000). *Dynamic capabilities: what are they? Strategic Management Journal. 21*, 105–1121.

Es-Sajjade, A., Pandza, K., & Volberda, H. (2021). Growing pains: Paradoxical tensions and vicious cycles in new venture growth. *Strategic Organization, 19*(1), 37–69.

Felin, T., Foss, N. J., Heimeriks, K. H., & Madsen, T. L. (2012). Microfoundations of routines and capabilities: Individuals processes, and structure. *Journal of Management Studies, 49*, 1351–1374.

Ganster, D. C., & Perrewé, P. L. (2011). Theories of occupational stress. In J. C. Quick & L. E. Tetrick (Eds.), *Handbook of occupational health psychology* (pp. 37–53). American Psychological Association.

Ganster, D. C., & Rosen, C. C. (2013). Work stress and employee health: A multidisciplinary review. *Journal of Management, 39*(5), 1085–1122. https://doi-org.www.remote.uwosh.edu/10.1177/0149206313475815

Griffin, M. A., & Clarke, S. (2011). Stress and well-being at work. In S. Zedeck (Ed.), *APA handbook of industrial and organizational psychology, Vol 3: Maintaining, expanding, and contracting the organization* (pp. 359–397). American Psychological Association.

Gruley, B., & Clough, R. (2020). How 3M plans to make more than a billion masks by end of year. *Bloomberg Businessweek.* https://www.bloomberg.com/news/features/2020-03-25/3m-doubled-production-of-n95-face-masks-to-fight-coronavirus#:~:text=How%203M%20Plans%20to%20Make,are%20a%20secret%20weapon%2C%20too

Halbesleben, J. R. B., Neveu, J.-P., Paustian-Underdahl, S. C., & Westman, M. (2014). Getting to the "COR" understanding the role of resources in conservation of resources theory. *Journal of Management, 40*(5), 1334–1364

Harms, P. D., Credé, M., Tynan, M., Leon, M., & Jeung, W. (2017). Leadership and stress: A meta-analytic review. *The Leadership Quarterly, 28*(1), 178–194.

Helfat, C. E., Finkelstein, S., Mitchell, W., Peteraf, M. A., Singh, H., Teece, D. J., & Winter, S. G. (2007). *Dynamic capabilities: Understanding strategic change in organizations.* John Wiley & Sons.

Hobfoll, S. E. (1989). Conservation of resources: A new attempt at conceptualizing stress. *American Psychologist, 44*(3), 513.

Hobfoll, S. E. (2001). The influence of culture, community, and the nested-self in the stress process: Advancing conservation of resources theory. *Applied Psychology: An International Review, 50*, 337–370.

Kammerlander, N., König, A., & Richards, M. (2018). Why do incumbents respond heterogeneously to disruptive innovations? The interplay of domain identity and role identity. *Journal of Management Studies, 55*(7), 1122–1165.

Lazarus, R. S., & Folkman, S. (1984). *Stress, appraisal, and coping.* Springer Publishing Company.

Leonard-Barton, D. (1992). Core capabilities and core rigidities: A paradox in managing new product development. *Strategic Management Journal, 13*(S1), 111–125.

LePine, J. A., LePine, M. A., & Jackson, C. L. (2004). Challenge and hindrance stress: Relationships with exhaustion, motivation to learn, and learning performance. *Journal of Applied Psychology, 89*(5), 883–891.

Makkonen, H., Pohjola, M., Olkkonen, R., & Koponen, A. (2014). Dynamic capabilities and firm performance in a financial crisis. *Journal of Business Research, 67*(1), 2707–2719.

Marion, R., & Uhl-Bien, M. (2001). Leadership in complex organizations. *The Leadership Quarterly, 12*, 389–418.

McEwen, B. S., & Seeman, T. E. (1999). Protective and damaging effects of mediators of stress. In N. E. Adler, M. Marmot, & B. S. McEwen (Eds.), *Socioeconomic status and health in industrial nations: Social, psychological and biological pathways* (pp. 30–47). Academic Sciences.

Meyer, A. D., Brooks, G. R., & Goes, J. B. (1990). Environmental jolts and industry revolutions: Organizational responses to discontinuous change. *Strategic Management Journal, 11*, 93–110.

Milosevic, I., Bass, A. E., & Combs, G. M. (2018). The paradox of knowledge creation in a high-reliability organization: A case study. *Journal of Management, 44*(3), 1174–1201.

Milosevic, I., Bass, A. E., & Uhl-Bien, M. (2022). The process of growing in small firms: Exploring dialectic adjustments to nonroutine disruptions. *Journal of Small Business Management.* doi:10.1080/00472778.2022.2152827

Moeen, M., Agarwal, R., & Shah, S. K. (2020). Building industries by building knowledge: Uncertainty reduction over industry milestones. *Strategy Science, 5*(3), 218–244.

Oh, C. H., & Oetzel, J. (2022). Multinational enterprises and natural disasters: Challenges and opportunities for IB research. *Journal of International Business Studies, 53*(2), 231–254.

Pearce, J. A., & Robbins, K. (1993). Toward improved theory and research on business turnaround. *Journal of Management, 19*(3), 613–636.

Perrewé, P. L., & Ganster, D. C. (2011). *The role of individual differences in occupational stress and well being.* Emerald Group Publishing.

Rindova, V., & Courtney, H. (2020). To shape or adapt: Knowledge problems, epistemologies, and strategic postures under Knightian uncertainty. *Academy of Management Review*, *45*(4), 787–807.

Riviere, M., & Bass, A. E. (2019). How dimensions of internationalization shape the MNE's renewal capability: Multidimensional and multilevel considerations. *Long Range Planning*, *52*(4), 101862. https://doi.org/10.1016/j.lrp.2018.12.002

Riviere, M., Suder, G., & Bass, A. E. (2018). Exploring the role of internationalization knowledge in fostering strategic renewal: A dynamic capabilities perspective. *International Business Review*, *27*(1), 66–77. https://doi.org/10.1016/j.ibusrev.2017.05.006

Romanelli, E., & Tushman, M. L. (1994). Organizational transformation as punctuated equilibrium: An empirical test. *Academy of Management Journal*, *37*(5), 1141–1166.

Salvato, C., & Vassolo, R. (2018). The sources of dynamism in dynamic capabilities. *Strategic Management Journal*, *39*, 1728–1752.

Sarkees, M., & Hulland, J. (2009). Innovation and efficiency: It is possible to have it all. *Business Horizons*, *52*(1), 45–55.

Schilke, O., Hu, S., & Helfat, C. E. (2018). Quo vadis, dynamic capabilities? A content-analytic review of the current state of knowledge and recommendations for future research. *Academy of Management Annals*, *12*, 390–439.

Schmitt, A., Raisch, S., & Volberda, H. W. (2018). Strategic renewal: Past research, theoretical tensions and future challenges. *International Journal of Management Reviews*, *20*(1), 81–98.

Seeman, T. E., Singer, B. H., Rowe, J. W., Horwitz, R. I., & McEwen, B. S. (1997). Price of adaptation—Allostatic load and its health consequences: MacArthur studies of successful aging. *Archives of Internal Medicine*, *157*(19), 2259–2268.

Shepherd, D. A., Douglas, E. J., & Shanley, M. (2000). New venture survival: Ignorance, external shocks, and risk reduction strategies. *Journal of Business Venturing*, *15*(5–6), 393–410.

Sheppard, J. P., & Chowdhury, S. D. (2005). Riding the wrong wave: Organizational failure as a failed turnaround. *Long Range Planning*, *38*(3), 239–260.

Simsek, Z., Veiga, J. F., Lubatkin, M. H., & Dino, R. N. (2005). Modeling the multilevel determinants of top management team behavioral integration. *Academy of Management Journal*, *48*(1), 69–84.

Singh, K., & Yip, G. S. (2000). Strategic lessons from the Asian crisis. *Long Range Planning*, *33*(5), 706–729.

Sonnentag, S., & Frese, M. (2013). Stress in organizations. In N. W. Schmitt, S. Highhouse, & I. B. Weiner (Eds.), *Handbook of psychology: Industrial and organizational psychology* (Vol. 12, pp. 560–592). Wiley.

Teece, D. J., Pisano, G., & Shuen, A. (1997). Dynamic capabilities and strategic management. *Strategic Management Journal*, *18*(7), 509–533. https://doi.org/10.1016/0167-2681(94)90094-9

Thomas, G. H., & Douglas, E. J. (2022). Resource reconfiguration by surviving SMEs in a disrupted industry. *Journal of Small Business Management*, 1–35.https://doi.org/10.1080/00472778.2021.2009489

Uhl-Bien, M., & Arena, M. (2018). Leadership for organizational adaptability: A theoretical synthesis and integrative framework. *The Leadership Quarterly*, *29*(1), 89–104.

Uhl-Bien, M., Marion, R., & McKelvey, B. (2007). Complexity leadership theory: Shifting leadership from the industrial age to the knowledge era. *The Leadership Quarterly*, *18*(4), 298–318.

Uhl-Bien, M. (2021). Complexity and COVID-19: Leadership and followership in a complex world. *Journal of Management Studies*, *58*(5), 1400–1404.

Volberda, H. W. (1996). Toward the flexible form: How to remain vital in hypercompetitive environments. *Organization Science*, *7*(4), 359–374.

Wenzel, M., Stanske, S., & Lieberman, M. B. (2020). Strategic responses to crisis. *Strategic Management Journal*, *41*, 7–18.

Zahra, S. A., Sapienza, H. J., & Davidsson, P. (2006). Entrepreneurship and dynamic capabilities: A review, model and research agenda. *Journal of Management Studies*, *43*, 917–955. https://doi.org/10.1111/j.1467-6486.2006.00616.x

THE RECIPROCAL RELATIONSHIP BETWEEN M&A STRATEGIC DECISION-MAKING AND WELL-BEING

Kris Irwin and Chris H. Willis

ABSTRACT

Strategic decisions leaders make involving organizational changes such as mergers and acquisitions (M&A), divestitures, and downsizing, which can influence and/or interact with other organizational factors. For example, within the context of M&A, changes impact financial performance, firm behaviors, and organizational culture. In addition, strategic decisions for these types of change can also interrelate with other more intrapersonal factors, including both leaders' and employees' health and well-being. Employee stress, also referred to as "merger syndrome," outlines individual negative impacts of the changes including, but not limited to, cynicism and distrust, change wariness, and burnout, all accumulating to psychological effects including increases in detachment to work, stress, and sick leave. In this chapter, the authors outline the different impacts M&A phases have on stress and well-being and how they interrelate with the strategic decisions leaders make. The authors also outline future research opportunities and practical implications for how leaders and employees could better manage future major changes such as M&A activities.

Keywords: M&A; strategic decision-making; well-being; leadership; stress; organizational change

Stress and Well-Being at the Strategic Level
Research in Occupational Stress and Well-Being, Volume 21, 17–43
Copyright © 2024 by Emerald Publishing Limited
All rights of reproduction in any form reserved
ISSN: 1479-3555/doi:10.1108/S1479-355520230000021002

INTRODUCTION

Strategic decisions leaders make involving organizational changes, such as M&A, divestitures, and downsizing, which can influence and/or interact with other organizational factors. For example, within the context of M&A, changes impact financial performance (e.g., King et al., 2021), firm behaviors (e.g., Devers et al., 2020), and organizational culture (e.g., Sarala et al., 2016). In addition, strategic decisions for these types of change can also interrelate with other more intrapersonal factors, including both leaders' and employees' health and well-being (Gunkel et al., 2015; Huy, 2002; Makri & Ntalianis, 2015). Employee stress, also referred to as "merger syndrome" (e.g., Marks & Mirvis, 1997), in response to an M&A integration, outlines individual negative impacts of the changes, including, but not limited to cynicism and distrust, change wariness, and burnout, all accumulating to psychological effects including increases in detachment to work, stress, and sick leave (Cartwright & Cooper, 1993; Marks & Mirvis, 1997; Sluiter et al., 2003).

Strategic decisions are defined as being "important, in terms of the actions taken, the resources committed, or the precedents set" (Mintzberg et al., 1976, p. 246), including both intended and unintended outcomes (see Elbanna et al., 2020). For the purposes of this study, we explore the M&A events as the resulting context of the strategic decision processes. Building upon the strategic decision-making literature (Eisenhardt & Zbaracki, 1992; Elbanna et al., 2020), we look to capture how individuals make strategic decisions in relation to individual well-being, extending our knowledge about how individuals (and firms) manage an M&A event. Exploring prior research that examines the effect of emotions on decision-making (e.g., Neumann, 2017; Seo & Barrett, 2007), we complement a novel stream of research that explores the antecedents of the M&A decision-making process (Nadkarni & Chen, 2014; Souitaris & Maestro, 2010). The CEO's managerial discretion over the organization is large and growing (Quigley & Hambrick, 2015), especially over the M&A process (Zacharias et al., 2015). We also know that CEO decisions are often led by their "gut feel" of the best option (e.g., Beim & Lévesque, 2006; Boisot & MacMillan, 2004). Given the major implications, M&A may have on both the organization and the individuals involved (Ager, 2011; Huy, 2011; Welch et al., 2020), we feel that it is important to understand not only the strategic decision-making process but also the underlying effects of and on the CEO and subsequently the employees.

We propose that individual well-being serves as a foundation for M&A success, where success is broadly defined and relies on the organization's talent. The variety of responses and level of support provided by both individual managers and leaders, enabled by prior organizational support systems, provides a systematic perspective for us to understand better the interconnectivity of an individual's well-being and that of the organization. Through our discussion of the strategic decision-making, M&A, and well-being literatures, we further outline and propose a reciprocal relationship between the decision-making process and individual well-being and identify opportunities for further research. In our focus on M&A as a context for change, which involves multiple phases and levels of decision-making, we highlight the many ways leader and employee stress, and well-being can play an integral role in firm success and the impacts they can have across the organization.

STRATEGIC DECISION-MAKING AND M&A

The study of decision-making within strategy has a long tradition (Rajagopalan et al., 1993). A review of past research indicates that scholars have focused on three critical dimensions of strategic decision-making: comprehensiveness, speed, and risk (e.g., Atuahene-Gima & Li, 2004; Eisenhardt, 1989). Strategic decisions tend to be unstructured, characterized by uncertain outcomes, and involve the processing of complex information cues (Bourgeois, 1985). Thus, strategy scholars have examined how various aspects of strategic decision-making, such as risk, comprehensiveness, and speed (Eisenhardt, 1989) impact firm outcomes.

The issue of risk associated with strategic decisions involves firm environments, characterized by ambiguous information and high levels of uncertainty (e.g., Knight, 1921), which is considered a critical component for executive decisions (Bourgeois, 1985). Studies on firm risk and performance remain a vital area of research within the strategy (Ruefli et al., 1999). However, how individual managers view risk remains quite intractable and complex (March & Shapira, 1987). Risk can be defined as the uncertainty about the nature of outcomes of a decision and is influenced by the framing of the decisions and the personal consequence of the decision to the individual (Williams & Voon, 1999). Kahneman and Tversky (1979) and others (Lovallo & Kahneman, 2000) illustrate how assumptions of the rational model are compromised as individuals make choices when uncertainty and risk are involved. The M&A process introduces a new level of organizational uncertainty and can have downstream effects on the individual leaders and employees throughout the process across all M&A phases.

Background on M&A Phases

Within the M&A literature, many strategic decisions are required throughout the M&A process. We define the M&A process into three phases: planning, announcement, and post-merger integration (PMI). Each phase introduces different types and levels of decision-making and uncertainty, which can have various effects on an individual and, subsequently, the organization (Calipha et al., 2010; Table 1).

The strategic decisions organizational leaders make for each M&A phase are complex and can have compounding impacts on the organization as well as the leaders themselves and the employees. For example, across all phases, the potential for high-level risk and uncertainty can have an impact on the stress and well-being of the CEO and other top management team members (TMT). Activities during different M&A phases can result in changes in the organizational culture, leadership team, and downstream impacts on functions such as marketing, finance, legal, and information technology. A high-level assessment of those impacts is detailed in Table 2. We further explore by phase the specific decisions and activities as they relate to the potential impacts on the stress and well-being of the leaders and employees.

Table 1. Background on M&A Phases.

Phase	Definition	Example Activities	Timeframe	Individual-level Antecedents
Planning	"period of a transaction that precedes the final closure of the deal" (Welch et al., 2020, p. 844)	Initiation Target selection Bidding and negotiation Valuation and Financing	Varies, one month to one year	CEO compensation Hubris Network ties Acquisition experience (Haleblian et al., 2009; Welch et al., 2020)
Announcement	Marks the end of the private pre-deal planning phase and begins with public announcement and usually deal closure (Welch et al., 2020)	Press release SEC filings Signed legal contracts Employee announcement Initial transaction agreements	One–three months, dependent on SEC approval (if public) and deal with complexity	CEO confidence Board confidence CEO tenure, gender, and turnover (Devers et al., 2013; Gamache et al., 2019)
PMI	The integration period of two firms post-M&A closure, which "processes tend to generate unintended consequences" including problems and opportunities for value creation" (Monin et al., 2013, p. 257)	Communications IT systems integration Knowledge sharing Product integration Sales & marketing	Six months to three years (e.g., Homburg & Bucerius, 2006)	Managerial experience CEO ownership and compensation CEO cognition and personality TMT turnover (Haleblian et al., 2009; Zollo & Singh, 2004)

Planning

The M&A planning phase involves multiple activities and sub-phases such as initiation, target selection, bidding and negotiations, and valuation and due diligence (Welch et al., 2020). When an organization decides to engage in an M&A, it needs to consider multiple levels of factors (Caiazza & Volpe, 2015). For example, many organizational-level factors are inputs into the process, including "investment rules, antitrust, protectionism, labor, local regulations, cultural and human resources management issues" (Caiazza & Volpe, 2015, p. 207). In addition, other antecedents include value creation opportunities (e.g., market power, efficiency, resource synergies), environmental characteristics (e.g., environmental uncertainty, regulation), and other firm-level factors such as acquisition experience and strategic position (see Haleblian et al., 2009 for full review).

In addition to these macroeconomic and organizational-level factors, other individual factors can drive M&A activity, such as CEO compensation aspiration,

Table 2.   Phases: Strategic M&A Decisions and Well-being Impacts.

	Planning	Announcement	PMI
Individuals affected	Key leadership	All employees	All employees
Example decisions	• Changes in benefits	• On-boarding	• Culture
	• Pre-layoffs	• Employee contracts	• Re-organization
	• Changes in costs/sales	• Turnover	• Branding
			• Technologies
Well-being impacts	• Physical energy	• Stages of grief	• Physical energy
	• Mental health	• Shock	• Stress
		• Physical effects	• Non-work impacts

hubris, and personality (Chatterjee & Hambrick, 2007, 2011; Haleblian et al., 2009; Rovenpor, 1993; Welch et al., 2020). Many CEO characteristics are associated with a higher likelihood of their organization engaging in an M&A, including overconfidence, narcissism, extraversion, and promotion focus (Welch et al., 2020). Further, some CEOs' self-serving focus and behaviors run in contrast to risk aversion behaviors demonstrated by CEOs who have experienced disasters or are more sensitive to risk (Welch et al., 2020).

Once organizations make the initial decision to engage in an M&A, the assessment of targets as part of the target selection process starts. Target selection encompasses all activities regarding assessing the fit of potential targets based on the motive behind the M&A. The identification, research on potential targets, and value assessment can take weeks to months to complete and require organizational resources and leadership attention. The risk of selecting an inappropriate target, which results in either the M&A not to close (Ten Brug & Sahib, 2018) or an acquisition failure, which can cause undue stress on leadership resulting in CEO departures (Park et al., 2018).

Announcement

The Announcement phase of an M&A consists of the timeframe upon which a contractual agreement has been reached and signed, and for publicly traded firms, the Security and Exchange Commission (SEC, 2018) requires a press release detailing the M&A agreement. The announcement phase also accounts for specific activities involving communicating with both the acquirer and target stakeholders, including employees, suppliers, buyers, and other external relations, for which M&A initial plans and timelines for activities may impact them. Specifically, within the target and acquirer organizations, human resources (HR) and communication functions work with leadership to coordinate communications and documentation for employees for any necessary information to ensure the continued operations of the firms (Bastien, 1987; Bagdadli et al., 2014). As outlined in Table 1, a few individual-level antecedents have been discussed in academic journals, which primarily focus on the CEO and Board of Directors. As an example, CEO and director confidence in the M&A, as displayed through the words and expressions used during announcements, including press releases and investor call transcripts, are associated with how both investors and other stakeholders perceive the M&A status and process may progress (Devers et al., 2013; Gamache et al., 2019).

Post-merger Integration

As this M&A phase receives the most scholarly attention, PMI encompasses all the activities post-announcement and final closure of the deal. These activities typically include leadership decisions and activities around different integration components, including communications, finance, marketing, manufacturing/ services, product management, and information technology. In some cases, a dedicated function is created to help with the M&A learning process (Trichterborn et al., 2016). The HR function is also usually highly involved in all reorganization and employee transitions, including employee mobility within the firm or voluntary turnover (Bagdadli et al., 2014). This phase usually takes the longest, from six months to up to three years or more (e.g., Homburg & Bucerius, 2006), and given the numerous organizational changes usually associated with an M&A, the level of uncertainty, and stress can be quite high (Cartwright & Cooper, 1993; Coff, 1999; Marks & Mirvis, 1997; Sluiter et al., 2003).

Identified individual-level factors such as CEO ownership and compensation, managerial experience, cognition, and personality traits can moderate PMI success (Haleblian et al., 2009). However, prior leader and employee experience and well-being from the planning and announcement phases on the effect on PMI has yet to have much discussion, including both PMI success and individual factors such as employee decision-making process on well-being. The typical leadership decisions made during PMI are under high scrutiny as investors assess if the acquisition will meet the value creation benefits previously promised (e.g., Aktas et al., 2013; Bruner, 2004; Yakis-Douglas et al., 2017). Beyond the everyday demands on leaders to make decisions regarding quarterly earnings and stock performance, the added pressure, risk, and uncertainty involving an M&A could have an additive, adverse effect on their stress and well-being (Walsh, 1988). Current research on CEO turnover post-M&A assesses PMI failure as an important causal factor. However, other individual factors such as CEO well-being and family conflicts are not addressed or only controlled for rather than theorized (e.g., Bauer et al., 2021; Bilgili et al., 2017; Cannella & Hambrick, 1993; Hambrick & Cannella, 1993). In addition, their employees face their own decisions during the PMI phase, including whether to voluntary leave and how much extra work effort they choose to commit to the PMI activities, which are usually beyond expected prior job expectations (Bauer et al., 2021). In the following sections, we review the multi-level factors that can influence leader decision-making and, subsequently, leader and employee well-being.

Leader Factors Impacting Decision-Making

While many differing organizational-level factors that can influence the M&A decision-making process, it is important to highlight current research on individual leader factors. Individual leaders' prior experiences, personalities, emotions, and other factors can influence what potential M&A decisions are made.

For example, prior experiences can help leaders make complicated decisions even under heavy cognitive loads and operating under uncertain information (Mitchell et al., 2011). However, this experience does not impact better decision-making when managers operate in a hostile environment (Mitchell et al., 2011). While prior experience can temper the stress created by ambiguity, when the firm and, by extension, the leader is threatening, the individual micro-level cognitive factors can have a larger impact. For example, Bennedsen et al. (2008) found that the impact of a death of a family member of the CEO is associated with negative firm performance, with the impact on the firm being higher in magnitude when the death was of a more immediate family member (e.g., spouse or child). Recent articles by *Deloitte* (Bhatt, 2022; Hatfield et al., 2022) highlight the importance of health-savvy executives and how leaders need to pay attention to both their and their employees' well-being. Below we discuss the background of different individual-level leader factors that can influence decision-making, highlighting the connection of these factors to individual well-being.

CEO Personality
CEO personality and religiosity are associated with their temporal focus (Kooij et al., 2018; Pieper et al., 2020) and associated short- or long-term decision-making. This temporal focus is important for understanding some CEOs' opportunistic impulses and for the firm's long-term growth and survivability. Also, Pieper et al. (2020) demonstrate that the CEO's temporal focus is associated with the firm time horizon. The individual temporal focus and firm time horizon both influence the strategic decision process and can be key in a lengthy M&A process. Most strategic decisions have potentially positive and negative outcomes, resulting in a risk-reward paradigm, which is shown to be influenced by organizational time horizon (e.g., Chen & Miller, 2015).

CEO personality also directly influences risk through the CEO's cognition or perception of the environment, which the CEO then portrays to their employees. (Nadkarni & Herrmann, 2010) Also, risk, both at an individual and corporate level, is shown to be driven by the CEO's five-factor model of personality (Benischke et al., 2018). Risk can potentially influence time horizons through wanting to maximize wealth. The opportunism and wish for short-term profits over long-term shareholder maximization is an interesting and important consideration for the firm and M&A decision-making. Firm temporal focus is also associated with CEO personality, with several studies showing the CEO micro-factors on firm strategic changes (e.g., Chen & Nadkarni, 2017; DesJardine & Shi, 2021). The personality traits of Openness, Conscientiousness, and Neuroticism have been shown to have the strongest influence on individual time horizon (Kooij et al., 2018). While the psychological literature (see Kooij et al., 2018) shows that "The ability to foresee, anticipate, and plan for future desired outcomes is crucial for well-being, motivation, and behavior" and has a relationship with personality, these key components affecting decision-making has received limited consideration in the M&A literature (p. 867).

CEO personality is "the enduring configuration of characteristics and behavior that comprises an individual's unique adjustment to life, including major traits, interests, drives, values, self-concept, abilities, and emotional patterns" (VandenBos, 2007, p. 1). CEO personality is known to impact the firm's M&A activities (Malhotra et al., 2018). With the CEO power large and growing over firm decisions (Zacharias et al., 2015), there likely are also direct ties between the CEO's personality and strategic decision-making process. Several studies have also shown the impact of the CEO's personality on strategic change, demonstrating that this strategic change is both independent and in combination with their firm performance (Herrmann & Nadkarni, 2014; Harrison et al., 2019). Harrison et al. (2019) find that a –1 to +1 standard deviation of managerial trait of openness is positively associated with a 21% increase in strategic change like M&As, and this relationship is negatively moderated by firm performance. Those authors further find that CEO conscientiousness or neuroticism are negatively associated with strategic change in high-performing firms, and positively associated in low-performing firms. The trait of Hubris, or overconfidence, is shown to be associated with lower levels of strategic change (Kowalzick & Appels, 2022). Narcissism, which is the trait that goes beyond mere overconfidence into grandiosity and attention-seeking, is associated with both more M&A activities along with overpaying for these targets (Cragun et al., 2020; Chatterjee & Hambrick, 2011). These changes may be through the impact of the personality factors on the TMT group dynamics (Peterson et al., 2003), resulting in these changes stemming from the strategic decision-making process.

CEO Emotions

The importance of the antecedents and impacts of emotions on the strategic decision process has been recognized by scholars resulting in a growth of recent studies (Neumann, 2017). Managers' emotions impact their perception of risk, with anger associated with a lower perception or judgment of risk (Podoynitsyna et al., 2012). One interesting finding of Podoynitsyna et al. (2012) is that with greater experience, positive emotions like happiness or hope become significantly associated with better risk awareness. Likewise, Wake et al. (2020) showed that emotions are associated with risk, with those experiencing a positive emotional state more likely to see positive or optimistic possible outcomes. With strategic decision-making under time constraints, negative emotions are linked to a less comprehensive decision process while considering fewer possibilities, resulting in a non-optimum decision (Treffers et al., 2020). In the M&A context, Vuori et al. (2018) showed that when either party suppresses their negative emotions during a post-acquisition process, neither the acquirer nor target could sense correctable issues. As the integration process continued, these initially correctable issues grew, resulting in an M&A failure. The CEO's emotional intelligence and ability to manage their emotions throughout the M&A process can thus be a differentiator in M&A success for an organization.

Other Factors

Other individual factors can impact leader decision-making, including its comprehensiveness as well as the level of stress and anxiety those decisions may cause.

For example, Talaulicar et al. (2005) discuss that debate is important for decision comprehensiveness. We know managers are less likely to debate when tired (Schilpzand et al., 2018). Tiredness is associated with long M&A deals (Birollo et al., 2018). The group dynamics and relationships between the TMT also impact debate (Simons et al.,1999), and the CEO's personality characteristics impact both the relationship between the CEO and the TMT and the intra-team dynamics also (Colbert et al., 2014; Peterson et al., 2003). Additionally, tiredness is negatively tied to appropriate levels of risk-taking behaviors, with these necessary risks which should be taken to improve the firm (Schilpzand, 2018). Job Anxiety also affects strategic decision-making (Mannor et al., 2016), with managers focusing on avoiding potential threats. This prevention focus is due to lower strategic risk-taking, and surrounding themselves with close supporters, possibly limiting the debate between alternative opinions.

Reciprocal Interactions of Well-being and M&A Strategic Decisions

Leaders' decision-making and well-being can impact employees' health and well-being. The consequences of M&A occur around several themes, including health and well-being impacts of emotional labor (e.g., Sarala et al., 2019; Vuori et al., 2018), talent retention (Younge et al., 2015), and work-family conflicts (Schriber et al., 2019) and are associated with different types of strategic decisions and events. For example, the feelings of loss for both the job and the organization through reflection and caring for others and curiosity into how others were coping with the new organization by both leaders and employees can have downstream impacts on their decisions (Vuori et al., 2018). Executives making M&A decisions not only face the uncertainty of the situation but also experience negative impacts on their health.

Uncertainty is an important context to incorporate when discussing both leader and employee reactions, which can include stress-related outcomes like emotional labor and work-family issues. The transactional model of stress (Lazarus & Folkman, 1984) and uncertainty management theory (Lind & Van den Bos, 2022) provide theoretical insights into how uncertainty can be a key factor in how individuals' well-being is affected by an M&A event. According to the transactional model of stress (Folkman, 2008; Griffin & Clarke, 2011; Lazarus, 2006; Lazarus & Folkman, 1984), whether to be determined to be challenging or threatening, is dependent on an individual's assessment of the situation within their environment. While leaders who choose to undertake M&A activities may believe it is purposeful and for the good of the company, they still may perceive the activity as a threat stressor if there are other environmental factors, such as a higher level of uncertainty. This same negative reaction to M&A is seen in employees who may worry about factors outside their control, like layoffs. This increase in uncertainty could lead to other negative well-being outcomes, such as emotional labor and work-life conflicts.

In addition, if employees perceive an M&A is somehow unfair, whether it be contra to prior leadership promises for the company's future or leads to an uncertain future for job benefits or promotions, employees will experience stress as threatening, resulting potentially in a decrease in overall well-being. Assessment of fairness matters, and employees undertake fairness judgments more often during times of uncertainty (Lind & Van den Bos, 2002). How leaders present and communicate the M&A engagement within the context of historical and cultural components can influence employees' assessment of fairness and consequently impact their reactions. The prior history and culture of the company are also important factors of the environment that can provide a temporal view of conditions (Lind & Van den Bos, 2002) for how "uncertain" the M&A event will be perceived as well as the fairness of the decision made by the leaders. Furthermore, these perceptions can influence how well individuals can cope throughout the PMI process and what personal support resources are needed to help in the transition process. As discussed further in the next section, a leader's decision-making process needs to include an assessment of the readiness of leaders and employees prior to and during the M&A process to help leaders manage employee well-being and reduce the high failure rate of M&A (Christensen et al., 2011).

The emotion of letting go and reflection as part of handling an uncertain situation expands on the topic of uncertainty, providing some new depth to what employees may mean when they say, "*times were uncertain*." The expectations of what it is like to experience an M&A as one who "lives" it are different than what one can envision from seeing it from the perspective of a third party. This daily experience can be hard to capture and require additional research approaches such as daily diaries or a qualitative approach such as an ethnographic study to truly capture the emotion and impacts on well-being regarding the changes and uncertainty of the M&A. The reciprocal relationship between the well-being of leaders while making decisions and the subsequent decisions' impacts on both the leaders' and the employees' well-being need further exploration. As we show in Fig. 1, this reciprocal relationship could impact the forward momentum of an

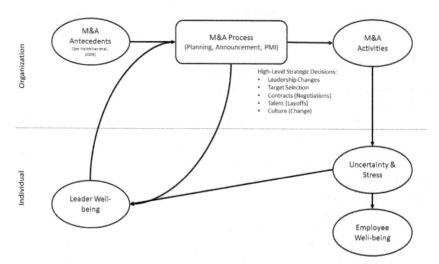

Fig. 1.   Reciprocal Interactions of M&A Strategic Decisions and Well-being.

organization, either dramatically through a 'death spiral' of decisions to M&A failure (e.g., Friedman et al., 2016), or forward to increased firm performance and future growth (Bauer et al., 2021).

Well-being as an Antecedent and an Outcome
While the effect of cognitive biases and heuristics (Bateman & Zeithaml, 1989) on decision-making is well-researched, the impact of well-being on strategic decision-making has not received enough attention (Hakonsson et al., 2016). Recent articles highlight the effect a major event can have on leaders' and employees' well-being. For example, the COVID-19 pandemic impacted employees' well-being (Craig & Churchill, 2020; Wu et al., 2020). In addition, the challenges of work/life balance suggest that gender and parental status affect how individuals manage work-life transitions and stress (Vaziri et al., 2020). These impacts on an individual's well-being and non-work life also be seen well during a major event like M&A (Graebner et al., 2017). Research of the effects of stress and coping on employees (Cartwright & Cooper, 1993) and their interactions with changes in job roles and organization identity is predominantly linked to micro-level outcomes such as voluntary turnover (Sung et al., 2017). The micro-effects of managers and individuals during the PMI stage show the influence of micro-level variables such as emotion, which can influence a manager's ability to perform their job and make decisions (Vuori et al., 2018).

One consideration is that the stress of an event is determined by employees' perceptions during an M&A, not by objective reality (Marks & Mirvis, 1997). For example, even if there is no indication that an employee's job is at risk objectively, if an employee perceives the potential negative impact of displays of unhappiness with the M&A, this can result in a negative effect on the employee's well-being and health (Danna & Griffin, 1999). This idea also aligns with uncertainty management theory on the importance of perception of fairness (Lind & Van den Bos, 2002). Ager (2011) highlights an emotional contagion effect, like change or stress saturation, but in this case, heightened emotions are affected by individual social setting and colleagues sharing their experiences. In relation to emotional labor stress, similar impacts of a reciprocating spiral of demotivation and unhealthy outcomes could result from a hostile and uncertain work environment. Suppose a leader or employee is already under duress prior to the M&A; the M&A event may negatively exacerbate their well-being. Thus, the context of the organization and M&A event are contributing factors to individuals' and individual groups' decision-making and perceptions necessitating consideration.

Emotional Labor
Emotional labor stressor, originally termed by Arlie Hochschild (1979), is triggered due to the discrepancy between the emotions an employee experiences and displays. For example, suppose an employee is already feeling other threats like job loss. In that case, the pressure to appear happy when instead, the employee is struggling with the uncertainty of the situation, that is, surface acting, could lead to emotional dissonance (Festinger, 1957). Emotional dissonance, considered a

source of strain threatening well-being, is similar to a poor person-environment fit (Pugh et al., 2011), and is also found to be associated with negative mood, emotional exhaustion, and job satisfaction (Gross, 1998). As Pugh et al. (2011) discuss perceived individual differences in the importance of the display of authenticity and level of self-efficacy, we would predict this would also be reflected in the circumstances of PMI activities, like when employees help integrate two companies knowing their future job role is uncertain.

The different M&A phases introduce additional complexities to how leaders, managers, and employees handle the decisions and stress of the situation. The relationship between emotional labor stress and the ability of one to do his/her job, including making good decisions during these stressful phases, appears pronounced. Reactions by individuals extend beyond mental health to negative effects on physical health. For example, we see from the decision-making literature that the negative impact on physical health raises the potential for poor decisions, which in a circularly reinforcing fashion, can have additional negative impacts on well-being (Cartwright & Cooper, 1994; Makri & Ntalianis, 2015).

Talent Retention

Given the nature of an M&A event, both voluntary and potentially involuntary turnover is expected (Holtom et al., 2005). Talent retention has been shown to impact firm performance. For example, Cannella and Hambrick (1993) show that manager turnover post-M&A is negatively associated with the acquisition. Additionally, an expected amount of TMT and manager turnover from the target firm due to an M&A can have positive impacts (Zollo & Meier, 2008). The current M&A turnover research has primarily focused on TMTs and appears to be lacking consideration of the linkage of employee-level turnover to performance. The impact on firm performance can be seen from unexpected and unplanned retention issues such that the knowledge transfer process is not completed at the executive level (Zollo & Meier, 2008), but this also needs to be accounted for at the employee level. Additionally, as employee turnover exceeds the slack or amount of human capital resources, the firm needs to continue operations sufficiently, this can lead to increases in employee strain. The resulting increased strain on employees could potentially create a death spiral of employee burnout and turnover, ultimately resulting in M&A failure. Overall, the linkage of individual experiences with organizational outcomes can help lead to practical applications for organizations for handling future changes like M&A.

Work-Family Conflict

One key element missing in current micro-level M&A literature is the impact on non-work elements like the stress of managing family and outside work commitments, which can affect turnover. In fact, in a recent analysis of work/non-work conflict, the impact of stress on family cohesion is related to the perceived fairness of the division of labor and a lack of fairness, which can cause psychological distress (Huffman et al., 2017). In addition to the uncertainty and loss of a job and connections with co-workers, the increased stress is reflected in the increased time commitments experienced. For example, research shows that leaders' and employees' experience with work-family conflict results in difficult personal and professional trade-off decisions (e.g., Reina et al., 2017; Rothman et al., 2017). This example highlights that the increase in workload often associated with an M&A can trickle down and affect an employee's home life, supporting the notion of work/non-work conflict, which can lead to increased stress and lower well-being.

ASSESSMENT OF WELL-BEING

One important challenge in the effort to address any potential negative impacts on leader and employee well-being during the difficult M&A process is in the assessment of whether well-being is impacted or if any intervention used successfully helps increase an individual's well-being. Many measures exist for both organizational and individual well-being. Scholars use survey instruments such as WHO-5 Well-Being Index (Topp et al., 2015) and measures of genuine progress indicators (Barrington-Leigh & Escande, 2018, p. 896) as well as individual items such as asking individuals how well they are managing the M&A experience. The interaction between the difficult decisions both leaders and employees make during the M&A process and how it relates to their overall stress and well-being has been assumed at a high level to mostly have a negative impact (Brahma & Srivastava, 2007; Huy, 2011; Makri & Ntalianis, 2015). However, as shown in Fig. 2, well-being may be more variable. Constant and consistent measurements throughout the M&A process, including during difficult decisions and tracking reactions to subsequent outcomes, could provide more insights into the effects on well-being. While well-being at the organizational level, as described below, is important, measuring how individuals respond to M&A decisions further extends our understanding of the M&A phenomenon.

Organizational Well-being Assessment

While organizational well-being is not our focus, we do want to highlight some overlap in terminology as well as uses of well-being assessment at the organizational level. For example, one activity of the M&A planning phase organizations enact is an organizational readiness assessment. The assessment includes activities such as a review of organizational culture and employee surveys, and the assessments usually include any prior annual employee surveys and potential for talent loss, leadership succession planning, financial planning, and legal preparations (e.g., Sarala et al., 2019; Welch et al., 2020). The assessment is then used in planning and preparation activities prior to the announcement, including leadership departures and addressing any areas of concern, for instance, initiating HR projects for needed employee interventions. This assessment can be referred to as a readiness (or well-being) scorecard for the organization in preparation for the M&A activities ahead.

Other organizational well-being assessments often include a more financial-focused lens. For example, a financial assessment often conducted by strategic

advisors and investment firms can outline specific guidelines for the organization's current and future financial health if an M&A is undertaken (Devers et al.,
2020). A balanced scorecard is also usually included to help ensure the strategic
alignment of future goals and activities gets met in some way by the M&A proposed (Rumelt, 2022). While these may be helpful at the organizational level, individual readiness, including leaders' and employees' situations, is rarely captured
within this broader set of data. However, the literature can refer to the meaning
of organizational well-being as a comprehensive view of the well-being of all
employees (Cartwright & Cooper, 2009). It is important to note this reference
when accounting for how an organization or academic scholar may utilize and
measure well-being.

Individual Well-being Assessment

Assessment and measures of individual well-being both within academic and
practice settings are typically conducted through individual surveys. The surveys
consist of self-reported or supervisor-reported assessment of how an individual
is doing on several different facets that can compromise a holistic assessment
of well-being. For example, psychological or subjective well-being (also referred
to as life satisfaction or quality of life; see Barrington-Leigh & Escande, 2018
for overview) plays a prominent role in many research areas, including income
(Leana & Meuris, 2015), job satisfaction (e.g., Wright & Bonett, 2007), and turnover (e.g., Erdogan et al., 2012), and scholars utilize a variety of survey instruments to assess this well-being construct (see Barrington-Leigh & Escande, 2018;
Diener et al., 2018; Topp et al., 2015; Sonnentag, 2015 for examples).

While current M&A micro-focused research does some assessment of employees' and leaders' reactions to M&A, opportunities exist to utilize newer technologies to enable more real-time and ongoing longitudinal assessments of how
individuals are responding to different M&A strategic decisions and activities.
For example, as outlined in Fig. 2, stress and well-being measurements during
times of change can be highly misleading, whether measured by a survey or a
physical measure discussed below. Accurate measures of individuals' well-being
can be conducted across all M&A phases. For example, a survey assessment of
individual well-being as part of the pre-M&A deal phase can be an input into the
leaders' decision-making process on whether the leaders and individual employees have the coping capacity to undertake such an uncertain and risky endeavor
(Christensen et al., 2011). In addition, assessing leaders' and employees' well-
being throughout the PMI process can provide critical information to the integration and HR teams for what supportive resources to deploy to help frame the
event as a challenge stressor rather than a threat. Early indicators of stress can
lead to the introduction of mitigation plans to help prevent additional negative
stressor outcomes such as increased emotional labor or turnover. However, scholars need a way to monitor ongoing individual well-being that is not intrusive or
time consuming.

The validity of well-being measures is limited by their temporal aspect (the
frequency of which they are measured) and common method bias if only one

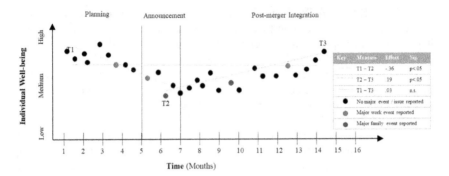

Fig. 2.   Example M&A Phases and Well-being Measurements.

assessment method is utilized. One potential opportunity is the option to physically measure health and well-being by utilizing newer technologies such as wearable devices, which allow for per-minute, hourly, and daily readings, in conjunction with other traditional mechanisms such as surveys to provide a more comprehensive assessment of well-being and what interventions organizations might utilize going forward during the different M&A phases. The surveys or other mechanisms that can capture details of the employees' experiences are still required to assess what may be impacting their stress and well-being, such as whether it be a work or family event contributing to a positive or negative physical response. Below we discuss the benefits and challenges of a few options for consideration that might provide more physical well-being data less obtrusively.

Well-being as a Measure of Physical Health

While the study of physical responses to work conditions like stress and emotion is not new to organizational research (e.g., Darrow, 1933, 1936), the new ease of access to this information, such as through wearable devices, allows for more exhaustive research and opportunities for field research. Physical individual responses to stress include increased blood pressure, increased resting heart rate and decrease in heart rate variability, and changes in skin conductance provide an additional metric for an individual's assessment of stress. One advantage of including a physical health assessment of well-being is that it allows for the monitoring of physical stress potentially beyond the individual's conscious awareness. We discuss below the types of physical signs of stress, how each physical stress indicator can be measured, and how scholars can incorporate additional physical health data for a more holistic composite for individual well-being.

Physical Signs of Stress

Individuals may have a decrease in overall well-being but may not be cognitively aware of their bodies. In the discussion of stress and coping, the employment of mindfulness, including body awareness, is necessary for an individual to fully comprehend the impact of a stressful event on their body and mind (see Good et al., 2016; Kossek & Perrigino, 2016). To increase the transparency and accuracy of the level of stress an individual may be experiencing, temporally accounting for physical responses to stress such as an increase in blood pressure, changes in heart rate variability, and skin conduction, in addition, typical survey measures can increase measure validation and triangulation for the level of stress. The measures briefly described below can be utilized across many stressful and uncertain contexts and are not limited to just M&A activities.

Blood pressure is the measurement of systolic blood pressure (the pressure in your blood vessels when your heart beats) over diastolic blood pressure (the pressure in your blood vessels when your heart rests between beats) (CDC.gov, 2018). Within organizational research, scholars have utilized the change in blood pressure as an indication of stress. For example, Heaphy and Dutton (2008) showed that blood pressure is associated with positive social interactions. In assessing the job demands–job control model of stress, the objective measure of blood pressure was used in conjunction with other subjective measures to show the impact of workload (Fox et al., 1993).

Heart rate variability (HRV) is a measure of bodily experienced stress (Schellhammer et al., 2013). When a person is under stress, the heart rate typically rises, but the heart rate variability diminishes (Schellhammer et al., 2013). The measurement of HRV reflects bodily experienced stress due to an event as it is apparent immediately in the body's reaction (Keller et al., 2011). The use of HRV has been utilized in understanding surgeon's reactions during a shift (Langelotz et al., 2008), investigating the effects of technostress on knowledge workers (Schellhammer et al., 2013), and in understanding the effect of violent games on boys (Ivarsson et al., 2009). Practically, HRV is one component utilized by consumer wearable device manufacturers to provide an exercise readiness score (e.g., Fitbit, n.d.; higher HRV means higher readiness for intense exercise).

Skin conductance response (SCR) is a measurement of the nonconscious reaction of an individual's sweat glands that can represent peripheral (bodily) signals associated with emotions, decisions, and eventual behavior (Christopoulos et al., 2019). While the measurement of physical responses like skin conductance is of interest to researchers, the tool also applies to practitioners and individuals in general. For example, psychologists utilize changes in skin temperature and heart rate (biofeedback) to assess physical responses during therapy sessions (Yucha & Montgomery, 2008). In the measurement of skin conductance for emotional reactions, researchers call out the need for heart rate, respiration, and electromyography (Christopoulos et al., 2019). Heart rate responses can help in indexing autonomic responses, respiration helps identify where a deep breath generated a large SCR (i.e., introduces potential for error), and electromyography provides an index to the startle response (Christopoulos et al., 2019).

Measurement Devices
The capturing of multiple data points of biological responses allows for their triangulation and increased confidence in the reported findings (Chaffin et al., 2017; Kayhan et al., 2018). Utilizing new technology that allows for the unobtrusive

measurement of multiple indicators of physical stress, which may not be fully accounted for or even understood by an individual's survey responses, and allows for a more holistic individual well-being. Wearable devices that monitor responses like heart rate and skin conductance (Christopoulos et al., 2019) give researchers access to more direct, unobtrusive data on what an individual may be experiencing, including unconscious physical reactions.

Individual users have purchased over-the-counter technology products such as the Apple Watch and Google Fitbit, which utilize four main measurement components: (1) accelerometer, (2) heat flux, (3) galvanic skin response, and (4) skin temperature to estimate a more accurate calorie burn for physical health monitoring and benefits. While the primary purpose of devices is for commercial profit, researchers can use these types of wearable devices in their research. Other types of wearable devices, including GPS monitors, RFID chips, and new visual capturing and eye movement tracking devices (e.g., Tobii Pro Glasses), can help triangulate the data measures. For example, in trying to understand what caused an employee's heart rate to increase, if the employee is wearing both a heart rate monitor and tracking glasses with video recording, the subject of stress (or excitement) is likely identifiable. While manual effort by the researcher would be required to help ensure the data triangulation mapping and conclusions are valid, future technologies, including using machine learning to interpret the context, may provide more efficient data interpretation (Zhou et al., 2017).

As scholars look to incorporate additional physical data in research, understanding the meaning behind the measurements will require additional work to ensure the individual responses measured accurately reflect the construct under study, such as well-being in response to an organizational change like M&A. Some potential disadvantages of using wearable devices include issues with the interpretation of the measures from the devices (Chaffin et al., 2017; Kayhan et al., 2018), interference of the measurement due to other external factors (Braeutigam et al., 2019), and the need to develop a new skill set including interfacing and programming languages for the use of the devices. In addition, two potential disadvantages related to the use of human subjects include the potential for interference or harm from wearing or using the device unsafely (Piwek et al., 2016) and possible ethical concerns about the collection and use of data related to protected health-related data (Rosen et al., 2015).

In addition, while wearables offer new data sources to researchers, a few cautions are needed regarding the output of the devices. For example, suppose a researcher is monitoring the anxiety level of a study participant through the measurement of heart rate and skin conductance and notices a spike during a scheduled meeting, one potential conclusion is that the meeting caused a reaction typical of anxiety. However, additional data collected for that same period may note the participant drank and reacted to a 64oz Mountain Dew with its high caffeine content, which suggests a different conclusion. Thus, similar to other research measures, context needs to be considered, and confounding variables are still possible with physical responses (Chaffin et al., 2017; Johns, 2006). Scholars also need to ensure proper measurement and data triangulation which requires additional time and expertise to handle multiple devices and measurement analyses.

Incorporation of Physical Health Data

The inclusion of physical health data, along with other measurement options such as individual and organizational-level surveys, can provide a more holistic view of the impacts an M&A event or other stress organizational or environmental event can have. Throughout all M&A phases, utilizing a readiness assessment with all data inputs can provide new insights for both leaders and supporting resources for any needed mitigation activities. As shown in Fig. 2, the drop in well-being between time one and time two could be due to an M&A process or other non-related activities. More accurate measurement of well-being, including physical data combined with ongoing touchpoints with leaders and employees, would provide more in-depth information for the decrease (increase) and how that might interrelate or affect future decision-making. The physical indicators, triangulated with other measures, may also show how individuals manage or recover from stress. For example, not unique to individuals' reactions to the uncertainty of an M&A event, the timing of HRV recovery after a stressful period may align with an individual's coping strategy. In the transactional model of stress where a stressor is deemed to be a challenge stressor, individuals' HRV may recover more quickly than those facing a threat stressor. Firms need additional research and discussion about appropriateness and when and how to incorporate physical health data into readiness assessments.

With the incorporation of physical data, several factors can influence the results of the impact of physical stress on well-being. For example, a participant's awareness, placement, and use of a wearable measurement device during a study may influence their reactions (Qi et al., 2020). Within the context of wearable textiles, researchers also assessed participants' varying comfort levels interfacing with the on-body technology, which depending on various factors like culture and gender, could influence participation and correct execution in the study (Kuru & Erbuǧ, 2013). While no research currently appears to address the issue of potential invalid measurement due to individuals purposefully manipulating their physical reactions like heart rate (e.g., faking on a lie detector test), other issues of concern include the potential hardware or software failure (Chaffin et al., 2017).

Another challenge in assessing physical health is the need to ensure the privacy of participants' data. For example, the capturing, transmitting, and storing of data related to heart rate and skin responses (health-related data) in combination with other data like GPS location could be viewed as an invasion of privacy (Rosen et al., 2015). While not considered medical research, if the data are associated with any personally identifiable information, the risks for potential harm to human subjects may be considered high. While institutional review boards may vary and be unclear on how to treat these types of studies (Wenzel & Van Quaquebeke, 2017), researchers utilizing medical devices will need to take additional precautions in the collection, storage, and use of the data above and beyond what might have been traditionally required in management research.

DISCUSSION

In taking a multi-level view of leader decision-making, we assess the precursors and impacts on individual well-being within the M&A context. Previous qualitative studies have explored employees' reactions to change, including changes to organizational identification (Ullrich et al., 2005), leadership, and change management strategies (Kavanagh & Ashkanasy, 2006). However, given the relationship of work and non-work in employee well-being (e.g., Danna & Griffin, 1999), more information is needed to fully assess the potential impact of large or simultaneously occurring changes like M&As on individuals within organizations. Before and during each M&A phase, organizations can assess their readiness and have some potential responses to help leaders and employees manage their well-being during each phase. Support for leadership and the PMI team's mental health and ongoing resilience can be key in ensuring the success of an M&A implementation. This support extends to the early planning phase, where initial assessments of organizational readiness can feed the development of support structures and proactive planning (Hutzschenreuter et al., 2014; Welch et al., 2020).

Broader issues currently facing organizations, such as the ongoing COVID-19 pandemic and the opportunities for practice regarding well-being, introduce a new level of complexity of how organizations must manage their talent and the available resources to support their employees (Hancock & Schaninger, 2020; Maddox-Daines, 2021). Therefore, future M&A research should continue its current progress to account for its multi-level nature and multiple outcome goals. For example, the expansion on the topic of specific human capital creation and capture looks promising, including opportunities to expand on the focus of HR professionals and managers' roles as key resources in the PMI process (e.g., Huy, 2011; Meglio et al., 2015) by targeting and capturing strategic human capital value and minimizing value leakage (Teerikangas et al., 2011). In addition, given the relationship between higher job satisfaction and lower levels of intention to leave, organizations undertaking an M&A that have or introduce policies focused on well-being may help mitigate the increased issues of work/non-work conflict (Butts et al., 2013).

While no M&A studies to our knowledge have assessed the work–family support system, assessing employees' experience and need for such policies as they undergo a stressful event like M&A seems warranted. As the power of the CEO grows (Zacharias et al., 2015), the direct and indirect ties between the CEO's personality and strategic decision-making process plus their overall well-being need further exploration. Their influence on the organization and, subsequently, the employees' well-being could serve as a differentiator as firms look to compete in a dynamically changing environment. In addition, given the discussed impacts stress saturation has on employees experiencing M&A, a logical trickle-down effect needs further explanation, given the recent research showing there is less and less distinction between work and non-work time (Owens et al., 2016; Spieler et al., 2017). Additional studies are needed to assess the M&A daily experience of both leaders and employees, requiring expanded research approaches such as daily diaries, qualitative approaches such as an ethnographic study, as well as incorporating physical measures of stress to truly capture the emotion and impacts on well-being regarding the changes and uncertainty of the M&A.

Our discussion is not without limitations. In our focus on the M&A context, we do not capture other non-M&A management strategic decisions that could also impact well-being. Future research studies may want to utilize multiple methods, including experimental design, which can help capture the directionality of the impact of decisions on well-being. The use of wearables and other new technology to allow for multiple physical and subjective measures of well-being throughout the M&A process could provide much-needed insights into how both leaders and employees are managing.

CONCLUSION

In this chapter, we examined the role of stress and well-being on leaders and employees' decision-making. We outline how a stressful and potentially very risky organizational event such as M&A can have both a mental and physical toll on an individual, which can subsequently have multi-level impacts on the individual and the organization. In conclusion, how leaders' decision-making relates to and potentially influences and/or impacts their own as well as employee well-being provides insights into how contextual elements, prior experience, and personal situations provide theoretical and practical insights for future M&A research.

REFERENCES

Ager, D. L. (2011). The emotional impact and behavioral consequences of post-M&A integration: An ethnographic case study in the software industry. *Journal of Contemporary Ethnography, 40*(2), 199–230.

Aktas, N., de Bodt, E., & Roll, R. (2013). MicroHoo: Deal failure, industry rivalry, and sources of overbidding. *Journal of Corporate Finance, 19*, 20–35.

Atuahene-Gima, K., & Li, H. (2004). Strategic decision comprehensiveness and new product development outcomes in new technology ventures. *Academy of Management Journal, 47*(4), 583–597.

Bagdadli, S., Hayton, J. C., & Perfido, O. (2014). Reconsidering the role of HR in M&As: What can be learned from practice. *Human Resource Management, 53*(6), 1005–1025.

Barrington-Leigh, C., & Escande, A. (2018). Measuring progress and well-being: A comparative review of indicators. *Social Indicators Research, 135*(3), 893–925.

Bastien, D. T. (1987). Common patterns of behavior and communication in corporate mergers and acquisitions. *Human Resource Management, 26*(1), 17–33.

Bateman, T. S., & Zeithaml, C. P. (1989). The psychological context of strategic decisions: A model and convergent experimental findings. *Strategic Management Journal, 10*(1), 59–74.

Bauer, F., King, D. R., Schriber, S., & Kruckenhauser, C. (2021). Navigating challenging contexts: Costs and benefits of codified acquisition experience. *Long Range Planning, 54*(6), 102088.

Beim, G., & Lévesque, M. (2006). Country selection for new business venturing: A multiple criteria decision analysis. *Long Range Planning, 39*(3), 265–293.

Benischke, M. H., Martin, G. P., & Glaser, L. (2018). CEO equity risk bearing and strategic risk taking: The moderating effect of CEO personality. *Strategic Management Journal, 40*(1), 153–177.

Bennedsen, M., Perez-Gonzalez, F., & Wolfenzon, D. (2008, October). *Do CEOs Matter?* [NYU Working Paper No. FIN-06-032]. https://ssrn.com/abstract=1293659

Bhatt, J. (2022, June 21). Employee health contributes to organizational health. *Deloitte Insights Magazine*, 38–40.

Bilgili, T. V., Calderon, C. J., Allen, D. G., & Kedia, B. L. (2017). Gone with the wind: A meta-analytic review of executive turnover, its antecedents, and postacquisition performance. *Journal of Management, 43*(6), 1966–1997.

Birollo, G., Rouleau, L., & Teerikangas, S. P. (2018). Middle managers' interactions at the heart of the strategy-adaptation process in acquisitions. *Academy of Management Proceedings* (Vol. 2018, No. 1, p. 12954). Academy of Management.

Boisot, M., & MacMillan, I. C. (2004). Crossing epistemological boundaries: Managerial and entrepreneurial approaches to knowledge management. *Long Range Planning, 37*(6), 505–524.

Bourgeois, L. J. (1985). Strategic goals, perceived uncertainty, and economic performance in volatile environments. *Academy of Management Journal, 28*, 548.

Braeutigam, S., Lee, N., & Senior, C. (2019). A role for endogenous brain states in organizational research: Moving toward a dynamic view of cognitive processes. *Organizational Research Methods, 22*(1), 332–353.

Brahma, S. S., & Srivastava, K. B. (2007). Communication, executive retention, and employee stress as predictors of acquisition performance: An empirical evidence. *ICFAI Journal of Mergers & Acquisitions, 4*(4), 7–26.

Bruner, R. (2004). Where M&A pays and where it strays: A survey of the research. *Journal of Applied Corporate Finance, 16*(4), 63–76.

Butts, M. M., Casper, W. J. & Yang, T. S. (2013). How important are work–family support policies? A meta-analytic investigation of their effects on employee outcomes. *Journal of Applied Psychology, 98*, 1–25.

Caiazza, R., & Volpe, T. (2015). M&A process: A literature review and research agenda. *Business Process Management Journal, 21*(1), 205–220.

Calipha, R., Tarba, S., & Brock, D. (2010). Mergers and acquisitions: A review of phases, motives, and success factors. In C. L. Cooper & S. Finkelstein (Eds.), *Advances in mergers and acquisitions* (Vol. 9, 1–24). Emerald Group Publishing Limited.

Cannella, A. A., Jr, & Hambrick, D. C. (1993). Effects of executive departures on the performance of acquired firms. *Strategic Management Journal, 14*(S1), 137–152.

Cartwright, S., & Cooper, C. L. (1993). The psychological impact of merger and acquisition on the individual: A study of building society managers. *Human Relations, 46*(3), 327–347.

Cartwright, S., & Cooper, C. L. (1994). The human effects of mergers and acquisitions. In C. L. Cooper & D. M. Rousseau (Eds.), *Trends in organizational behavior* (Vol. 1, pp. 47–61). John Wiley & Sons.

Cartwright, S., & Cooper, C. L. (Eds.). (2009). *The Oxford handbook of organizational well-being*. Oxford Handbooks.

CDC.gov. (2018). *Measuring blood pressure*. https://www.cdc.gov/bloodpressure/measure.htm

Chaffin, D., Heidl, R., Hollenbeck, J. R., Howe, M., Yu, A., Voorhees, C., & Calantone, R. (2017). The promise and perils of wearable sensors in organizational research. *Organizational Research Methods, 20*(1), 3–31.

Chatterjee, A., & Hambrick, D. C. (2007). It's all about me: Narcissistic chief executive officers and their effects on company strategy and performance. *Administrative Science Quarterly, 52*(3), 351–386.

Chatterjee, A., & Hambrick, D. C. (2011). Executive personality, capability cues, and risk taking: How narcissistic CEOs react to their successes and stumbles. *Administrative Science Quarterly, 56*(2), 202–237.

Chen, M. J., & Miller, D. (2015). Reconceptualizing competitive dynamics: A multidimensional framework. *Strategic Management Journal, 36*(5), 758–775.

Chen, J., & Nadkarni, S. (2017). It's about time! CEOs' temporal dispositions, temporal leadership, and corporate entrepreneurship. *Administrative Science Quarterly, 62*(1), 31–66.

Christensen, C. M., Alton, R., Rising, C., & Waldeck, A. (2011). The new M&A playbook. *Harvard Business Review, 89*(3), 48–57.

Christopoulos, G. I., Uy, M. A., & Yap, W. J. (2019). The body and the brain: Measuring skin conductance responses to understand the emotional experience. *Organizational Research Methods, 22*(1), 394–420.

Coff, R. W. (1999). How buyers cope with uncertainty when acquiring firms in knowledge-intensive industries: Caveat emptor. *Organization Science, 10*(2), 144–161.

Colbert, A. E., Barrick, M. R., & Bradley, B. H. (2014). Personality and leadership composition in top management teams: Implications for organizational effectiveness. *Personnel Psychology, 67*(2), 351–387.

Cragun, O. R., Olsen, K. J., & Wright, P. M. (2020). Making CEO narcissism research great: A review and meta-analysis of CEO narcissism. *Journal of Management, 46*(6), 908–936.

Craig, L., & Churchill, B. (2020). Dual-earner parent couples' work and care during COVID-19. *Gender, Work & Organization, 28*(51), 66–79.

Danna, K., & Griffin, R. W. (1999). Health and well-being in the workplace: A review and synthesis of the literature. *Journal of Management, 25*(3), 357–384.

Darrow, C. (1933). The functional significance of the galvanic skin reflex and perspiration on the backs and palms of the hands. *Psychological Bulletin, 30*(4), 712.

Darrow, C. W. (1936). The galvanic skin reflex (sweating) and blood-pressure as preparatory and facilitative functions. *Psychological Bulletin, 33*(2), 73.

DesJardine, M. R., & Shi, W. 2021. How temporal focus shapes the influence of executive compensation on risk taking. *Academy of Management Journal, 64*(1), 265–292.

Devers, C. E., McNamara, G., Haleblian, J., & Yoder, M. E. (2013). Do they walk the talk? Gauging acquiring CEO and director confidence in the value creation potential of announced acquisitions. *Academy of Management Journal, 56*(6), 1679–1702.

Devers, C. E., Wuorinen, S., McNamara, G., Haleblian, J., Gee, I. H., & Kim, J. (2020). An integrative review of the emerging behavioral acquisition literature: Charting the next decade of research. *Academy of Management Annals, 14*(2), 869–907.

Diener, E., Oishi, S., & Tay, L. (2018). Advances in subjective well-being research. *Nature Human Behaviour, 2*(4), 253–260.

Eisenhardt, K. M. (1989). Making fast strategic decisions in high-velocity environments. *Academy of Management Journal, 32*(3), 543–576.

Eisenhardt, K. M., & Zbaracki, M. (1992) Strategic decision making. *Strategic Management Journal, 13*(S2), 17–37.

Elbanna, S., Thanos, I. C., & Jansen, R. J. (2020). A literature review of the strategic decision-making context: A synthesis of previous mixed findings and an agenda for the way forward. *M@n@gement, 23*(2), 42–60.

Erdogan, B., Bauer, T. N., Truxillo, D. M., & Mansfield, L. R. (2012). Whistle while you work: A review of the life satisfaction literature. *Journal of Management, 38*(4), 1038–1083.

Festinger, L. (1957). *A theory of cognitive dissonance*. Row, Peterson.

Fitbit. (n.d.). *Daily readiness score with fitbit premium.* https://www.fitbit.com/global/us/technology/daily-readiness-score

Folkman, S. (2008). The case for positive emotions in the stress process. *Anxiety, Stress, and Coping, 21*(1), 3–14.

Fox, M. L., Dwyer, D. J., & Ganster, D. C. (1993). Effects of stressful job demands and control on physiological and attitudinal outcomes in a hospital setting. *Academy of Management Journal, 36*(2), 289–318.

Friedman, Y., Carmeli, A., Tishler, A., & Shimizu, K. (2016). Untangling micro-behavioral sources of failure in mergers and acquisitions: A theoretical integration and extension. *The International Journal of Human Resource Management, 27*(20), 2339–2369.

Gamache, D. L., McNamara, G., Graffin, S. D., Kiley, J., Haleblian, J., & Devers, C. E. (2019). Impression offsetting as an early warning signal of low CEO confidence in acquisitions. *Academy of Management Journal, 62*(5), 1307–1332.

Good, D. J., Lyddy, C. J., Glomb, T. M., Bono, J. E., Brown, K. W., Duffy, M. K., Baer, R. A., Brewer, J. A., & Lazar, S. W. (2016). Contemplating mindfulness at work: An integrative review. *Journal of Management, 42*(1), 114–142.

Graebner, M. E., Heimeriks, K. H., Huy, Q. N., & Vaara, E. (2017). The process of postmerger integration: A review and agenda for future research. *Academy of Management Annals, 11*(1), 1–32.

Griffin, M. A., & Clarke, S. (2011). Stress and well-being at work. In S. Zedeck, (Ed.) *APA handbook of industrial and organizational psychology: Maintaining, expanding, and contracting the organization* (Vol. 3). American Psychological Association.

Gross, J. J. (1998). The emerging field of emotion regulation: An integrative review. *Review of General Psychology, 2*(3), 271–299.

Gunkel, M., Schlaegel, C., Rossteutscher, T., & Wolff, B. (2015). The human aspect of cross-border acquisition outcomes: The role of management practices, employee emotions, and national culture. *International Business Review, 24*(3), 394–408.

Hakonsson, D. D., Eskildsen, J. K., Argote, L., Monster, D., Burton, R. M., & Obel, B. (2016). Exploration vs. exploitation: Emotion and performance as antecedents and consequences of team decisions. *Strategic Management Journal, 37*(6), 985–1001.

Haleblian, J., Devers, C. E., McNamara, G., Carpenter, M. A., & Davison, R. B. (2009). Taking stock of what we know about mergers and acquisitions: A review and research agenda. *Journal of Management, 35*(3), 469–502.

Hambrick, D. C., & Cannella, A. A., Jr. (1993). Relative standing: A framework for understanding departures of acquired executives. *Academy of Management Journal, 36*(4), 733–762.

Hancock, B., & Schaninger, B. (2020). HR says talent is crucial for performance-and the pandemic proves it. *McKinsey & Company, 27*, 1–7.

Harrison, J. S., Thurgood, G. R., Boivie, S., & Pfarrer, M. D. (2019). Measuring CEO personality: Developing, validating, and testing a linguistic tool. *Strategic Management Journal, 40*(8), 1316–1330.

Hatfield, S., Fisher, J., & Silverglate, P. H. (2022). The C-suite's role in well-being. How health-savvy executives can go beyond workplace wellness to workplace well-being—for themselves and their people. *Deloitte Insights Magazine*. https://www2.deloitte.com/us/en/insights/topics/leadership/employee-wellness-in-the-corporate-workplace.html

Heaphy, E. D., & Dutton, J. E. (2008). Positive social interactions and the human body at work: Linking organizations and physiology. *Academy of Management Review, 33*(1), 137–162.

Herrmann, P., & Nadkarni, S. (2014). Managing strategic change: The duality of CEO personality. *Strategic Management Journal, 35*(9), 1318–1342.

Hochschild, A. R. (1979). Emotion work, feeling rules, and social structure. *American Journal of Sociology, 85*(3), 551–575.

Holtom, B. C., Mitchell, T. R., Lee, T. W., & Inderrieden, E. J. (2005). Shocks as causes of turnover: What they are and how organizations can manage them. *Human Resource Management, 44*(3), 337–352.

Homburg, C., & Bucerius, M. (2006). Is speed of integration really a success factor of mergers and acquisitions? An analysis of the role of internal and external relatedness. *Strategic Management Journal, 27*(4), 347–367.

Huffman, A., Matthews, R., & Irving, L. (2017). Family fairness and cohesion in marital dyads: Mediating processes between work–family conflict and couple psychological distress. *Journal of Occupational and Organizational Psychology, 90*(1), 95–116.

Hutzschenreuter, T., Kleindienst, I., & Schmitt, M. (2014). How mindfulness and acquisition experience affect acquisition performance. *Management Decision, 52*(6), 1116–1147.

Huy, Q. N. (2002). Emotional balancing of organizational continuity and radical change: The contribution of middle managers. *Administrative Science Quarterly, 47*(1), 31–69.

Huy, Q. N. (2011). How middle managers' group-focus emotions and social identities influence strategy implementation. *Strategic Management Journal, 32*(13), 1387–1410.

Ivarsson, M., Anderson, M., Åkerstedt, T., & Lindblad, F. (2009). Playing a violent television game affects heart rate variability. *Acta Paediatrica, 98*(1), 166–172.

Johns, G. (2006). The essential impact of context on organizational behavior. *Academy of Management Review, 31*(2), 386–408.

Kahneman, D., & Tversky, A. (1979). On the interpretation of intuitive probability: A reply to Jonathan Cohen. *Cognition, 7*(4), 409–411.

Kavanagh, M. H., & Ashkanasy, N. M. (2006). The impact of leadership and change management strategy on organizational culture and individual acceptance of change during a merger. *British Journal of Management, 17*(S1), S81–S103.

Kayhan, V. O., Chen, Z. C., French, K. A., Allen, T. D., Salomon, K., & Watkins, A. (2018). How honest are the signals? A protocol for validating wearable sensors. *Behavior Research Methods*, 1–27.

Keller, J., Bless, H., Blomann, F., & Kleinböhl, D. (2011). Physiological aspects of flow experiences: Skills-demand-compatibility effects on heart rate variability and salivary cortisol. *Journal of Experimental Social Psychology, 47*(4), 849–852.

King, D. R., Wang, G., Samimi, M., & Cortes, A. F. (2021). A meta-analytic integration of acquisition performance prediction. *Journal of Management Studies, 58*(5), 1198–1236.

Knight, F. H. (1921). *Risk, uncertainty and profit* (Vol. 31). Houghton Mifflin.

Kowalzick, M., & Appels, M. (2022). To change or not to change? Evidence on the steadiness of more hubristic CEOs. *Journal of Management*, 01492063221104398.

Kooij, D. T., Kanfer, R., Betts, M., & Rudolph, C. W. (2018). Future time perspective: A systematic review and meta-analysis. *Journal of Applied Psychology, 103*(8), 867.

Kossek, E. E., & Perrigino, M. B. (2016). Resilience: A review using a grounded integrated occupational approach. *Academy of Management Annals, 10*(1), 1–69.

Kuru, A., & Erbuğ, Ç. (2013). Explorations of perceived qualities of on-body interactive products. *Ergonomics, 56*(6), 906–921.

Langelotz, C., Scharfenberg, M., Haase, O., & Schwenk, W. (2008). Stress and heart rate variability in surgeons during a 24-hour shift. *Archives of Surgery, 143*(8), 751–755.

Lazarus, R. S. (2006). *Stress and emotion: A new synthesis*. Springer Publishing Company.

Lazarus, R. S., & Folkman, S. (1984). *Stress, appraisal, and coping*. Springer Publishing Company.

Lind, E. A., & Van den Bos, K. (2002). When fairness works: Toward a general theory of uncertainty management. *Research in Organizational Behavior, 24*, 181–223.

Leana, C. R., & Meuris, J. (2015). Living to work and working to live: Income as a driver of organizational behavior. *Academy of Management Annals, 9*(1), 55–95.

Lovallo, D., & Kahneman, D. (2000). Living with uncertainty: Attractiveness and resolution timing. *Journal of Behavioral Decision Making, 13*(2), 179–190.

Maddox-Daines, K. L. (2021). Delivering well-being through the coronavirus pandemic: The role of human resources (HR) in managing a healthy workforce. *Personnel Review*.

Makri, E., & Ntalianis, F. (2015). Post M&A ill-health: Main, moderating and mediating effects of job stressors and perceived organizational support. *Employee Relations, 37*(2), 176–191.

Malhotra, S., Reus, T. H., Zhu, P., & Roelofsen, E. M. (2018). The acquisitive nature of extraverted CEOs. *Administrative Science Quarterly, 63*(2), 370–408.

Mannor, M. J., Wowak, A. J., Bartkus, V. O. & Gomez-Mejia, L. R. (2016). Heavy lies the crown? How job anxiety affects top executive decision making in gain and loss contexts. *Strategic Management Journal, 37*(9), 1968–1989.

March, J. G., & Shapira, Z. (1987). Managerial perspectives on risk and risk taking. *Management Science, 33*(11), 1404–1418.

Marks, M., & Mirvis, P. H. (1997). Revisiting the merger syndrome: Dealing with stress. *Mergers and Acquisitions, 31*(1), 21–27.

Meglio, O., King, D. R., & Risberg, A. (2015). Improving acquisition outcomes with contextual ambidexterity. *Human Resource Management, 54*(S1), s29–s43.

Mintzberg, H., Raisinghani, D., & Theoret, A. (1976). The structure of "unstructured" decision processes. *Administrative Science Quarterly*, 246–275.

Mitchell, J. R., Shepherd, D. A., & Sharfman, M. P. (2011). Erratic strategic decisions: when and why managers are inconsistent in strategic decision making. *Strategic Management Journal, 32*(7), 683–704.

Monin, P., Noorderhaven, N., Vaara, E., & Kroon, D. (2013). Giving sense to and making sense of justice in postmerger integration. *Academy of Management Journal, 56*(1), 256–284.

Nadkarni, S., & Chen, J. (2014). Bridging yesterday, today, and tomorrow: CEO temporal focus, environmental dynamism, and rate of new product introduction. *Academy of Management Journal, 57*(6), 1810–1833.

Nadkarni, S., & Herrmann, P. (2010). CEO personality, strategic flexibility, and firm performance: The case of the Indian business process outsourcing industry. *The Academy of Management Journal, 53*(5), 1050–1073.

Neumann, F. (2017). Antecedents and effects of emotions in strategic decision-making: a literature review and conceptual model. *Management Review Quarterly, 67*(3), 175–200.

Owens, B. P., Baker, W. E., Sumpter, D. M., & Cameron, K. S. (2016). Relational energy at work: Implications for job engagement and job performance. *Journal of Applied Psychology, 101*(1), 35.

Park, K., Gould, A., & King, D. R. (2018, July). CEO status and turnover in the market for corporate control. *Academy of Management Proceedings, 2018*(1), 14628.

Peterson, R. S., Smith, D. B., Martorana, P. V., & Owens, P. D. (2003). The impact of chief executive officer personality on top management team dynamics: one mechanism by which leadership affects organizational performance. *Journal of Applied Psychology, 88*(5), 795.

Pieper, T. M., Williams Jr, R. I., Manley, S. C., & Matthews, L. M. (2020). What time may tell: An exploratory study of the relationship between religiosity, temporal orientation, and goals in family business. *Journal of Business Ethics, 163*(4), 759–773.

Piwek, L., Ellis, D. A., Andrews, S., & Joinson, A. (2016). The rise of consumer health wearables: promises and barriers. *PLoS Medicine, 13*(2), e1001953.

Podoynitsyna, K., Van der Bij, H., & Song, M. (2012). The role of mixed emotions in the risk perception of novice and serial entrepreneurs. *Entrepreneurship Theory and Practice, 36*(1), 115–140.

Pugh, S. D., Groth, M., & Hennig-Thurau, T. (2011). Willing and able to fake emotions: a closer examination of the link between emotional dissonance and employee well-being. *Journal of Applied Psychology, 96*(2), 377.

Qi, J., Yang, P., Newcombe, L., Peng, X., Yang, Y., & Zhao, Z. (2020). An overview of data fusion techniques for Internet of Things enabled physical activity recognition and measure. *Information Fusion, 55,* 269–280.

Quigley, T. J., & Hambrick, D. C. (2015). Has the "CEO effect" increased in recent decades? A new explanation for the great rise in America's attention to corporate leaders. *Strategic Management Journal, 36*(6), 821–830.

Rajagopalan, N., Rasheed, A. M., & Datta, D. K. (1993). Strategic decision processes: Critical review and future directions. *Journal of Management, 19*(2), 349–384.

Reina, C. S., Peterson, S. J., & Zhang, Z. (2017). Adverse effects of CEO family-to-work conflict on firm performance. *Organization Science, 28*(2), 228–243.

Rosen, M. A., Dietz, A. S., Yang, T., Priebe, C. E., & Pronovost, P. J. (2015). An integrative framework for sensor-based measurement of teamwork in healthcare. *Journal of the American Medical Informatics Association, 22*(1), 11–18.

Rothman, N. B., Pratt, M. G., Rees, L., & Vogus, T. J. (2017). Understanding the dual nature of ambivalence: Why and when ambivalence leads to good and bad outcomes. *Academy of Management Annals, 11*(1), 33–72.

Rovenpor, J. L. (1993). The relationship between four personal characteristics of chief executive officers (CEOs) and company merger and acquisition activity (MAA). *Journal of Business and Psychology, 8*(1), 27–55.

Ruefli, T. W., Collins, J. M., & Lacugna, J. R. (1999). Risk measures in strategic management research: auld lang syne? *Strategic Management Journal, 20*(2), 167–194.

Rumelt, R. (2022). *The Crux. How leaders become strategists.* Public Affair.

Sarala, R. M., Junni, P., Cooper, C. L., & Tarba, S. Y. (2016). A sociocultural perspective on knowledge transfer in mergers and acquisitions. *Journal of Management, 42*(5), 1230–1249.

Sarala, R. M., Vaara, E., & Junni, P. (2019). Beyond merger syndrome and cultural differences: New avenues for research on the "human side" of global mergers and acquisitions (M&As). *Journal of World Business, 54*(4), 307–321.

Schellhammer, S., Haines, R., & Klein, S. (2013). *Investigating technostress in situ: Understanding the day and the life of a knowledge worker using heart rate variability* [Paper presentation]. 2013 46th Hawaii international conference on system sciences (HICSS) (pp. 430–439). IEEE.

Schilpzand, P., Houston, L., Cho, J., (2018). Not too tired to be proactive: Daily empowering leadership spurs next-morning employee proactivity as moderated by nightly sleep quality. *Academy of Management Journal, 61,* 2367–2387. https://doi.org/10.5465/amj.2016.0936

Schriber, S., Bauer, F., & King, D. R. (2019). Organisational resilience in acquisition integration—Organisational antecedents and contingency effects of flexibility and redundancy. *Applied Psychology, 68*(4), 759–796.

SEC. (2018). *Form 8-K Current Report Pursuant to Section 13 OR 15(d) of the Securities Exchange Act of 1934.* Securities and Exchange Commission. https://www.sec.gov/files/form8-k.pdf

Seo, M. G., & Barrett, L. F. (2007). Being emotional during decision making—Good or bad? An empirical investigation. *Academy of Management Journal, 50*(4), 923–940.

Simons, T., Pelled, L. H., & Smith, K. A. (1999). Making use of difference: Diversity, debate, and decision comprehensiveness in top management teams. *Academy of Management Journal*, *42*(6), 662–673.

Sluiter, J. K., De Croon, E. M., Meijman, T. F., & Frings-Dresen, M. H. W. (2003). Need for recovery from work related fatigue and its role in the development and prediction of subjective health complaints. *Occupational and Environmental Medicine*, *60*(suppl 1), i62–i70.

Sonnentag, S. (2015). Dynamics of well-being. *Annual Review of Organizational Psychology and Organizational Behavior*, *2*(1), 261–293.

Souitaris, V., & Maestro, B. M. (2010). Polychronicity in top management teams: The impact on strategic decision processes and performance of new technology ventures. *Strategic Management Journal*, *31*(6), 652–678.

Spieler, I., Scheibe, S., Stamov-Roßnagel, C., & Kappas, A. (2017). Help or hindrance? Day-level relationships between flextime use, work–nonwork boundaries, and affective well-being. *Journal of Applied Psychology*, *102*(1), 67.

Sung, W., Woehler, M. L., Fagan, J. M., Grosser, T. J., Floyd, T. M., & Labianca, G. J. (2017). Employees' responses to an organizational merger: Intraindividual change in organizational identification, attachment, and turnover. *Journal of Applied Psychology*, *102*(6), 910.

Talaulicar, T., Grundei, J., & Werder, A. V. (2005). Strategic decision making in start-ups: The effect of top management team organization and processes on speed and comprehensiveness. *Journal of Business Venturing*, *20*(4), 519–541.

Ten Brug, H., & Sahib, P. R. (2018). Abandoned deals: the merger and acquisition process in the electricity and gas industry. *Energy Policy*, *123*, 230–239.

Teerikangas, S., Véry, P., & Pisano, V. (2011). Integration managers' value-capturing roles and acquisition performance. *Human Resource Management*, *50*(5), 651–683.

Topp, C. W., Østergaard, S. D., Søndergaard, S., & Bech, P. (2015). The WHO-5 well-being index: A systematic review of the literature. *Psychotherapy and Psychosomatics*, *84*(3), 167–176.

Treffers, T., Klarner, P., & Huy, Q. N. (2020). Emotions, time, and strategy: The effects of happiness and sadness on strategic decision-making under time constraints. *Long Range Planning*, *53*(5), 101954.

Trichterborn, A., Zu Knyphausen-Aufseß, D., & Schweizer, L. (2016). How to improve acquisition performance: The role of a dedicated M&A function, M&A learning process, and M&A capability. *Strategic Management Journal*, *37*(4), 763–773.

Ullrich, J., Wieseke, J., & Dick, R. V. (2005). Continuity and change in mergers and acquisitions: A social identity case study of a German industrial merger. *Journal of Management Studies*, *42*(8), 1549–1569.

VandenBos, G. R. (2007). *APA dictionary of psychology*. American Psychological Association.

Vaziri, H., Casper, W. J., Wayne, J. H., & Matthews, R. A. (2020). Changes to the work–family interface during the COVID-19 pandemic: Examining predictors and implications using latent transition analysis. *Journal of Applied Psychology*, *105*(10), 1073.

Vuori, N., Vuori, T. O., & Huy, Q. N. (2018). Emotional practices: How masking negative emotions impacts the post-acquisition integration process. *Strategic Management Journal*, *39*(3), 859–893.

Wake, S., Wormwood, J., & Satpute, A. B. (2020). The influence of fear on risk taking: A meta-analysis. *Cognition and Emotion*, *34*(6), 1143–1159.

Walsh, J. P. (1988). Top management turnover following mergers and acquisitions. *Strategic Management Journal*, *9*(2), 173–183.

Welch, X., Pavićević, S., Keil, T., & Laamanen, T. (2020). The pre-deal phase of mergers and acquisitions: A review and research agenda. *Journal of Management*, *46*(6), 843–878.

Wenzel, R., & Van Quaquebeke, N. (2017). The double-edged sword of big data in organizational and management research: A review of opportunities and risks. *Organizational Research Methods*, *21*(3), 548–591.

Williams, S., & Voon, Y. W. W. (1999). The effects of mood on managerial risk perceptions: Exploring affect and the dimensions of risk. *The Journal of Social Psychology*, *139*(3), 268–287.

Wright, T. A., & Bonett, D. G. (2007). Job satisfaction and psychological well-being as nonadditive predictors of workplace turnover. *Journal of Management*, *33*(2), 141–160.

Wu, M., Xu, W., Yao, Y., Zhang, L., Guo, L., Fan, J., & Chen, J. (2020). Mental health status of students' parents during COVID-19 pandemic and its influence factors. *General Psychiatry, 33*(4), 1–9.

Yakis-Douglas, B., Angwin, D., Ahn, K., & Meadows, M. (2017). Opening M&A strategy to investors: predictors and outcomes of transparency during organisational transition. *Long Range Planning, 50*(3), 411–422.

Younge, K. A., Tong, T. W., & Fleming, L. (2015). How anticipated employee mobility affects acquisition likelihood: Evidence from a natural experiment. *Strategic Management Journal, 36*(5), 686–708.

Yucha, C., & Montgomery, D. (2008). *Evidence-based practice in biofeedback and neurofeedback*: AAPB Wheat Ridge, CO.

Zacharias, N. A., Six, B., Schiereck, D., & Stock, R. M. (2015). CEO influences on firms' strategic actions: A comparison of CEO-, firm-, and industry-level effects. *Journal of Business Research, 68*(11), 2338–2346.

Zhou, L., Pan, S., Wang, J., & Vasilakos, A. V. (2017). Machine learning on big data: Opportunities and challenges. *Neurocomputing, 237*, 350–361.

Zollo, M., & Meier, D. (2008). What is M&A performance? *Academy of Management Perspectives, 22*(3), 55–77.

Zollo, M., & Singh, H. (2004). Deliberate learning in corporate acquisitions: post-acquisition strategies and integration capability in US bank mergers. *Strategic Management Journal, 25*(13), 1233–1256.

WORK–NONWORK POLICIES AND PRACTICES: THE STRATEGIC OPPORTUNITY TO CONSIDER ORGANIZATIONAL BOUNDARY MANAGEMENT STRATEGIES

Haley R. Cobb and Bradley J. Brummel

ABSTRACT

Work–nonwork policies and practices provide support for employee well-being, as well as a competitive advantage that can help differentiate organizations. However, not all work–nonwork policies and practices are effective, utilized, or relevant. In this chapter, the authors introduce "organizational boundary management strategy" as a way to leverage these policies and practices, making them more widely adopted and more effective. Organizational boundary management strategy refers to how an organization as a whole tends to support workers' work–nonwork boundaries (i.e., via segmentation, integration, or somewhere in between). Although boundary management has historically tended to focus on how individuals navigate distinctions between work and personal life, the authors extend boundary management to the organization to suggest how understanding and aligning the organization's overall boundary management strategies can support worker well-being. To expound on this, the authors present a model suggesting how organizational boundary management can be used to support worker well-being.

Keywords: Work–nonwork; work–family; boundary management; organizational policy; well-being; strategy

Stress and Well-Being at the Strategic Level
Research in Occupational Stress and Well-Being, Volume 21, 45–64
Copyright © 2024 by Emerald Publishing Limited
All rights of reproduction in any form reserved
ISSN: 1479-3555/doi:10.1108/S1479-355520230000021003

INTRODUCTION

A consultant once mentioned to the authors how great it was working for a prestigious external consulting firm, so long as one realized that the "three Ps" – pets, plants, and partners – would need to be cared for by someone other than the consultant. Over time, the large salary allowed the consultant to outsource care while they were working, which was often. Any occupational health psychology scholar hearing this story may respond with disapproval, but this specific arrangement was embraced by the consultant and was a strategic choice of the organization to cultivate workers who were primarily dedicated to work.

One can infer from this story that the organization asks their workers to minimize the boundary from work-to-nonwork, where work and work-related responsibilities take precedence over personal life (e.g., responding to e-mail late at night or on the weekends), and nonwork-to-work interruptions are mostly unacceptable (e.g., answering a call from a partner during the work day). Boundary management refers to the maintenance, navigation, and management of the distinctions between work and nonwork (e.g., Ashforth et al., 2000; Clark, 2000), and the boundaries between work and personal life are a critical linking mechanism that describes how work and nonwork should be structured on a day-to-day-basis (e.g., Ashforth et al., 2000; Edwards & Rothbard, 2000). The consulting firm in this anecdote likely attracts workers who can put their work above all other life roles and responsibilities, such as those who embody the ideal worker (e.g., Dumas & Sanchez-Burks, 2015) or prefer to integrate work into nonwork (Rothbard et al., 2005). The strategic advantage of this approach is that the organization can promise clients that workers will be available to fulfill their requests as needed, including being on-site at a moment's notice and meeting deadlines by moving any and all workers wherever and whenever needed to meet company priorities.

A notable feature of this anecdote is that the consultant offers no information about *how* workers were expected to manage any nonwork responsibilities, other than to outsource them. The organization signals to the worker what is valued (i.e., work), how they should behave (e.g., outsource care), and how daily life should be structured (e.g., prioritize work-related tasks and responsibilities) – all without mentioning work–nonwork policies or practices. Work–nonwork policies and practices have received substantial attention across the organizational sciences, with literature discussing human resources systems and their outcomes (e.g., Boon et al., 2019), the generally positive outcomes associated with worker well-being (e.g., the benefits of working flexibly, Allen et al., 2013), how formal and informal policies and practices support the work–family interface (e.g., French & Shockley, 2020), and strategic human resource management (e.g., Schuler, 1992). In this chapter, we describe how work–nonwork policies and practices additionally signal to workers how they can (and perhaps should) structure their daily work and nonwork lives, including managing the boundaries between roles, identities, domains, and responsibilities. In other words, when organizations adopt work–nonwork policies and practices that workers can use, organizations also signal how they expect work–nonwork boundaries to be managed, maintained, and navigated.

Despite its relevance, work–nonwork boundary management may be an over-looked facet of this dynamic. For example, when an organization adopts univer-sal policies that allow nonwork-related responsibilities to be outsourced without considering the individual worker's needs or preferences, the work–nonwork boundary can be overlooked, violated, and disrespected for the organization's strategic gain. A more strategic approach might involve intentional choice and transparent communication of what boundaries are supported and expected. This chapter highlights the strategic opportunity of an organization's explicit understanding and creation of what we term organizational boundary manage-ment strategy, and we focus on strategies that support integration (e.g., the blend-ing of work and nonwork) or segmentation (e.g., the separation of work and nonwork) to highlight the two extremes within boundary management. Finally, recommendations are made for leaders, managers, and other relevant stakehold-ers to adopt the policies and practices that work best for their organization as a whole and to make the implications of those choices clear for the boundary man-agement preferences of each member of their workforce. It should be noted that the focus here is on the organization's actions around organizational boundary management strategies such as identifying the strategy, supporting that strategy using policies and practices, clearly marketing and advertising the strategy and policies and practices that support it, and identifying and monitoring well-being-related outcomes. We posit that the organization should be explicit with their expected boundary management practices so as to attract and retain a work-force that reflects the values of the organization; the work–nonwork policies and practices that are marketed, adopted, and created should reflect the culture of the organization, resulting in a workforce with clearly articulated and respected work–nonwork boundaries.

ORGANIZATIONAL BOUNDARY MANAGEMENT STRATEGIES

Fig. 1 depicts the organizational boundary management strategy process described in this chapter, as it is integrated with strategic decisions regarding policy and well-being. This chapter begins with a summary of organizational boundary man-agement strategies, followed by the importance of leader buy-in, how to attract new workers that reflect the internal organizational boundary management strat-egy, and proposed well-being-related outcomes of these processes at both the individual and organizational levels. Several leverage points are also discussed, which indicate how to strengthen the link between each element. The figure also indicates that the organizational boundary management strategy must be con-tinuously tended to and leveraged at various points to maintain its effectiveness.

Stage 1: Organizational Boundary Management Strategy

Organizations can adopt a variety of work–nonwork policies and practices (see Table 1), including working flexibly (e.g., Allen et al., 2013), personalized work

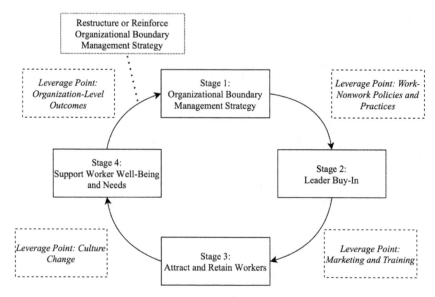

Fig. 1. Conceptual Model of Organizational Boundary Management Strategy Process.

arrangements like idiosyncratic deals (e.g., Tang & Hornung, 2015), and "bundles" of such policies and practices (e.g., Perry-Smith & Blum, 2000). The availability of work–nonwork policies and practices is used as a strategic marketing advantage, signaling to prospective and current workers that their well-being, family, and job satisfaction are valued (e.g., Ali et al., 2015; Rodríguez-Sánchez et al., 2020). According to signaling theory (e.g., Spence, 1973), organizations can "signal" their values, such as valuing gender diversity (Ali et al., 2015) and that the organization and leaders support family needs (French & Shockley, 2020) by adopting relevant policies (e.g., Casper & Harris, 2008). These work–nonwork policies and practices may also signal to potential and current workers that their well-being is valued, therefore providing a strategic advantage, especially when competitors are less likely to promote worker well-being.

However, the existence of more policies is not always better (Perry-Smith & Blum, 2000), and understanding the culture of the organization in which one works may be more informative than knowing the availability of work–nonwork policies and practices. For example, work–family cultures or family sacrifice climates can provide workers with a sense of how their personal lives may be (de) valued by the organization (e.g., French & Shockley, 2020; Kossek et al., 2001). Another way that workers can begin to understand how their personal life might be (de)valued is through the organization's expectations for boundary management. Without attending to the underlying values of worker well-being and work–nonwork boundaries, organizations may experience implementation gaps, where there is a "failure to implement [these marketed policies] and that these policies are really more window dressing than real support" (Kossek et al., 2011, p. 356). In addition to implementation gaps, certain workers may be more or less able to access flexibility policies (e.g., workers in lower-paying jobs as less able to access policy, Kossek & Lautsch, 2018) and using certain policies can result in stigma (Williams et al., 2013, 2016) or discrimination (Bobbitt-Zeher, 2011). For example, Reid (2015) found that workers who were able to hide their nonwork responsibilities received better performance evaluations; yet more men than women hid their nonwork responsibilities, partly due to men's ability to use more informal practices than women, who tended to need formal work-nonwork accommodations.

Another issue with focusing on the availability of work–nonwork policies and practices is that many of these accommodations may be better suited for major life events, such as taking parental leave during the first few months after a family has grown. Conversely, boundary management focuses on the daily micro-transitions between work and nonwork (e.g., Ashforth et al., 2000) and may have greater implications for understanding well-being in everyday life. Workers differ in their needs and preferences for segmentation or integration of work–nonwork boundaries (e.g., Kreiner, 2006), partly due to their career or family role prioritization (Ashforth et al., 2000). Workers who prioritize their work roles and responsibilities strive to protect that identity by segmenting their nonwork roles (Capitano et al., 2017), which may be strategic in a work environment where the work role should be kept separate from the nonwork role. However, workers might integrate the role they identify more strongly with (e.g., Olson-Buchanan & Boswell, 2006), meaning that workers who prioritize the work role may integrate this self into the nonwork self. This type of role prioritization may be beneficial in a workplace that values the ideal worker norm or requires organizational boundary control; it would not be strategic in a more family-supportive environment and may be considered aligned with the family sacrifice climates (e.g., Kossek et al., 2001; Nsair & Piszczek, 2021).

Given these differences at the individual level, there is a need to understand boundary management as it pertains to larger groups, such as organizations.[1] There is some scholarship on boundary management in organizations, such as boundary management norms and practices (e.g., Park et al., 2011; Richardson & Benbunan-Fich, 2011; Stanko & Beckman, 2015), and we extend this research to consider *organizational boundary management strategy*, defined as how an organization as a whole tends to support workers' work–nonwork boundaries. Organizational boundary management strategy is different from organizational norms for boundary management (e.g., Park et al., 2011) in that these strategies are enacted and supported using the explicit policies and practices available to the organization as a whole while norms are more informal and can develop slowly or out of necessity (e.g., Feldman, 1984). We suggest that organizations can, as a whole, promote either integration (e.g., allowing workers to conduct paid work in their homes) or segmentation (e.g., limiting the use of social media sites while at work) using the work–nonwork policies and practices that the organization adopts.

Leverage Point: Work–Nonwork Policies and Practices

Boundary management theories suggest that boundaries fall somewhere along the segmentation-integration continuum, where segmented boundaries are inflexible, impermeable, and keep work and nonwork separate, and integrated boundaries are more flexible, permeable, and allow work and nonwork to blend together (e.g., Ashforth et al., 2000; Clark, 2000). It is important to note neither segmenting nor integrating is overall "better" but it is accurate that individuals have their own preferences for one or the other (e.g., Kreiner, 2006). Segmentation simply means that the two domains do not influence each other, and integration can be enhancing *or* conflicting (e.g., Edwards & Rothbard, 2000). Preferences for segmentation or integration can converge with organizational supports, such as work–nonwork policies and practices, to elicit an experience of fit (e.g., Rothbard et al., 2005). Similarly, organizations themselves may have overall needs or preferences for segmenting or integrating work and nonwork (e.g., Stanko & Beckman 2015).

Table 1 highlights several work–nonwork policies and practices that an organization may use, and organizations should align these policies and practices with their organizational boundary management strategy. Organizations that require sustained worker attention and cannot afford interdomain transitions (e.g., taking a phone call from a child's school, leaving to go to a dentist appointment in the middle of the day) may wish to exert organizational boundary control. Organizational boundary control has been studied in the United States Navy and refers to the organization's attempts to control attention by tracking or limiting technology use on the job (Stanko & Beckman, 2015). This type of organizational boundary management strategy, beyond implications for worker well-being at the individual level, is applied to promote safety and security along with productivity, which would ultimately relate to organizational effectiveness. One category of policy and practice that align or could support organizational boundary control may be social media use policies. For workplaces that do not require segmentation to this degree, integration may be better suited, and integrating work and nonwork is easier, and perhaps expected, among white-collar office workers (e.g., Poppleton et al., 2008).

Flexible work arrangements are a type of organizational policy and practice that makes accommodations for workers to better manage work–nonwork responsibilities (e.g., Perlow & Kelly, 2014) and allow workers to choose where and when they complete their paid work (e.g., Allen et al., 2013; Rau & Hyland, 2002). This organizational boundary management strategy has been shown to relate to job satisfaction and organizational commitment among workers (e.g., Chen & Fulmer, 2018) and allows workers to be "always-on," which benefits organizations that are part of the global workforce. This is the first "leverage point" in the proposed model, where the organization must choose work–nonwork policies and practices that align with the identified or chosen organizational boundary management strategy. This must be done to provide workers with organizational support to enact the type of boundary best suited for success within the organization, as well as to signal to workers what is valued and supported.

Stage 2: Leader Buy-in

One limitation of the current literature on approaches to either making accommodations or creating more stringent boundaries between work and nonwork is the focus on the individual worker (e.g., Perlow & Kelly, 2014). When individuals

Table 1. Boundary Management Strategy Examples.

Work–Nonwork Policy or Practice	Definition or Main Feature	Integration/Segmentation Strategy	Work/Nonwork Prioritization
Flexplace	Changing the location in which one works (Allen et al., 2013)	Supports integration of work into nonwork (e.g., work from home)	Supports prioritization of both work and nonwork roles and responsibilities
Flextime	Changing the times at which one works (Allen et al., 2013)	Supports segmentation of nonwork into work	Supports prioritization of both work and nonwork roles and responsibilities
Organizational Boundary Control	"[T]he various ways managers at multiple levels of the organization work to capture and shape employee attention during the daily flow of work/non-work interactions" (Stanko & Beckman, 2015, p. 38)	Supports segmentation of nonwork into work	Supports prioritization of work roles and responsibilities
Flexibility i-deals	"i-deals [that] involve not only the quantity of time, i.e. numbers of working hours, but also qualitative dimensions such as where to work and when to start and stop working" (Tang & Hornung, 2015, p. 942)	Supports integration or segmentation, depending on employee's unique needs and i-deal	Supports prioritization of both work and nonwork roles and responsibilities, depending on employee's unique needs and i-deal
On-site Childcare or Caregiving	"Caregiving centers that are on site or very close to a company location and can be used by employees, often at a discounted rate" (French & Shockley, 2020, p. 210)	Supports integration of nonwork into work	Supports prioritization of both work roles and responsibilities
Reduced Work Hours	"Working fewer hours than full-time at a commensurate compensation rate" (French & Shockley, 2020, p. 210)	Supports segmentation of work into nonwork	Supports prioritization of both work and nonwork roles and responsibilities
Social Media Policies	Policies about what employers can do with respect to an employee's use of personal social media	Supports segmentation of nonwork into work	Supports prioritization of work roles and responsibilities
Drug Use	Prohibitions of drug use both during work and outside of work based on enforcement mechanisms and rules	Supports segmentation of nonwork into work	Supports prioritization of work roles and responsibilities
Political or Social Position Statements	Organization position statements on what it believes should be legal in society or what political activism workers can engage in	Supports both segmentation and integration, depending on the statement or policy	Typically supports prioritization of work roles and responsibilities

Note. The policies and practices listed here are not exhaustive, and this table does not include work–nonwork policies and practices that assist with large life transitions, such as parental leave (e.g., for supporting workers at the birth of a child) or the Family and Medical Leave Act (e.g., for supporting workers who need to tend to personal or family medical issues). Aligned with boundary management theories, the policies and practices listed here support the *daily* work–nonwork transitions that workers engage in, rather than major or temporary life changes.

are slated to make their own accommodations, such as by working from home when they need to care for a sick child, the organization may not actually support these choices, and their policy uptake may be stigmatized or discriminated against (e.g., Bobbitt-Zeher, 2011). Aligned with signaling theory (Spence, 1973), top management and leaders signal to current and future workers what organizational boundary management strategies should be adopted, leading to culture change, value congruence, and relevant organization-level well-being indicators, and leaders must be consistent in their support of these policies (Salas-Vallina et al., 2021). Signaling theory, while originally applied to job applicants, suggests that overt behaviors that organizations engage in (e.g., making certain work–nonwork policies available) demonstrate what they inherently value (e.g., value workers' well-being), which is less explicit or visible (Spence, 1973).

As stated, making these policies and practices available to workers is only one piece of the puzzle; French and Shockley (2020) suggest that workers are "more likely to use family-friendly policies when their organization and supervisors are supportive of family needs … and when employees feel they can use policies without negative career consequences" (p. 211). Piszczek and Berg (2020) suggest that source attribution additionally influences the experience of fit between work–family practices and individual preferences, meaning *who* provides access to the work–nonwork policy or practice and *why* it is being offered are important moderators. Similarly, Casper and Harris (2008) use signaling theory to suggest that policy availability is related to increased organizational commitment and decreased turnover intentions through perceived organizational support. Both models suggest that policy availability is only one piece of the puzzle relating to desired well-being-related outcomes; the leader is a critical component in both models. We posit that the policies and practices that an organization implements must align with their organizational boundary management strategy *and* be supported by leadership.

Leaders can also demonstrate their support and mitigate policy use backlash (e.g., stigma and discrimination) by understanding their own boundary management preferences and strategies and how their personal needs align with the organization's overall boundary management strategies. One of the authors of this chapter worked with a company that told their workers that they had the flexibility to handle family and life issues as they arose, meaning that workers could come in late or leave early if there was a need. However, when a leader in this company utilized their own need for working flexibly, he snuck in the side door upon coming to work so that no one would see him. The message that is signaled by the leader is that it is not acceptable to invest in one's personal life. In an organization where the organizational boundary management strategy is supported by leadership, the leader would not have felt the need to hide their use of the flexibility policy.

Leverage Point: Marketing and Training

After identifying the organization's boundary management strategy and the work–nonwork policies and practices that support it, leaders must uphold the balance between the two. This allows organizations to go beyond adopting work–nonwork policies and practices to having leaders that signal and align with what is valued regarding the work–nonwork interface. Marketing the organizational boundary management strategy is an important leverage point, which includes more than simply marketing what work–nonwork policies and practices would be available to prospective workers. Prospective workers should know what policies and practices would be available to them, how to access them, who among the current workforce uses the policies, and what organization-level outcomes are associated with policy use. This is also important for the current workforce so that all workers, both prospective and incumbent, are aware of the work–nonwork policies and practices that are available to them and how their use of these will align with the organizational boundary management strategy. Marketing is further supported by leader buy-in and leaders signaling that these policies are used, that work–nonwork is valued (in some capacity), and what that looks like for workers on a day-to-day basis. When leaders do not know that a policy exists or how to help workers use the practice, then the strategy is undermined at the implementation point. By understanding policies and practices to this degree, job applicants and current workers should be better able to decide how their daily work–nonwork lives will be managed at this particular organization, which will relate to the need and uptake of these formal or informal organizational supports.

Stage 3: Attract and Retain Workers

As the prior stages in our proposed model are fulfilled, attracting new workers and retaining those who align with the organizational boundary management strategy will be more effective. Classically, work and nonwork were considered separate domains, although this distinction has largely been dispelled (e.g., Kanter, 1977). Research has shown that boundary management has implications for the attraction of individuals to certain workplaces or jobs (e.g., Rothbard et al., 2005), and the attraction-selection-attrition framework suggests that individuals are attracted to certain organizations, selected for specific jobs, and leave the job when the organization no longer supports their individual needs (e.g., Schneider, 1987). When this occurs on a large scale, "the people make the place" and shape the organization's culture and overall behavior (Schneider, 1987). By marketing the organization's boundary management strategy, organizations will be more transparent than their variety of work–nonwork policies and practices allows them to be.

For example, Rothbard et al. (2005) found that workers who prefer to integrate experienced greater job satisfaction and organizational commitment when their workplace offered on-site childcare, yet those who preferred to segment did not experience the same improvements in well-being. Unfortunately, Casper and Harris (2008) found that having access to, but not using, dependent care or flexible scheduling can result in negative attitudes among workers, which may contribute to the aforementioned stigma and discrimination associated with certain policy use. Thus, in order to effectively attract and retain workers who will use and benefit from these policies, as well as minimize backlash of policy use, organizations should strategically market their organizational boundary management strategies, therefore maintaining the cyclical nature of this process.

Leverage Point: Culture Change

At the time of this writing, Tesla recently announced that workers in supervisory positions will need to work in-office for a minimum of 40 hours per week, stating that they ask their factory workers to work *more* hours than that (Franklin, 2022), and this is seen as a strategic decision (Main, 2022). This decision to allow flexibility only after workers have reached a certain threshold of work in the physical office is counter to many other companies' strategic decisions, with recent estimates suggesting over two-thirds of the global workforce desiring more flexibility (Richardson & Antonello, 2022). However, the cultural statement is clear for the workers and the leaders. They can make individual choices and leadership demands that are aligned with the organization as a whole without wondering if someone in a different unit is doing something else. The choice becomes to stay in the culture or find a different organization.

This chapter was also written as the Supreme Court of the United States overturned the federal right to an abortion that was based in *Roe* v. *Wade*. This change has the potential to influence many workers' personal *and* professional lives as laws are likely to vary based on states (Harmon, 2022). Workers may turn to their organization for support, such as relocating to a state that provides comprehensive reproductive healthcare (e.g., Cerullo, 2022), or workers may choose to work for companies that better align with their personal values, as the ruling is intertwined with religion, philosophy, and spirituality (Crary, 2022). Some organizations have publicly stated their support for the previous legal protections of women's reproductive rights, thereby signaling their values in this political turmoil. Some workers may find these statements to be supportive, while others may find them to be work–nonwork boundary violations regardless of their personal values and beliefs. Having public organizational statements on political issues forces the integration of work and nonwork, which may be unappealing for workers who prefer segmentation. Overall, these statements or organizational supports, while signaling the values of the organization, should also align with transparency and other work–nonwork policies and practices.

The broader notion of personal life as *private* begs the question of how much an organization can encroach upon that boundary. The need for privacy may be due to individual differences and preferences, but it may also be due to their need to hide a stigmatized identity and avoid discrimination (Khachatryan et al., 2022). For others, a chronic health condition may require the treatment of a stigmatized drug, such as marijuana (e.g., Reinarman et al., 2011), and organizations may take away religious freedoms, including indigenous workers' drug usage for spiritual reasons (e.g., Farris & Lorence, 1995). Political beliefs and affiliation can be censured by organizations (e.g., Zilber, 2022), and legal cases such as *Barbulescu* v. *Romania* demonstrate how far organizations will go when encroaching on workers' personal, private lives overall (e.g, Jervis, 2018). These examples all point to the organizational boundary management strategy as critical to worker well-being, including physical, psychological, and social well-being. In these instances, organizations have the opportunity to create boundaries that might support or hurt their workers; for example, an organization could destigmatize medical marijuana use by allowing workers with a legitimate medical need to avoid penalties. Yet, some workers may find this type of explicit statement an overreach of the workplace and may also be unfairly put into place.

It is crucial that the organization understands the needs and preferences of their workers such that these elements are in alignment. By implementing the recommendations outlined in this chapter, an organization can avoid potential missteps when the organization, its leaders, and its members understand and support the organization's boundary management strategy. Upholding privacy in certain situations, such as family planning, medical treatment and conditions, and political affiliation, organizations allow workers to bring their best professional self to work, including one that is supported by the work–nonwork policies and practices available to them when they are needed. By making these expectations explicit and transparent on a day-to-day basis via organizational boundary management strategy, workers will be better able to use formal and informal support systems with minimal backlash.

Stage 4: Support Worker Well-being and Needs

It may be a strategic decision for the organization to incorporate organizational boundary management strategies and work–nonwork policies and practices that minimize the boundary between work-to-nonwork by effectively reducing workers' nonwork lives (e.g., not having time for personal life, outsourcing care). Workers in an organization like this will likely be engaged in work-related responsibilities for more hours of the day and spend more time thinking about work. It is possible that this is a strategic decision for organizations that require workers to be consistently engaged with work, such as management consultants who respond to client needs at all hours of the day, active members of the military who are deployed, or on-call medical doctors. However, this need may only be temporary, and it is an untruth that any worker is devoid of a personal life, requiring no time away from work.

Similarly, reducing one's personal life may also have detrimental effects on well-being. Extending the workday is related to increased stress and reduced recovery experiences from work (e.g., Dettmers et al., 2016); overwork culture is related to decreased work engagement and increased workaholism (e.g., Mazzetti et al., 2016), with workaholism itself being related to a host of negative outcomes (e.g., Clark et al., 2016); and long work hours reduces firm-level productivity (e.g., Delmez & Vandenberghe, 2018). Similarly, having a life outside of work means that workers have an opportunity to experience work–nonwork enrichment, which is related to various beneficial work-related outcomes (e.g., job satisfaction, affective commitment, McNall et al., 2010). Therefore, while it may seem like a strategic decision to minimize workers' personal lives, protecting the workers' personal lives may be *more* beneficial, and therefore more strategic, especially in the long term.

The strategic decision to minimize nonwork lives will do more than harm worker well-being; it is also likely to undermine other strategic initiatives, such as diversity, equity, and inclusion efforts, as expecting minimal nonwork involvement will disproportionately (and negatively) affect workers with childcare responsibilities, women, and lower-income workers, including those workers with intersectional identities (e.g., women in lower-paying jobs with childcare responsibilities, e.g., Acker, 1990; Coltrane et al., 2013; Kossek et al., 2021; Williams et al., 2016). For example, Kossek and Lautsch (2018) found that lower-status workers (e.g., lower wages) may experience many benefits from working flexibly yet have few opportunities to access policies that allow them to work flexibly. Additionally, while reviewing over 200 sex discrimination cases, Bobbitt-Zeher (2011) found that "discretionary policy application and enforcement" (p. 781) led to unequal treatment of women and men workers. Organizations should be able to recognize and cultivate the organizational boundary management strategy that attracts and retains workers that reflect their most productive, healthy workforce, which differs from the notion that eliminating personal life would serve as a strategic decision or providing subsets of workers with access to policies and practices.

Outsourcing care of the "three Ps," as suggested by the organization described at the beginning of this chapter, upholds the ideal worker norm, and transparency regarding organizational boundary management strategy should not be used to maintain harmful work–nonwork relationships. The expectation that work should come before all else in the ideal worker norm does not appear to yield long-term benefits to workers or organizations and should be forgotten (Peters & Blomme, 2019). This type of work–nonwork arrangement can also perpetuate workplace inequities that undermine women's involvement in the workforce (e.g., Bobbitt-Zeher, 2011, Reid, 2015) and other less-privileged workers (e.g., lower-status workers, Kossek & Lautsch, 2018). By being transparent, organizations should be able to reduce these workplace inequities, reduce policy implementation gaps, and minimize the stigma and discrimination of those who need to use these work–nonwork policies. Those workers who criticize or look unfavorably upon policy use should consider the larger organizational boundary management strategy and determine if policy use detracts from that strategy – or is it their own personal biases about who the "ideal worker" should be that contributes to their negative perceptions of policy use.

Leverage Point: Organization-level Outcomes

This also necessitates the evaluation of policy and practice use and implementation. For organizations to evaluate whether their choices in this space are having the desired strategic effects they will need to measure if organization-level outcomes improve as workers have available policies and use these policies. Deciding what organization-level outcomes should be measured over what time frame when considering these strategies is necessary to support the decisions. These are important questions that each organization must answer for themselves, but organizations should think beyond the bottom line. Unfortunately, the lack of strong "business case" evidence [for work–nonwork policies] is worrisome because organizations may decide to back away from work–family policies and initiatives if the [return on investment] evidence is not clear. (Kelly et al., 2008, p. 14)

This type of evidence is not always the goal of occupational health psychology, as this literature boasts that "happy workers are productive workers" (e.g., Taris & Schreurs, 2009). Certainly, occupational health psychology scholars understand the financial costs associated with an unhealthy workforce. Recent estimates suggest that over $225 billion are spent on worker illness and injury in the United States (Stinson, 2015). But workers spend close to nine hours a day on the weekdays on work-related activities (Bureau of Labor Statistics, 2022), and workers in the United States work more than most workers in the industrialized West (US workers are only surpassed in their annual working hours by Mexico, Costa Rica, Chile, South Korea, Greece, and Poland; Organization for Economic Co-Operation and Development, 2022). Thus, the workplace is a key instigator shaping the work–nonwork interface, ultimately structuring how workers enact their everyday lives. By understanding each stage of this model, including the benefits to worker well-being, organizations will also be informed to reinforce their organizational boundary management strategies or restructure those boundaries to better align with the needs of their workforce.

THE STRATEGIC OPPORTUNITY

The model in Fig. 1 is cyclical in nature, meaning that understanding organizational boundary management strategy should be an ongoing task where the organizational boundary management strategy is either reinforced or restructured. This effort can be supported by strategic human resources management and other leaders. The components of the proposed model should be carefully monitored, as workers will turnover, worker needs will change, and other strategic initiatives will develop. It is also possible that an organization will learn from this process and determine that new work–nonwork policies and practices should be implemented or that a new organizational boundary management strategy is required to meet other strategic decisions. Thus, the organizational boundary management strategy is dynamic and must be tended to as such.

There are many ways that the proposed model could benefit organizations, including return on investment for policies that may have costs associated with them (e.g., costs for on-site childcare) and improvements to worker and workplace well-being, both in the short and long term. Table 2 provides a depiction of what could go right – and wrong – for an organization that does (not) pay attention to its organizational boundary management strategy. We use this simply to illustrate our main points in a creative manner, and the stories are mostly fiction. In these stories, we demonstrate the benefit of identifying the organizational boundary management strategy, as well as the opportunity costs of avoiding such efforts. Fig. 2 also provides example policies and practices that can be adopted to promote either segmentation or integration. This chart can be used to help

Table 2.   Jane and John's Work–Nonwork Boundaries.

Jane and John: Scenario A	Jane and John: Scenario B
Jane and John are marketing specialists at a mid-size company in the Midwest United States. They were hired with the same skillset, for the same position, on the same day. They have both successfully worked for this company for five years. Both are committed to their careers and are high work role identity salience and work long hours. They both also enjoy personal time away from work with friends and family, and they enjoy talking about personal life with many of their coworkers. They, like many of their coworkers, prefer integrating work into nonwork	

In Scenarios A and B, Jane and John's employer recently worked with an organizational development (OD) consultant who helped the company develop their five-year strategic plan.

The leaders of the company working with the consultant take their advice to learn the organization's boundary management strategy. After several weeks of data collection, the company learns that their workers appreciate flexibility (e.g., working remotely three days a week, being able to start and stop work based on productivity and other life demands). Findings from the data also suggest that the organization should adopt new work–nonwork policies and practices, as the ones they have in place aren't used or don't meet the needs of their workforce. They also learn that a large portion of the workforce appreciates learning about their coworkers' personal lives, such as their hobbies, volunteer opportunities, and families, but the workers do not feel that they are able to discuss their personal lives with leadership, as leaders tend to focus only on work-related tasks and do not allude to their own personal lives. Overall, the OD consultant recommends that the organization adopt an organizational boundary management strategy that facilitates integration of both work into nonwork *and* nonwork into work

In *Scenario A*, leadership takes the OD consultant's information and suggestions to heart. Based on this information, leadership works with the Human Resources Department to create new work–nonwork policies and practices that support the needs of their workforce, and the leaders include all workers in this endeavor, including full-time and hourly staff. Day to day, leaders start working from home more regularly, and they are open with their subordinates about how they spent their weekend – not working. They also celebrate their subordinates' nonwork achievements and respect when an employee would rather not share details about their personal life	In *Scenario B*, leadership scoffs at the OD consultant's information and suggestions. Leadership staunchly believes that they should not be responsible for their workforces' personal lives, and that their workers should be "at work when they are working, which should be often." The company doesn't make any changes and continues to market their vast array of work–nonwork policies and practices, despite knowing that those supports don't actually help their workers. They continue business as usual, but now the organization has explicitly seen their leadership ignore their needs and desires for shaping their daily work and nonwork lives
Six months after this change, both Jane and John need to take time away from work: John and his partner are adopting a baby and Jane has been diagnosed with breast cancer. Both of their supervisors had recently used formal policies to take time away from work. Both employees felt equally comfortable when asking their supervisors about what organizationally sponsored support they could use to manage this growing nonwork responsibility. At their comfort and discretion, both Jane and John share the reasons for their needs with their coworkers and are met with growing social support and concern for their well-being	Six months after this event, both Jane and John need to take time away from work: John and his partner are adopting a baby and Jane has been diagnosed with breast cancer. John talks to his supervisor and is able to use two weeks of paid time off to accommodate his nonwork need. His supervisor asks few questions, preferring to know as little as possible about John's personal needs. Jane, meanwhile, cannot have her personal life needs met with informal support and needs to use formal policy. Her supervisor scoffs at this need and asks if she can take meetings from her chemotherapy appointments

(Continued)

Table 2.   (*Continued*)

Jane and John: Scenario A	Jane and John: Scenario B
Six months after their use of formal policy, Jane and John both feel that they are able to meet the everyday demands of the work and personal lives. They also know their coworkers and supervisors on a more personal level, which improves their interpersonal work relationships. They both serve on hiring committees within their departments, and both employees are able to respond confidently when job applicants ask about their work culture	Six months after their use of formal and informal policy, Jane and John both feel devalued and burned out. After missing out on a promotion because she "regularly leaves five minutes early" – which is due to her doctor's office closing at 5 PM on weekdays – Jane quickly accepts new employment at a larger, more successful competitor. John remains at the marketing company and climbs the corporate ladder; under the guise of "success," he chooses to ignore personal life needs

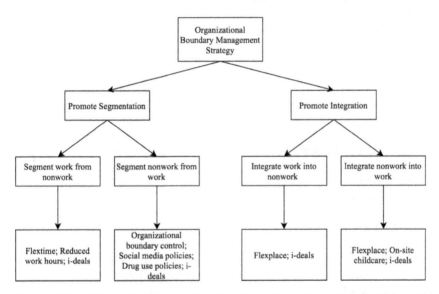

Fig. 2.   Work–Nonwork Policy and Practice Chart. *Note.* Examples of policies and practices listed; this is a non-exhaustive diagram.

leaders determine which boundary management strategy could be supported by several policies and practices. For example, an organization that determines that integration may be a strategic opportunity may identify various policies and practices pertaining to the flexibility that their organization would benefit from.

IMPLICATIONS AND FUTURE DIRECTIONS

There are several implications that our chapter details, including work–nonwork policy and practice use, boundary management at the organization-level, worker well-being, and organization-level outcomes. While much of the work–family literature focuses on individuals, as does boundary management scholarship, we extend this thinking to the organization. Overall, by making organizational boundary management strategy transparent, organizations should be better able to adopt the work–nonwork policies and practices that best support their workforce, marketing these supports to future job incumbents and therefore creating and upholding an organizational culture that supports a particular boundary management strategy. This can only be done by leader buy-in; therefore, this implication also affects leadership and other decision-making persons in the organization. We hope that this also reduces policy implementation gaps and mitigates any stigma or discrimination associated with policy use, as policies should be intended to support worker well-being, not thwart it. Ultimately, then, worker well-being should improve overall, which would improve organization-level outcomes. As we have stated, these outcomes are unique for each organization, but may include outcomes such as increased organizational effectiveness, decreased healthcare costs, and decreased turnover (and its associated costs).

There are also missed opportunity costs of not aligning work–nonwork policies and practices with organizational boundary management strategy. When workers cannot use – or feel that they will be penalized for using – work–nonwork policies and practices, the organization is paying for support that go unused. Additionally, this misalignment may cause workers to seek their own respite from work without policies or without the proper policies; when the organization does not address any specific plans for boundary management, they are leaving it to the employee and supervisor to figure out without organizationally sponsored support. If there is no specific culture, policies, or procedures, or these policies are not universally celebrated, then people with privilege, such as those workers with access to support systems and resources that may be outside of the scope of what the organization formally provides, are most likely to arrange the best deals for them. Lastly, turnover is known to be incredibly costly to the organization; recent estimates suggest that turnover costs almost twice that of the individual workers' annual salary (McFeely & Wigert, 2022). While it is a small facet of the work–nonwork interface, providing transparency around expectations for boundary management, including values, tolerated behaviors, and the daily structuring of work and nonwork life, we posit that organizations will be better able to avoid these opportunity costs.

Future research must corroborate our suggestions and propositions. While based on the literature, the proposed model is not based on primary data collected by the authors, and we recommend that organization-level and multilevel research will be best suited to test the model, determining how strategically including boundary management can support the organization's strategic management. This can also be linked to strategic human resources management (e.g., Schuler, 1992). Regardless of the work–nonwork-friendly policy or practice being adopted by an organization, it is important to recognize that each worker will have their own boundary management preferences, and organizations must respect and support these individual differences. It is unrealistic to assume that all workers in an organization will be able to adhere to the organization's boundary management strategy at all times, but by being transparent, strategically marketing, and using leaders to signal what boundary management strategies are generally supported, organizations may be better suited to support their workers and create healthier workplaces. We hope that this chapter has provided actionable recommendations, as well as highlighted potential backlash to be aware of, for organizations, top management, and leaders to create an environment where work–nonwork boundaries can be respected, supported, and valued.

CONCLUSION

Extending boundary management to the organization-level is a useful future direction, and we have presented a conceptual model describing how organizational boundary management strategy can be used to support worker well-being. As research has detailed how work–nonwork policies and practices do not always have the intended outcomes (i.e., supporting well-being), we hope that this chapter has provided readers with a novel way to consider how organizations can better support worker well-being and bring a new level of effectiveness to these policies and practices.

NOTE

1. While this chapter focuses on the organization as the focal group for a boundary management strategy, it is worth noting that many organizations have subsets of workers with different working arrangements and needs due to the work that they perform. Therefore, organizations will want to consider whether they need different strategies for these different categories of workers and how to clearly communicate those differences to the workers. Often there are different expectations for hourly and salaried workers in work–nonwork boundaries. For example, one of the authors experienced an organization that only applied drug testing policies to workers in the shop and not to those who worked in the office. When considering the organizational boundary management strategy, it is therefore important to consider the universality of this position.

REFERENCES

Acker, J. (1990). Hierarchies, jobs, bodies: A theory of gendered organizations. *Gender & Society, 4*(2), 139–158.

Ali, M., Metz, I., & Kulik, C. T. (2015). The impact of work–family programs on the relationship between gender diversity and performance. *Human Resource Management, 54*(4), 553–576.

Allen, T. D., Johnson, R. C., Kiburz, K. M., & Shockley, K. M. (2013). Work–family conflict and flexible work arrangements: Deconstructing flexibility. *Personnel Psychology, 66*(2), 345–376. https://doi.org/10.1111/peps.12012

Ashforth, B. E., Kreiner, G. E., & Fugate, M. (2000). All in a day's work: Boundaries and micro-role transitions. *Academy of Management Review, 25*(3), 472–491. https://doi.org/10.5465/amr.2000.3363315

Bobbitt-Zeher, D. (2011). Gender discrimination at work: Connecting gender stereotypes, institutional policies, and gender composition of workplace. *Gender & Society, 25*(6), 764–786. https://doi.org/10.1177/0891243211424741

Boon, C., Den Hartog, D. N., & Lepak, D. P. (2019). A systematic review of human resource management systems and their measurement. *Journal of Management, 45*(6), 2498–2537.

Bureau of Labor Statistics. (2022, June 23). *American Time Use Survey – 2021 Survey Results*. Retrieved July 19, 2022, from https://www.bls.gov/news.release/pdf/atus.pdf

Capitano, J., DiRenzo, M. S., Aten, K. J., & Greenhaus, J. H. (2017). Role identity salience and boundary permeability preferences: An examination of enactment and protection effects. *Journal of Vocational Behavior, 102*, 99–111. https://doi.org/10.1016/j.jvb.2017.07.001

Casper, W. J., & Harris, C. M. (2008). Work-life benefits and organizational attachment: Self-interest utility and signaling theory models. *Journal of Vocational Behavior, 72*(1), 95–109. https://doi.org/10.1016/j.jvb.2007.10.015

Cerullo, M. (2022, June 27). Google tells U.S. workers they can move to States where abortion is legal: Report. *CBS News*. Retrieved July 18, 2022, from https://www.cbsnews.com/news/abortion-google-workers-can-move-to-states-where-abortion-is-legal-roe-v-wade/

Chen, Y., & Fulmer, I. S. (2018). Fine-tuning what we know about employees' experience with flexible work arrangements and their job attitudes. *Human Resource Management, 57*(1), 381–395. https://doi.org/10.1002/hrm.21849

Clark, S. C. (2000). Work/family border theory: A new theory of work/family balance. *Human Relations, 53*(6), 747–770. https://doi.org/10.1177/0018726700536001

Clark, M. A., Michel, J. S., Zhdanova, L., Pui, S. Y., & Baltes, B. B. (2016). All work and no play? A meta-analytic examination of the correlates and outcomes of workaholism. *Journal of Management, 42*(7), 1836–1873. https://doi.org/10.1177/0149206314522301

Coltrane, S., Miller, E. C., DeHaan, T., & Stewart, L. (2013). Fathers and the flexibility stigma. *Journal of Social Issues, 69*(2), 279–302. https://doi.org/10.1111/josi.12015

Crary, D. (2022, June 24). Faith leaders react with joy, anger to Roe's reversal. *PBS*. Retrieved July 18, 2022, from https://www.pbs.org/newshour/politics/faith-leaders-react-with-joy-anger-to-roes-reversal

Delmez, F., & Vandenberghe, V. (2018). Long working hours make us less productive but also less costly. *Labour, 32*(4), 259–287. https://doi.org/10.1111/labr.12128

Dettmers, J., Vahle-Hinz, T., Bamberg, E., Friedrich, N., & Keller, M. (2016). Extended work availability and its relation with start-of-day mood and cortisol. *Journal of Occupational Health Psychology, 21*(1), 105–118. https://doi.org/10.1037/a0039602

Dumas, T. L., & Sanchez-Burks, J. (2015). The professional, the personal, and the ideal worker: Pressures and objectives shaping the boundary between life domains. *Academy of Management Annals, 9*(1), 803–843. https://doi.org/10.5465/19416520.2015.1028810

Edwards, J. R., & Rothbard, N. P. (2000). Mechanisms linking work and family: Clarifying the relationship between work and family constructs. *Academy of Management Review, 25*(1), 178–199.

Farris, M. P., & Lorence, J. W. (1995). *Employment Division v. Smith and the need for the Religious Freedom Restoration Act. Regent University Law Review, 6*. 65–102.

Feldman, D. C. (1984). The development and enforcement of group norms. *Academy of Management Review, 9*(1), 47–53. https://doi.org/10.2307/258231

Franklin, J. (2022, June 2). Elon Musk tells employees to return to the office 40 hours a week – or quit. *NPR*. Retrieved July 19, 2022, from https://www.npr.org/2022/06/01/1102513281/elon-musk-tesla-return-to-work

French, K. A., & Shockley, K. M. (2020). Formal and informal supports for managing work and family. *Current Directions in Psychological Science, 29*(2), 207–216.

Harmon, S. (2022, July 6). *U.S. Supreme Court takes away the constitutional right to abortion*. Center for Reproductive Rights. Retrieved July 18, 2022, from https://reproductiverights.org/supreme-court-takes-away-right-to-abortion/

Jervis, C. E. (2018). Barbulescu v Romania: Why there is no room for complacency when it comes to privacy rights in the workplace. *Industrial Law Journal, 47*(3), 440–453. https://doi.org/10.1093/indlaw/dwy002

Kanter, R. M. (1977). *Work and family in the United States: A critical review and agenda for research and policy*. Russell Sage Foundation.

Kelly, E. L., Kossek, E. E., Hammer, L. B., Durham, M., Bray, J., Chermack, K., Murphy, L. A., & Kaskubar, D. (2008). Getting there from here: research on the effects of work–family initiatives on work–family conflict and business outcomes. *Academy of Management Annals, 2*(1), 305–349. https://doi.org/10.1080/19416520802211610

Khachatryan, K., Graml, R., Hagen, T., Ziegler, Y., & Herman, R. A. (2022). Sexual identity management of working lesbian women. *Organization Management Journal*, *19*(3), 99–109. https://doi.org/10.1108/OMJ-01-2021-1133

Kossek, E. E., Baltes, B. B., & Matthews, R. A. (2011). How work–family research can finally have an impact in organizations. *Industrial and Organizational Psychology*, *4*(3), 352–369. https://doi.org/10.1111/j.1754-9434.2011.01353.x

Kossek, E. E., Colquitt, J. A., & Noe, R. A. (2001). Caregiving decisions, well-being, and performance: The effects of place and provider as a function of dependent type and work–family climates. *Academy of Management Journal*, *44*(1), 29–44. https://doi.org/10.5465/3069335

Kossek, E. E., & Lautsch, B. A. (2018). Work–life flexibility for whom? Occupational status and work–life inequality in upper, middle, and lower level jobs. *Academy of Management Annals*, *12*(1), 5–36. https://doi.org/10.5465/annals.2016.0059

Kossek, E. E., Perrigino, M., & Rock, A. G. (2021). From ideal workers to ideal work for all: A 50-year review integrating careers and work–family research with a future research agenda. *Journal of Vocational Behavior*, *103504*, 1–18. https://doi.org/10.1016/j.jvb.2020.103504

Kreiner, G. E. (2006). Consequences of work–home segmentation or integration: A person–environment fit perspective. *Journal of Organizational Behavior*, *27*(4), 485–507. https://doi.org/10.1002/job.386

Main, K. (2022, June 7). Elon Musk used the 3 C's rule to give Tesla staff an ultimatum. It's a crucial lesson in leadership. *Inc.com*. Retrieved July 19, 2022, from https://www.inc.com/kelly-main/elon-musk-leadership-3-cs-rule.html

Mazzetti, G., Schaufeli, W. B., Guglielmi, D., & Depolo, M. (2016). Overwork climate scale: Psychometric properties and relationships with working hard. *Journal of Managerial Psychology*, *31*(4), 1–17. https://doi.org/10.1108/JMP-03-2014-0100

McFeely, S., & Wigert, B. (2022, June 10). *This fixable problem costs U.S. businesses $1 trillion*. Gallup.com. https://www.gallup.com/workplace/247391/fixable-problem-costs-businesses-trillion.aspx

McNall, L. A., Nicklin, J. M., & Masuda, A. D. (2010). A meta-analytic review of the consequences associated with work–family enrichment. *Journal of Business and Psychology*, *25*(3), 381–396. https://doi.org/10.1007/s10869-009-9141-1

Nsair, V., & Piszczek, M. (2021). Gender matters: The effects of gender and segmentation preferences on work-to-family conflict in family sacrifice climates. *Journal of Occupational and Organizational Psychology*, *94*(3), 509–530. https://doi.org/10.1111/joop.12361

Olson-Buchanan, J. B., & Boswell, W. R. (2006). Blurring boundaries: Correlates of integration and segmentation between work and nonwork. *Journal of Vocational behavior*, *68*(3), 432–445. https://doi.org/10.1016/j.jvb.2005.10.006

Organization for Economic Co-Operation and Development. (2022). *Average annual hours actually worked per worker*. OECD.Stat. Retrieved July 19, 2022, from https://stats.oecd.org/index.aspx?DataSetCode=ANHRS

Park, Y., Fritz, C., & Jex, S. M. (2011). Relationships between work–home segmentation and psychological detachment from work: The role of communication technology use at home. *Journal of Occupational Health Psychology*, *16*(4), 457–467. https://doi.org/10.1037/a0023594

Perlow, L. A., & Kelly, E. L. (2014). Toward a model of work redesign for better work and better life. *Work and Occupations*, *41*(1), 111–134. https://doi.org/10.1177%2F0730888413516473

Perry-Smith, J. E., & Blum, T. C. (2000). Work–family human resource bundles and perceived organizational performance. *Academy of Management Journal*, *43*(6), 1107–1117.

Peters, P., & Blomme, R. J. (2019). Forget about 'the ideal worker': A theoretical contribution to the debate on flexible workplace designs, work/life conflict, and opportunities for gender equality. *Business Horizons*, *62*(5), 603–613. https://doi.org/10.1016/j.bushor.2019.04.003

Piszczek, M. M., & Berg, P. (2020). HR policy attributions: Implications for work–family person–environment fit. *Human Resource Management Review 30*(2), 1–12. https://doi.org/10.1016/j.hrmr.2019.100701

Poppleton, S., Briner, R. B., & Kiefer, T. (2008). The roles of context and everyday experience in understanding work–non-work relationships: A qualitative diary study of white- and blue-collar workers. *Journal of Occupational and Organizational Psychology*, *81*, 481–502. https://doi.org/10.1348/096317908X295182

Rau, B. L., & Hyland, M. A. M. (2002). Role conflict and flexible work arrangements: The effects on appli-
cant attraction. *Personnel Psychology*, *55*(1), 111–136. https://doi.org/10.1111/j.1744-6570.2002.
tb00105.x

Reid, E. (2015). Embracing, passing, revealing, and the ideal worker image: How people navigate expected
and experienced professional identities. *Organization Science*, *26*(4), 997–1017.

Reinarman, C., Nunberg, H., Lanthier, F., & Heddleston, T. (2011). Who are medical marijuana
patients? Population characteristics from nine California assessment clinics. *Journal of
Psychoactive Drugs*, *43*(2), 128–135. https://doi.org/10.1080/02791072.2011.587700

Richardson, N., & Antonello, M. (2022). *People at work 2022: A global workforce view* (pp. 1–47). ADP
Research Institute. https://www.adpri.org/wp-content/uploads/2022/04/PaW_Global_2022_
GLB_US-310322_MA.pdf

Richardson, K., & Benbunan-Fich, R. (2011). Examining the antecedents of work connectivity
behavior during non-work time. *Information and Organization*, *21*(3), 142–160. https://doi.
org/10.1016/j.infoandorg.2011.06.002

Rodríguez-Sánchez, J. L., González-Torres, T., Montero-Navarro, A., & Gallego-Losada, R. (2020).
Investing time and resources for work–life balance: The effect on talent retention. *International
Journal of Environmental Research and Public Health*, *17*(6), 1920–1934. https://doi.org/10.3390/
ijerph17061920

Rothbard, N. P., Phillips, K. W., & Dumas, T. L. (2005). Managing multiple roles: Work–family policies and individuals' desires for segmentation. *Organization Science*, *16*(3), 243–258. https://doi.
org/10.1287/orsc.1050.0124

Salas-Vallina, A., Alegre, J., & López-Cabrales, Á. (2021). The challenge of increasing employees' well-
being and performance: How human resource management practices and engaging leadership
work together toward reaching this goal. *Human Resource Management*, *60*(3), 333–347.

Schneider, B. (1987). The people make the place. *Personnel Psychology*, *40*(3), 437–453.

Schuler, R. S. (1992). Strategic human resources management: Linking the people with the strategic
needs of the business. *Organizational Dynamics*, *21*(1), 18–32.

Spence, A. M. (1973). Job market signaling. *The Quarterly Journal of Economics*, *87*(3), 335–374.

Stanko, T. L., & Beckman, C. M. (2015). Watching you watching me: Boundary control and capturing
attention in the context of ubiquitous technology use. *Academy of Management Journal*, *58*(3),
712–738. https://doi.org/10.5465/amj.2012.0911

Stinson, C. (2015, January 28). *Worker illness and injury costs U.S. employers $225.8 billion annually*.
CDC Foundation. https://www.cdcfoundation.org/pr/2015/worker-illness-and-injury-costs-
us-employers-225-billion-annually-:~:text=Worker Illness and Injury Costs U.S. Employers
%24225.8 Billion Annually,-January 28, 2015&text=The Centers for Disease Control,States,
or %241,685 per employee

Tang, Y., & Hornung, S. (2015). Work–family enrichment through i-deals: Evidence from Chinese
employees. *Journal of Managerial Psychology*, *30*(8), 940–954. https://doi.org/10.1108/JMP-02-
2013-0064

Taris, T. W., & Schreurs, P. J. (2009). Well-being and organizational performance: An organizational-
level test of the happy-productive worker hypothesis. *Work & Stress*, *23*(2), 120–136. https://doi.
org/10.1080/02678370903072555

Williams, J. C., Berdahl, J. L., & Vandello, J. A. (2016). Beyond work-life "integration". *Annual Review
of Psychology*, *67*, 515–539. https://doi.org/10.1146/annurev-psych-122414-022710

Williams, J. C., Blair-Loy, M., & Berdahl, J. L. (2013). Cultural schemas, social class, and the flexibility
stigma. *Journal of Social Issues*, *69*(2), 209–234. https://doi.org/10.1111/josi.12012

Zilber, A. (2022, June 16). New York Times boss to journalists: Don't use Twitter to 'vet grievances'.
New York Post. Retrieved July 18, 2022, from https://nypost.com/2022/06/15/nyt-boss-to-jour-
nalists-dont-use-twitter-to-vet-grievances/

PUBLICLY INVULNERABLE, PRIVATELY LONELY: HOW THE UNIQUE INDIVIDUAL AND STRUCTURAL CHARACTERISTICS OF THEIR ORGANIZATIONAL ROLE CONTRIBUTE TO CEO LONELINESS

Sarah Wright, Anthony Silard and Alaric Bourgoin

ABSTRACT

In this chapter, the authors explore the notion of loneliness in the CEO role. Traditionally, leaders are portrayed as possessing plentiful personal and social resources whereas lonely people are portrayed as socially and personally lacking, and so the notion of being lonely in a leadership position seems counterintuitive. The authors explore the elements of the CEO role and discuss the various ways the position can induce or perpetuate loneliness. The authors review the research on loneliness in relation to the CEO role and lay the foundation for future research in this underdeveloped area. The authors propose that loneliness is likely to develop when CEOs either are new to the leadership role or enact negative individual behaviors and might be felt more acutely during times of poor performance, criticism, and difficult decisions. The authors discuss implications and suggestions for future research.

Keywords: CEO role; loneliness; leadership; social isolation; CEO relationships; lonely at the top

Stress and Well-Being at the Strategic Level
Research in Occupational Stress and Well-Being, Volume 21, 65–79
Copyright © 2024 by Emerald Publishing Limited
All rights of reproduction in any form reserved
ISSN: 1479-3555/doi:10.1108/S1479-355520230000021004

INTRODUCTION

Traditionally, the literature on organizational leadership portrays leaders in a strong and positive light. Chief Executive Officers (CEOs), in particular, are expected to influence people to achieve objectives, work to maintain cooperative relationships, enlist support from others, and have a broad and influential social network (Yukl, 2012). The traits required to achieve these outcomes include possessing high self and social confidence, self and other awareness, and social adeptness (Humphrey, 2012; Yukl, 2018). Individuals in CEO positions are therefore typically highly interconnected in their social networks, and these networks are precisely what makes them powerful and influential. Therefore, the concept of loneliness among CEOs seems counterintuitive and antithetical to the notion of leadership. On the one hand, leaders are portrayed as having plentiful personal and social resources (and so should not be lonely), whereas lonely people are portrayed as socially and personally lacking (therefore, they are unlikely to be successful in leadership positions). Moreover, lonely people are likelier than non-lonely people to report shyness, low social competence, emotional instability, and low self-esteem (Cacioppo & Patrick, 2008). Given such socially counterproductive attributes, it would suggest that someone experiencing loneliness would be unlikely to obtain or sustain a senior executive role, as their personal qualities would inhibit their ability to maintain such a position.

Despite such contradictions, CEOs report feeling lonely and isolated in their roles (e.g., Daskal, 2022; Saporito, 2012) and it is this experiential aspect that we are interested in exploring. The purpose of this chapter is to explore the working conditions of CEOs and examine the emotional, social, political, and situational dimensions of the role that might help us better understand the connection between the CEO role and their experience of loneliness. We argue that researching and understanding CEO loneliness is a neglected area of research and requires attention to help raise awareness of the potentially harmful effects of loneliness in senior leadership roles.

UNDERSTANDING LONELINESS

Unlike social isolation, which is an objective and emotionally neutral experience, loneliness is the subjective, aversive, undesirable feeling derived from a lack of desired meaningful relationships (Wright & Silard, 2021). To be clear, the type of loneliness we are referring to throughout this chapter is the subjective feeling of social disconnectedness, not physical social isolation. Research suggests that loneliness has little to do with the quantity of a person's social interaction (Peplau & Perlman, 1982); instead, it reflects the perceived emotional and social deficiencies in a person's relationships that cause distress (Sergin & Kinney, 1995; Wright & Silard, 2021). We are focusing on the latter notion of perceived deficiencies in this chapter.

The deficiency model of loneliness purports that loneliness occurs when there is a discrepancy or mismatch between an individual's desired and actual social relations (Peplau & Perlman, 1982). That is, an individual yearns for more or better-quality relationships than they currently have. This model is represented in standardized measures of loneliness with items such as "I am unhappy doing so many things alone" and "I feel shut out and excluded by others." The deficiency model represents the foundation for most loneliness scholarship in general population studies. However, in terms of understanding CEO loneliness, it is important to recognize that social deficiency might not be felt as distressing or painful because of the expectation that social distance is inherent in the role. Rather, loneliness is more likely to be experienced as a subjective representation of a CEO's feelings of alienation and abandonment in times of need or duress than simply "not having people around." This important addendum to the deficiency model reminds us that in order to achieve relational fulfillment (i.e., a match between desired and actual relationships) we need to feel understood, authentically supported, heard, and valued by those with whom we want to be connected.

Wright and Silard (2021) propose a process model of loneliness to help understand the potential predictors of loneliness in organizational contexts. Within the model is the notion that there are various intrapersonal, interpersonal, and contextual factors that might contribute to an individual's feeling of relational fulfillment, such as personality factors, psychological safety, and organizational climate. While it is difficult to isolate any one potential trigger for loneliness, we can use this model – along with recent research on leader loneliness (Gabriel et al., 2021; Rokach, 2014; Silard & Wright, 2020) – to identify some of the individual and contextual factors that might create a pathway toward understanding relational deficiencies in the CEO role. Particular attention might be given to both the differences between how leader and follower loneliness are experienced (Silard & Wright, 2021) and cognitive and affective leadership strategies that effectively reduce loneliness and enable leaders to experience more meaningful social connections in the workplace (Gabriel et al., 2021).

CEO LONELINESS

Statistics about CEOs' levels of loneliness are scarce. There is literature on loneliness and occupational status (Bell et al., 1990; Silard & Wright, 2022) and conceptual research on leader loneliness (Silard & Wright, 2020), but such research is not specified to CEOs. Several decades ago, Katz and Kahn (1978) suggested that leaders at the top echelons of the organization are the most distant from the membership of the organization, contributing to a perception of psychological distance between leader and followers (Popper, 2013). Despite this line of theorizing, loneliness is largely absent from the leader distance literature. There is also very little anecdotal evidence beyond the saying that "it's lonely at the top," which assumes that loneliness is an inevitable byproduct of possessing positional authority. The scarcity of research may be due to the taboo nature of loneliness, particularly for those in prominent positions who are perceived to have more power and access to social resources. Indeed, loneliness carries a significant social stigma, as a lack of social connection is generally deemed an undesirable life condition. However, loneliness does not respect the boundaries of prominence nor any other contextual factor such as age, gender, race, marital status, or socio-economic standing. CEOs may not necessarily have a strong personal social network despite being well-networked because of their formal position. Therefore, a CEO's position might be experienced as a double-edged sword in that they have amplified social and political influence within the organization but also real or perceived isolation and alienation from others. Furthermore, the notion of the idealized leader in Western cultures as strong and independent may lead to pressure to conceal vulnerability and negative emotions from those around them (Rokach, 2004). Throughout this chapter, we explore how leader distance might be a loneliness-provoking factor in the practice of the CEO role.

THE CEO ROLE

Leaders often manage multiple conflicting demands, goals, and responsibilities – including many goals, tasks, and responsibilities that conflict with each other (Smith & Lewis, 2011) – and tend to experience more stress and time pressures than followers (Boyatzis et al., 2006; Mintzberg, 1973). As a result, they have less time to cognitively process and regulate complex emotions such as loneliness (Kaplan et al., 2014). Another challenge for leaders is that they must perform more varied forms of emotion regulation than followers (Humphrey, 2012; Vuori & Huy, 2020), including the emotion of loneliness. As leaders of their organizations, CEOs are tasked with influencing people to achieve specific goals and are responsible for coordinating others toward the pursuit and achievement of those goals. At times, the outcomes of CEOs are anticipated to produce are expected in the face of a highly competitive, turbulent, and rapidly changing environment dominated by interpersonal mistrust where relationships are used for personal gain (Avolio et al., 2009; Gittell & Douglass, 2012; Yukl, 2012). As such, a CEO might have to oscillate between diplomacy and aggression, thus "running with the hare and hunting with the hounds" on any given day. However, we also speculate whether CEO loneliness is experientially different from other types of loneliness. Although loneliness can affect anyone at any time, we believe the contextual nature of the CEO role may create greater vulnerability to suppressed feelings of loneliness.

WHY DO WE CARE ABOUT CEO LONELINESS?

Due to the stigma associated with voicing loneliness, it is often experienced without ever being verbalized (Rokach, 2012). This scenario may be especially true in positions of power and leadership, where discussions of psychological welfare are often private, masked, or taboo, with loneliness often being observed as a personal failure (Yalom, 1998). Furthermore, lonely leaders may conceal and avoid discussing their feelings with others, thus missing out on opportunities to learn from similar experiences. Paradoxically, however, despite the often private nature of loneliness, its effects can manifest in very public ways.

Loneliness can affect an individual's psychological, emotional, and physical health and can have a highly negative impact on existing relationships. The effects of loneliness on physical health are vast and unsettling and include less effective physiological repair mechanisms (Cacioppo et al., 2003); reduced sleep efficiency, and more time awake after the onset of sleep, which decreases resilience while awake (Cacioppo et al., 2002); augmented risk of heart attack (Brown et al., 2018); increased heart rate and cardiac contractility (Cacioppo et al., 2002); and lower functioning of the cardiovascular, immune, and endocrine systems, which leads to reduced blood pressure regulation (Hawkley et al., 2010; Uchino et al., 1996).

Psychologically, loneliness sufferers experience greater levels of depression, negative self-assessment, and poorer marital quality, and loneliness tends to precipitate a number of mental illnesses (Cacioppo et al., 2010). In a nutshell, loneliness is associated with many adverse outcomes and stands in great contrast to the physiological and psychological benefits of high-quality social connections (Heaphy & Dutton, 2008). Recognizing the conditions in which CEOs feel lonely will help contribute to a more nuanced understanding of some of the more severe consequences of loneliness, such as depression and anxiety (Baumeister & Tice, 1990).

Understanding the research on loneliness outcomes begs the question of whether such general correlates between psychological and physical health and loneliness apply to CEOs. Taken together, all of the factors identified by Rokach (1989) as the most common antecedents of loneliness, such as loss, inadequate social support, crisis, and personal shortcomings, can apply to a CEO because of the role they assume in the organization. Specifically, leaders often become less attuned to their followers over time (Hogg, 2001; Keltner et al., 2003), resulting in their being shifted into an outgroup where they are socially avoided, resulting in an increased sense of loneliness. In addition, adjusting to the CEO role often requires an internal existential crisis in which a leader's deeper values become subordinated to organizational norms, resulting in increased feelings of self-isolation and, potentially, loneliness (Silard & Wright, 2020).

LONELINESS-PROVOKING FACTORS IN THE CEO ROLE

For many CEOs, loneliness might be accepted as inherent to the role, and the phrase "it's lonely at the top" echoes their reality. For others, loneliness is a distant concept with which they do not personally identify. Although loneliness is not a binary concept, it would be helpful to know why some CEOs feel lonely in their role whereas others escape the feeling. Do individual characteristics perpetuate or help create an immunity to loneliness in the CEO role? Similarly, are there environmental and contextual factors that drive problematic relationships and loneliness, or conversely, provide relational protection?

Individual Characteristics

There is much literature, spanning several decades, on the individual antecedents of loneliness in the general population. We know, for example, that lonely people often have very negative self-perceptions and can be heavily impaired when it comes to establishing social ties. These two attributes suggest the lonely person may possess personal deficiencies, have psychological adjustment issues, interpersonal inadequacies, or socially undesirable attributes such as unlikable-ness (Lau & Gruen, 1992). On the other hand, CEOs typically possess high self-confidence, self-awareness, and social adeptness, which augurs well for their management of loneliness (Gabriel et al., 2021). Further, in the general population, the traits common to CEOs typically result in satisfying and meaningful relationships with others (Graen & Uhl-Bien, 2005). Therefore, we need to look more closely at the CEO role and how individual characteristics might contribute to loneliness in the presence of others.

Personality traits of CEOs such as rigidity, perfectionism, and the need to be in control – as well as the "Dark Triad" of leadership traits, which are Machiavellianism, narcissism, and psychopathy – might all contribute to social disconnection (Grijalva et al., 2015; Owens et al., 2015). People tend to avoid others who are self-interested and express low levels of empathy, which is characteristic of these Dark Triad traits (labeled as such because they often highly overlap; Harms et al., 2011). As a consequence, and given the tendency of individuals with Dark Triad traits to be drawn to leadership roles, CEOs often end up feeling socially isolated and lonely—in no small part because people tend to become less emotionally expressive around those who possess such traits. CEOs are typically highly self-monitoring (Eby et al., 2003) and conscious of the image they need to project in order to control the social dynamic of their organization.

At the same time, however, there is the leadership aspiration of being "truly authentic" to their peers and employees, which is at odds with managing others' perceptions of their image being one of control and confidence (Silard & Wright, 2020). In this respect, using their social adeptness to create and maintain at least some trusting and intimate relationships might be key to warding off feelings of disconnection. Such relationships might be with their board chair, key investors, other board members, and other top executives, although the impression management associated with such relationships, for some CEOs, may prohibit such close relationships from developing. Such a hypothesis favors the notion that whenever genuine feelings of friendship are present, loneliness is muted in consciousness (Mijuskovic, 1979).

We suggest the relationship between CEO personality traits and loneliness is moderated by the presence of a few close relationships that may provide a protective buffer. In terms of future research, we also propose that the expression of positive individual characteristics, such as social and emotional adeptness and relational skills associated with high-quality connections, may lead to more fulfilling and trusting relationships with colleagues that can help prevent loneliness. On the other hand, we believe a CEO who does not report feeling lonely but displays negative characteristics associated with the Dark Triad and is socially isolated, might be masking or suppressing loneliness.

Structural Characteristics

Another potential loneliness-provoking factor is the culture of the organization. The short-term focus of "blame and shame" of not reaching revenue or fundraising targets, for instance, might be isolating for some, especially in competitive, fear-driven cultures (Wright, 2005).

Economic Performance and Loneliness

There are several potential explanations for the connection between economic performance and loneliness. Most explanations derive from the foundation that because people are socially and emotionally interconnected in the workplace, their performance is also interconnected. Therefore, the firm's business and financial performance might be another dominant contextual factor determining CEOs' feelings of loneliness. Specifically, when the firm's performance is challenged and the CEO is the target of criticism, they might experience stronger feelings of loneliness.

Poor performance puts increased pressure on CEOs to uphold their responsibility in front of the organization's collective. They may feel a strong need to project an image of confidence to employees and shareholders despite their inner doubts and knowledge of upcoming risks. This projection puts CEOs in a "position of keeping secrets" – of feeling that they are the only ones who know the truth about the situation and cannot share such information with anyone without jeopardizing the group's morale and future performance. Such protection may create a sense of disconnection from their employees. Additionally, the need to maintain confidence in the face of negative performance may require CEOs to practice surface acting, a form of emotional labor that often results in isolation from self and others (Grandey et al., 2015; Humphrey et al., 2015). Such emotional performances accentuated in periods of low economic performance, are likely to accentuate loneliness (Silard & Wright, 2020). There seems to be, therefore, a specific sense of loneliness associated with projecting confidence in complex, challenging business, and economic situations.

Poor performance also puts pressure on the CEO's tenure as it increases the probability of them being judged as incompetent by their employees, board members, and investors, and ultimately, losing their jobs. CEOs may start doubting their ability to do the job, thus falling into a spiral of decreased self-confidence and social hypervigilance, resulting in a more significant social disconnection from those around them. Much more so than lower-status organizational actors, leaders may also become increasingly concerned about the impact a public failure will have on their "personal brand" and future employability. In this case, CEOs might start planning alternative career pathways, which reduces their identification with the organization and their sense of ownership and might lead to a disconnection between their trajectory and that of the collective. Once again, this dissociation with the firm puts CEOs in a position of keeping secrets and increases their likelihood of feeling compelled to engage in surface acting, augmenting their loneliness (Silard & Wright, 2020).

"Ivory Tower Syndrome" and the Difficulty of Obtaining Honest Feedback

Almost without exception, CEOs are performance-driven individuals concerned with being positively evaluated in the practice of their job by their employees, peer executives, and board members. CEOs, therefore, are continuously looking for feedback on their performance and more indirect cues of positive perception. Such feedback reinforces their self-image: it allows them to ascertain whether they are creating an appropriate work climate among their teams and whether they are "staying in touch with the field" and procuring information about market needs to make informed business decisions (Bourgoin & Harvey, 2018). However, leadership advancement often leads to non-reciprocal relationships with subordinates. As CEOs climb the corporate ladder, they may find it increasingly difficult to collect and receive transparent feedback, *both downwards and upwards*. This difficulty is because leaders are expected to provide support, although it is usually unavailable to them (Blake & Mouton, 1978; Moyle, 1998).

In addition, leaders are expected to provide empathy and emotional support to their employees, who usually do not reciprocate it (Toegel et al., 2013). This asymmetry of socio-emotional support often fosters the feeling within leaders as though their followers do not care about them. In practice, the disconnect often emerges because followers perceive leaders' empathy as in-role behavior – an attempt to motivate them in line with the first core mechanism of transformational leadership, individualized consideration (Avolio et al., 1991; Lehmann-Willenbrock et al., 2015). Leaders, on the other hand, deem their empathy toward followers as extra-role behavior – actions taken because they care about their followers (Toegel et al., 2013). As such, they expect reciprocation that, due to this perceptual disconnect, is not forthcoming. Given that social rejection is a well-researched antecedent of loneliness (Cacioppo & Patrick, 2008), with even a brief experience of social rejection at times propelling someone into a downward spiral that includes feelings of hopelessness, increased aggression, binge eating, and irrational, risky behaviors (Twenge et al., 2002), it should be no surprise that leaders end up feeling lonely after such organizational interactions.

This lack of feedback might be perceived as a vulnerability for CEOs, as it potentially creates a sense of disconnection from others and blindness to the reality of the field. This situation is metaphorically known as the "ivory tower syndrome," which describes how senior organizational leaders can become unaware and ignorant of their employees' demands and challenges. Such disconnection may be experienced as a sense of estrangement or rejection from others in the organization and create or reinforce feelings of loneliness.

Downwards, CEOs may experience employees who no longer dare say what they think in front of the "big boss" – due to concerns over not being relevant enough, being too operational, or that the CEO does not have time for such matters. Employees often reduce their willingness to voice concerns, for instance, when the leader is extraverted (Grant et al., 2011), as many leaders are given the social interaction pressures of their role (Yukl, 2018). This disconnect can shock those newly appointed to the CEO role and heighten the peerless nature of the position. Once again, CEOs' hierarchical positions produce asymmetric relations with employees that may increase their power/social distance and might create a sense that relationships are simply instrumental to achieving goals. In other words, the power dynamics of the superior-subordinate relationship may impede direct feedback and increase CEOs' general sense of loneliness.

Upwards, CEOs might notice an impoverishment of feedback merely based on the minimal circle of people available with whom to interact: the chairman, some board members, and a few top executives. Seeking feedback from these figures may be interpreted as a weakness or a lack of control, which CEOs are unlikely to want to project upwards. Seeking feedback can also interfere with the dynamics of the CEO-board relationship, which can be complex and perilous for CEOs. For example, seeking feedback from board members may negatively impact the CEOs managerial discretion, as board members might feel more entitled to give advice and intervene directly in the company's operations. The CEO role, therefore, can be impoverishing from a feedback perspective. This paucity of feedback may engender a lack of trust and vulnerability in relationships that creates a sense of isolation in the CEO role.

Unpacking the "Burden of Power" and the Loneliness of Making Difficult Decisions

One of the main contentions of this chapter is that CEOs tend to experience loneliness in relation to the specific dynamics and responsibilities of their role – including, among others, the "burden" of power and the need to make difficult strategic decisions. The formal power associated with the CEO role comes with a certain level of responsibility that puts pressure on the individual who occupies the role. The literature on power and the hierarchical position of the CEO suggests that the burden of power may create a social distance that increases the risk of loneliness (Keltner et al., 2003). At a macro level, power distance may influence the ability to attain satisfying relationships, with high power distance cultures accentuating the professional distance between leaders and followers (Hofstede et al., 1990). However, this cultural dimension may also reduce the desire for social relations, as the professional distance may be expected in high power distance cultures and, hence, experienced as less subjectively distressing. The quantity and quality of actual social relationships may be more directly influenced by a leader's psychological distance from subordinates. At the organizational level, social distance incorporates aspects of power distance and is referred to in the leadership literature as "perceived differences in status, rank, authority, social standing, and power, which affect the degree of intimacy and social contact that develop between followers and their leader" (Antonakis & Atwater, 2002, p. 682). Given that followers who have more frequent interactions with their leader are likely to have closer relationships, it is not surprising that the concept of social distance between leaders and their followers has been at the center of many leadership theories (see Bligh & Riggio, 2012). Some literature suggests that leader distance can be beneficial to an organization's culture by reducing "micromanagement" issues and other interpersonal problems (Howell et al., 2005). However, most of the literature points to leader distance fostering negative outcomes including poor relationship development and follower perceptions of leaders as uninvolved or disengaged (Erskine, 2012).

By necessity, most CEOs desire and embrace the power that comes with the role. However, power might be perceived as an opportunity, an unwelcome constraint, merely a requirement of the job, or a burden. As part of their role, CEOs are often required to broker power (Hambrick, 2007). Because there is a collective, strategic process to facilitate, they are often required to arbitrate between opposing views among top executives. Facilitating such arbitration can lead to fractious relationships and political divisiveness. A socially adept and emotionally skilled individual might be able to navigate the kind of political dynamics inherent in the role and protect new and existing relationships. Others might not possess the traits or skills to avoid relational fractures, such as a violation of trust and mismanaged loyalty.

The responsibility for making very difficult or high-stakes decisions can have an isolating effect on some CEOs, primarily when the outcomes of those decisions are complex, ambiguous, or have deleterious consequences for colleagues or employees. Decisions that challenge the organization's core values or threaten its identity may weigh on its future prosperity or imply a significant change in the business model. Such radical decisions can disrupt relationships and wreak havoc on relationship-building blocks such as trust, loyalty, mutuality, and respect, which in turn reduces the quality of relationships (Stephens et al., 2011). In the face of such decisions, some CEOs might have very few people to talk to. This limitation could exist because they need to preserve confidential or commercially sensitive information, and confessing their fears and vulnerabilities to their colleagues may be beyond the boundaries of those relationships. Despite the collective decision-making process of the Board, having the final say in these decisions often means the CEO bears the entire burden of the responsibility associated with their power role. This heightened accountability in and of itself may augment CEO loneliness, as moments in which an individual must make high-stakes decisions without adequate and attentive socioemotional support from others may be conducive of loneliness.

Perhaps one of the most difficult and potentially isolating decisions are those that affect employees and colleagues, such as layoffs or having to terminate the employment of a close colleague whose interests no longer serve the firm. Those CEOs who feel lonely in their role are potentially less likely to express doubt, vulnerability, or uncertainty in front of their board members which tends to produce tension and discourage high-quality relationships and a collective engagement in decision-making. Ultimately, bearing such heavy responsibility alone can leave CEOs feeling uncomfortable and isolated in this accountability, which is likely to induce loneliness.

OUTCOMES OF CEO LONELINESS

Along with individual psychological and physiological effects, CEO loneliness may also augur ill for organizations, as lonely individuals are less likely to make judicious social decisions (Cacioppo et al., 2015). In fact, research indicates that the lonelier one is the less able they are to perform complex cognitive tasks such as planning, decision-making, and abstract thinking (Cacioppo & Patrick, 2008). These research findings have implications for how we can understand CEO's performance in relation to social cognition and loneliness. However, like loneliness itself, the loneliness-performance connection is complex. We have discussed above how poor organizational performance can influence CEO loneliness. However, in a vicious cycle, poor performance can also be an outcome of loneliness. Decades of research, from a multitude of scholarly perspectives, indicate that loneliness can distort social cognition, influence an individual's interpersonal behavior (Baumeister et al., 2008), and adversely affect aspects of organizational performance (Lam & Lau, 2012; Ozcelik & Barsade, 2018). The central theoretical claim here is that loneliness reduces performance levels partly as a result of lowered executive functioning, such as reduced mental speed and accuracy. Empirical research has shown that perceived social isolation affects logical reasoning and concentration in that "isolates" attempt fewer problem-solving exercises and make more mistakes when doing so (Baumeister et al., 2002). Future research can help better understand the link between organizational performance and loneliness, and how loneliness itself might affect the quality of problem-solving and decision-making in the CEO role.

FUTURE RESEARCH DIRECTIONS

This chapter has outlined several contributing factors that may induce or perpetuate loneliness in the CEO role, and throughout we have appealed for future research. Much of our ideas are exploratory and therefore there is room for empirical work. To our knowledge, there is no empirical study that unpacks CEO loneliness beyond the anecdotal evidence of the popular press, and any research effort going in that direction is likely to provide original insights. Although doing empirical research with CEOs is a challenge in itself (Cycyota & Harrison, 2006; Ma et al., 2021), we encourage researchers to go beyond proxies and unobtrusive measures to gather primary data on CEO loneliness.

In particular, research on the link between CEO's personality traits – such as narcissism, or the "dark triad" – and loneliness could yield interesting results, as they may explain the counter-intuitive nature of loneliness for individuals who are deeply embedded in social networks. Another topic of crucial interest could be the relationship between hierarchical status as well as power/social distance and loneliness in the CEO population, as existing research on this topic in the leadership literature has yielded mixed results (Waytz et al., 2015; Wright, 2012). Also, the bulk of the popular press papers on CEO loneliness enumerate tactics through which CEOs can deal with their negative feelings by acknowledging their emotional vulnerability and finding appropriate support systems (e.g., Cooper & Quick, 2003; Kets de Vries, 2019; Saporito, 2012). However, the effects of these tactics on CEO loneliness have never been systematically tested empirically. Therefore, a promising avenue for future research could be to investigate the impact of self-disclosure and deep-acting, as well as the impact of various peer and support groups on CEO loneliness.

Finally, the elements put forth in this chapter suggest that CEOs loneliness may be largely induced by structural and contextual factors related to CEOs tasks and to the performance of their organization. This helps contextualize prior accounts and seminal definitions of loneliness which are dominantly embedded in the psychology and sociology literatures (e.g., Peplau & Perlman, 1982; Weiss, 1973). It may be that CEOs do not experience loneliness as subjective negative emotion deriving from a lack of meaningful relationships and a deprived need to belong, thereby offering a promising opportunity for future research to advance a more task-related and/or organizational approach to loneliness at the top.

CONCLUSION

Poor relationships marked by a lack of trust and mutuality can adversely affect health and well-being (Heaphy & Dutton, 2008). CEOs are more likely than the average working person to experience more harmful relational acts such as criticism, betrayal, rejection, or other social wounds. Thus, it stands to reason that leaders may be vulnerable and suffer negative consequences when the relationships they previously formed in organizations change or threaten to change as they move into the CEO role and cement the hierarchy (Mao, 2006). It is our hope that this chapter will prove useful to others intrigued with the individual and structural characteristics of the CEO role that can potentially produce loneliness.

REFERENCES

Antonakis, J., & Atwater, L. (2002). Leader distance: A review and a proposed theory. *Leadership Quarterly*, *13*(6), 673–704.

Avolio, B. J., Waldman, D. A., & Yammarino, F. J. (1991). Leading in the 1990s: The four I's of transformational leadership. *Journal of European Industrial Training*, *15*(4), 9–16.

Avolio, B., Walumbwa, F., & Weber, T. J. (2009). Leadership: Current theories, research, and future directions. *Management Department Faculty Publications*, *37*, 421–449.

Baumeister, R. F. (2008). Free will in scientific psychology. *Perspectives on Psychological science*, *3*(1), 14–19.

Baumeister, R. F., Twenge, J. M., & Nuss, C. K. (2002). Effects of social exclusion on cognitive processes: Anticipated aloneness reduces intelligent thought. *Journal of Personality and Social Psychology*, *83*(4), 817–827.

Baumeister, R. F., & Tice, D. M. (1990). Point-counterpoints: Anxiety and social exclusion. *Journal of Social and Clinical Psychology*, *9*(2), 165–195.

Bell, R. A., Roloff, M. E., Van Camp, K., & Karol, S. H. (1990). Is it lonely at the top? Career success and personal relationships. *Journal of Communication*, *40*(1), 9–23.

Blake, R. R., & Mouton, J. S. (1978). What's new with the grid?. *Training and Development Journal*, *32*(5), 3–8.

Bligh, M. C., & Riggio, R. E. (Eds.). (2012). *Exploring distance in leader–follower relationships: When near is far and far is near*. Routledge.

Bourgoin, A., & Harvey, J. F. (2018). Professional image under threat: Dealing with learning–credibility tension. *Human Relations*, *71*(12), 1611–1639.

Boyatzis, R., Smith, M., & Blaize, N. (2006). Developing sustainable leaders through coaching and compassion. *Academy of Management Learning & Education*, *5*(1), 8–24.

Brown, E. G., Gallagher, S., & Creaven, A. M. (2018). Loneliness and acute stress reactivity: A systematic review of psychophysiological studies. *Psychophysiology*, *55*(5), e13031.

Cacioppo, S., Grippo, A. J., London, S., Goossens, L., & Cacioppo, J. T. (2015). Loneliness: Clinical import and interventions. *Perspectives on Psychological Science, 10*(2), 238–249.

Cacioppo, J. T., Hawkley, L. C., & Berntson, G. G. (2003). The anatomy of loneliness. *Current Directions in Psychological Science, 12*(3), 71–74.

Cacioppo, J. T., Hawkley, L. C., Berntson, G. G., Ernst, J. M., Gibbs, A. C., Stickgold, R., & Hobson, J. A. (2002). Do lonely days invade the nights? Potential social modulation of sleep efficiency. *Psychological Science, 13*(4), 384–387.

Cacioppo, J. T., Hawkley, L. C., & Thisted, R. A. (2010). Perceived social isolation makes me sad: 5-year cross-lagged analyses of loneliness and depressive symptomatology in the Chicago Health, Aging, and Social Relations Study. *Psychology and Aging, 25*(2), 453.

Cacioppo, J. T., & Patrick, W. (2008). *Loneliness: Human nature and the need for social connection.* WW Norton & Company.

Cooper, C. L., & Quick, J. C. (2003). The stress and loneliness of success. *Counselling Psychology Quarterly, 16*(1), 1–7.

Cycyota, C. S., & Harrison, D. A. (2006). What (not) to expect when surveying executives: A meta-analysis of top manager response rates and techniques over time. *Organizational Research Methods, 9*(2), 133–160.

Daskal, L. (2022). *How to cope with the loneliness of leadership.* https://www.lollydaskal.com/leadership/how-to-cope-with-the-loneliness-of-leadership/.

Eby, L. T., Cader, J., & Noble, C. L. (2003). Why do high self-monitors emerge as leaders in small groups? A comparative analysis of the behaviors of high versus low self-monitors 1. *Journal of Applied Social Psychology, 33*(7), 1457–1479.

Ernst, J., & Cacioppo, J. (1998). Lonely hearts: Psychological perspectives on loneliness. *Applied & Preventative Psychology, 8*, 1–22.

Erskine, L., (2012). Defining relational distance for today's leaders. *International Journal of Leadership Studies, 7*(1), 96–113.

Gabriel, A. S., Lanaj, K., & Jennings, R. (2021). Is one the loneliest number? A within-person examination of the adaptive and maladaptive consequences of leader loneliness at work. *Journal of Applied Psychology, 106*(10), 15–17.

Gittell, J. H., & Douglass, A. (2012). Relational bureaucracy: Structuring reciprocal relationships into roles. *Academy of Management Review, 37*(4), 709–733.

Grandey, A., Rupp, D., & Brice, W. (2015). Emotional labor threatens decent work: A proposal to eradicate emotional display rules. *Journal of Organizational Behavior, 36*, 770–785.

Graen, G. B., & Uhl-Bien, M. (1995). Relationship-based approach to leadership: Development of leader-member exchange (LMX) theory of leadership over 25 years: Applying a multi-level multi-domain perspective. *The Leadership Quarterly, 6*(2), 219–247.

Grant, A. M., Gino, F., & Hofmann, D. A. (2011). Reversing the extraverted leadership advantage: The role of employee proactivity. *Academy of Management Journal, 54*(3), 528–550.

Grijalva, E., Harms, P. D., Newman, D. A., Gaddis, B. H., & Fraley, R. C. (2015). Narcissism and leadership: A meta-analytic review of linear and nonlinear relationships. *Personnel Psychology, 68*(1), 1–47.

Hambrick, D. C. (2007). Upper echelons theory: An update. *Academy of Management Review, 32*(2), 334–343.

Harms, P., Spain, S., & Hannah, S. (2011). Leader development and the dark side of personality. *The Leadership Quarterly, 22*, 495–509.

Hawkley, L. C., Thisted, R. A., Masi, C. M., & Cacioppo, J. T. (2010). Loneliness predicts increased blood pressure: 5-year cross-lagged analyses in middle-aged and older adults. *Psychology and Aging, 25*(1), 132.

Heaphy, E., & Dutton, J. (2008). Positive social interactions and the human body at work: Linking organizations and physiology. *The Academy of Management Review, 33*(1), 137–162.

Hofstede, G., Neuijen, B., Ohayv, D., & Sanders, G. (1990). Measuring organizational cultures: A qualitative and quantitative study across twenty cases. *Administrative Science Quarterly, 35*(2), 286–316.

Hogg, M. (2001). A social identity theory of leadership. *Personality and Social Psychology Review, 5*(3), 184–200.

Howell, J. M., Neufeld, D. J., & Avolio, B. J. (2005). Examining the relationship of leadership and physical distance with business unit performance. *The Leadership Quarterly*, *16*(2), 273–285.

Humphrey, R. H. (2012). How do leaders use emotional labor? *Journal of Organizational Behavior*, *33*(February), 740–744.

Humphrey, R. H., Ashforth, B. E., & Diefendorff, J. M. (2015). The bright side of emotional labor. *Journal of Organizational Behavior*, *36*(6), 749–769.

Kaplan, S., Cortina, J., Ruark, G., LaPort, K., & Nicolaides, V. (2014). The role of organizational leaders in employee emotion management: A theoretical model. *Leadership Quarterly*, *25*(3), 563–580.

Katz, L., & Kahn, P. (1978). *Leadership in action*. https://www.tlu.ee/~sirvir/Leadership/Leadership%20Models/skills_approach_robert_katz.html

Keltner, D., Gruenfeld, D., & Anderson, C. (2003). Power, approach, and inhibition. *Psychological Review*, *110*(2), 265–284.

Kets de Vries, M. F. R. (2019, March 14). *The cure for the loneliness of command*. INSEAD Knowledge. https://knowledge.insead.edu/leadership-organisations/cure-loneliness-command

Lau, S., & Gruen, G. E. (1992). The social stigma of loneliness: Effect of target person's and perceiver's sex. *Personality and Social Psychology Bulletin*, *18*(2), 182–189.

Lam, L. W., & Lau, D. C. (2012). Feeling lonely at work: Investigating the consequences of unsatisfactory workplace relationships. *The International Journal of Human Resource Management*, *23*(20), 4265–4282.

Lehmann-Willenbrock, N., Meinecke, A. L., Rowold, J., & Kauffeld, S. (2015). How transformational leadership works during team interactions: A behavioral process analysis. *The Leadership Quarterly*, *26*(6), 1017–1033.

Ma, S., Seidl, D., & McNulty, T. (2021). Challenges and practices of interviewing business elites. *Strategic Organization*, *19*(1), 81–96.

Mao, H. Y. (2006). The relationship between organizational level and workplace friendship. *The International Journal of Human Resource Management*, *17*(10), 1819–1833.

Mijuskovic, B. (1979). Loneliness and narcissism. *Psychoanalytic Review*, *66*(4), 479.

Mintzberg, H. (1973). *The nature of managerial work*. Harper & Row.

Moyle, P. (1998). Longitudinal influences of managerial support on employee well-being. *Work & Stress*, *12*(1), 29–49.

Owens, B. P., Walker, A. S., & Waldman, D. A. (2015). Leader narcissism and follower outcomes: The counterbalancing effect of leader humility. *Journal of Applied Psychology*, *100*(4), 1–11.

Ozcelik, H., & Barsade, S. G. (2018). No employee an Island: Workplace loneliness and job performance. *Academy of Management Journal*, *61*(6), 2343–2366.

Peplau, L., & Perlman, D. (1982). Perspectives on loneliness. In L. Peplau & D. Perlman (Eds.), *Loneliness: A sourcebook of current theory, research and therapy* (pp. 407–417). John Wiley & Sons.

Popper, M. (2013). Leaders perceived as distant and close: Some implications for psychological theory on leadership. *The Leadership Quarterly*, *24*(1), 1–8.

Rokach, A. (2004). Loneliness then and now: Reflections on social and emotional alienation in everyday life. *Current Psychology*, *23*(1), 24–40.

Rokach, A. (1989). Antecedents of loneliness: A factorial analysis. *The Journal of Psychology*, *123*(4), 369–384.

Rokach, A. (2012). Loneliness updated: An introduction. *The Journal of Psychology*, *146*(1–2), 1–6.

Rokach, A. (2014). Leadership and loneliness. *International Journal of Leadership and Change*, *2*(1), 46–58.

Saporito, T. J. (2012, February 15). It's time to acknowledge CEO loneliness. *Harvard Business Review*. https://hbr.org/2012/02/its-time-to-acknowledge-ceo-lo

Sergin, C., & Kinney, T. (1995). Social skills deficits among the socially anxious: Rejection from others and loneliness. *Motivation and Emotion*, *19*, 1–24.

Silard, A., & Wright, S. (2020). The price of wearing (or not wearing) the crown: The effects of loneliness on leaders and followers. *Leadership*, *16*(4), 389–410.

Silard, A., & Wright, S. (2021). Distinctly lonely: How loneliness at work varies by status in organizations. *Management Research Review*, *45*(7), 913–928,

Silard, A., & Wright, S. (2022). Distinctly lonely: How loneliness at work varies by status in organizations. *Management Research Review*, *45*(7), 913–928.

Smith, W. K., & Lewis, M. W. (2011). Toward a theory of paradox: A dynamic equilibrium model of organizing. *Academy of Management Review, 36*(2), 381–403.

Stephens, J., Heaphy, E., & Dutton, J. (2011). High quality connections. In K. Cameron & G. Spreitzer (Eds.), *Handbook of positive organizational scholarship* (pp. 385–399.). Oxford University Press.

Toegel, G., Kilduff, M., & Anand, N. (2013). Emotion helping by managers: An emergent understanding of discrepant role expectations and outcomes. *Academy of Management Journal, 56*(2), 334–357.

Twenge, J. M., Catanese, K. R., & Baumeister, R. F. (2002). Social exclusion causes self-defeating behavior. *Journal of Personality and Social Psychology, 83*(3), 606–615.

Uchino, B. N., Cacioppo, J. T., & Kiecolt-Glaser, J. K. (1996). The relationship between social support and physiological processes: a review with emphasis on underlying mechanisms and implications for health. *Psychological Bulletin, 119*(3), 488.

Vuori, T. O., & Huy, Q. (2020). Regulating top managers' emotions during strategy making: Nokia's socially distributed approach enabling radical change from mobile phones to networks in 2007–2013. *Academy of Management Journal, 65*(1), 331–361. https://doi.org/10.5465/amj.2019.0865

Waytz, A., Chou, E. Y., Magee, J. C., & Galinsky, A. D. (2015). Not so lonely at the top: The relationship between power and loneliness. *Organizational Behavior and Human Decision Processes, 130*, 69–78.

Weiss, R. S. (1973). *Loneliness: The experience of emotional and social isolation.* Cambridge, MA: The MIT Press.

Wright, S. (2012). Is it lonely at the top? An empirical study of managers' and nonmanagers' loneliness in organizations. *The Journal of Psychology, 146*(1–2), 47–60.

Wright, S. L. (2005). Organizational climate, social support and loneliness in the workplace. In N. Ashkanasy, W. Zerbe, & C. Hartel (Eds.), *Research on emotion in organizations*: The effect of affect in organizational studies (Vol. 1, pp. 123-142). Elsevier.

Wright, S., & Silard, A. (2021). Unravelling the antecedents of loneliness in the workplace. *Human Relations, 74*(7), 1060–1081.

Yalom, I. (1998). It's lonely at the top: Isolation as a problem for CEOs. Inc., *20*(5), 39–41.

Yukl, G. (2012). Effective leadership behavior: What we know and what questions need more attention. *Academy of Management Perspectives, 26*(4), 66–85.

Yukl, G. (2018). *Leadership in organizations* (9th ed.). Pearson.

CRACKING THE CEO'S BRAIN ON RISK: EXPLORING THE INTERPLAY BETWEEN CEO COGNITION AND AFFECT INTENSITY IN ORGANIZATIONAL DECISION-MAKING AND ITS OUTCOMES

Steven J. Hyde and Cameron J. Borgholthaus

ABSTRACT

Prior work has suggested that individual decision-making is influenced by the emotions and cognition of the decision-maker. Within the firm context, the chief executive officer (CEO) is required to make many decisions that will meaningfully impact the firm. However, little is known about how CEO emotions and cognition influence not only firm decision-making but also the performance consequences of those decisions. Within this chapter, the authors conceptually explore (1) how CEO affect intensity moderates the relationship between performance below aspirations and risk-taking; and (2) how CEO cognitive complexity determines the directional effect of the risk-performance relationship.

Keywords: Upper echelons theory; CEO; prospect theory; affect intensity; cognitive complexity; CEO emotions

Stress and Well-Being at the Strategic Level
Research in Occupational Stress and Well-Being, Volume 21, 81–93
Copyright © 2024 by Emerald Publishing Limited
All rights of reproduction in any form reserved
ISSN: 1479-3555/doi:10.1108/S1479-355520230000021005

INTRODUCTION

Scholars have repeatedly demonstrated that decision-making is neither an easy nor entirely rational process (Kahneman & Tversky, 1979). While decision-makers often lack relevant information to make decisions, research shows that both emotions and cognitive styles can directly influence how decisions are made (Andrade & Ariely, 2009; Bromiley & Rau, 2016; Loewenstein & Lerner, 2003). Indeed, a central premise within upper echelons (UE) theory (Hambrick & Mason, 1984) is that executives' characteristics – including their attitudes, beliefs, and values – can play a significant role in organizational decision-making, and therefore an organization's outcomes. Prior work has examined a number of these CEO characteristics including personality, political affiliation, and managerial discretion, and how they impact organizations (see Borgholthaus et al., 2023; Gupta et al., 2018, 2021; Holmes et al., 2021; Wangrow et al., 2015).

Despite calls for greater examination of CEO emotion and cognition (see Liu et al., 2018), little has been done to advance the strategic leadership literature in this area (see Delgado-García & De La Fuente-Sabaté, 2010; Malhotra & Harrison, 2022, for exceptions). Therefore, it is important to recognize the conditions under which CEO emotion and cognition have the greatest impact on organizational decision-making. To address the limitations of the extant literature, this study conceptually explores how CEO affect the intensity and cognitive complexity impact executive decision-making about risk and future performance. The CEO population is chosen for this framework because the decisions of these individuals have a widespread impact on the firm. In fact, prior work demonstrates that not only do CEOs serve as the public face of the firm (Busenbark et al., 2016; Love et al., 2017), but they also have the single greatest impact among individuals on organizational outcomes (Quigley & Graffin, 2017; Quigley & Hambrick, 2015).

Since the effects of affect intensity are more pronounced during stressful situations (Flett et al., 1996), we discuss the effects of affect intensity on CEO decision-making within the context of poor firm performance. Poor performance serves as a particularly salient stressor for a CEO because continued negative deviation from investor expectations increases the likelihood of dismissal (Crossland & Chen, 2013). Affect intensity refers to the degree to which an individual experiences emotion and can impact both negative (e.g., anger or anxiety) and positive (e.g., happiness) emotions (Larsen & Diener, 1987). Individuals who have low affect intensity will experience emotional stimuli mildly. As such, we expect that CEOs with low affect intensity will restrict themselves from allowing their emotions to impact decision-making (Tang et al., 2016). Conversely, CEOs with high affect intensity will experience much more extreme emotions from the same stimuli, thereby making it substantially more difficult to prevent their systematic biases from influencing decision-making, particularly as it pertains to risk.

We next address the performance consequences of risk-taking. The extant literature on risk-taking has demonstrated that risky actions often result in extreme outcomes, either positive (Dess et al., 1997) or negative (Quigley et al., 2019) for firm performance. This begs the question, what determines whether risky actions yield favorable outcomes for the firm versus unfavorable outcomes? To answer this, we investigate the boundary conditions of the risk-performance relationship, once again focusing on the firm's top manager. We theorize how CEO cognitive complexity is an important moderating factor within this relationship, as it reflects a CEO's ability to navigate complex situations into favorable outcomes. Cognitive complexity reflects an individual's ability to discern subtle differences and patterns within an event and then use this knowledge to make an optimal decision (Malhotra & Harrison, 2022). This construct has been shown to be associated with strategic planning, communication, and creativity (Charlton & Bakan, 1989; Judge & Speitzfaden, 1995; Rubin & Henzl, 1984). Thus, we expect that CEOs who have high levels of cognitive complexity will be able to process the complicated nature of risk-taking in such a way that their performance outcomes will exceed CEOs with low levels of cognitive complexity.

This study seeks to investigate the influence of CEO micro-level characteristics on macro-level relationships (see Fig. 1 for a full conceptual model). First, we explore how the relationship between firm performance and risk is moderated by a CEO's affect intensity. In doing so, we focus on how the primary tenets of the behavioral theory of the firm (e.g., performance relative to aspirations) and prospect theory (e.g., loss or gain frame) become more pronounced when CEO affect intensity is high. Specifically, we theorize that while failing to achieve performance aspirations – or being in a loss frame – leads to higher levels of firm risk-taking, this relationship is stronger when CEO affect intensity increases. Second, we examine the performance consequences of firm risk-taking. We posit that CEO cognitive complexity serves as an important boundary condition to the relationship and that it is critical in assessing whether or not performance outcomes will yield favorable or unfavorable results. In doing so, our study paves the way for additional empirical research on how executive-level individual differences impact organizational decision-making and its consequences.

THEORY AND HYPOTHESES

Prospect theory examines how individuals evaluate decisions involving risk (Kahneman & Tversky, 1979). According to the theory, losses loom larger than gains, meaning a potential loss has much greater salience to an individual than a

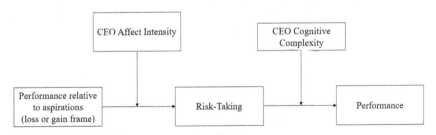

Fig. 1. Conceptual Model.

potential gain, even if the two are objectively equivalent in value. In other words, individuals are more likely to pay to protect against a potential loss rather than take a risk to gain the same value. For example, prospect theory suggests that an individual is more likely to pay $15 to purchase an insurance policy in order to protect against a 1% chance of losing $100,000 of assets than purchase a lottery ticket for $15 that has a 1% chance of winning $100,000. However, there are circumstances in which gains loom larger than losses, meaning the individual would be more likely to enter the lottery than to invest in insurance (Harinck et al., 2007; Mukherjee et al., 2017). For instance, individuals who have recently lost a significant amount of resources may be driven to become more risk-seeking because they have nothing to lose and everything to gain. This is referred to as a "loss frame." Conversely, when individuals have recently gained resources, they are considered to be in a "gain frame, " leading them to be risk averse, as they perceive the potential gains from taking a risk as minimal, or rather they have "everything to lose. "

The behavioral theory of the firm (BTF) argues that firms will strive to reach their performance aspiration levels, which is influenced by their historical performance and the performance of their competitors (Cyert & March, 1963). BTF has also examined how boundedly rational managers, such as CEOs, make decisions to address performance shortfalls (see Borgholthaus, 2021; Mount & Baer, 2022). By incorporating the assumptions of prospect theory into BTF, we can conceptualize the extent to which a firm fails to achieve its aspiration level as operating in a loss or gain frame (Fiegenbaum, 1990; Shimizu, 2007). Specifically, we argue that firms that have achieved their performance aspirations are in a gain frame – leading their managers to be risk averse – while firms that fail to reach their aspirations are in a loss frame – prompting their managers to be risk-seeking. We seek to refine prospect theory by examining its boundary conditions and argue that the affect intensity of the CEO is an important factor when considering how prior performance impacts future risk-taking.

Prospect theory generally neglects the emotional aspect of appraisal processes within decision-making and implicitly assumes that individuals will experience risk equally. However, research has consistently shown that individuals have different emotional reactions to risk and vary in the intensity with which they experience and express emotions (Loewenstein et al., 2001; Seo & Barrett, 2007). Specifically, we propose that a CEO's affect intensity will enhance the relationship between achieving the aspiration level (i.e., whether or not a firm is in a loss frame or gain frame) and risk-taking behavior. This is because individuals with high affect intensity will experience losses more intensely than those with low affect intensity.

UE Theory

Since Hambrick and Mason (1984) first proposed UE theory, scholarly interest in linking CEO attributes to firm decision-making and performance has substantially increased. Prior research has demonstrated that CEO age, tenure, and functional background (Andrews & Welbourne, 2000; Boeker, 1997) can have a considerable impact on firm outcomes, including performance. These findings are valuable for our understanding of the influence executives have on a firm. However, by investigating only the most surface level of constructs, it may be challenging for scholars to unlock the full potential of UE theory, which Carpenter et al. (2004, p. 750) described as centering on "executive cognitions, values, and perceptions and their influence on the process of strategic choice and resultant performance outcomes." This is because superficial level attributes such as age or sex provide limited information about what an individual thinks or feels.

Nevertheless, surface-level characteristics can still influence deeper-level traits (see White & Borgholthaus, 2022). For example, Finkelstein and Hambrick (1990) found that the tenure of top management teams was positively associated with risk aversion. They also observed that as CEOs increased in tenure, they became more reliant on intuitional logic when making decisions and were more committed to their prior decisions. Without examining this surface-level construct, scholars may not have identified the impact CEO tenure has on decision-making. Nonetheless, surface-level attributes are restricted in their capacity to predict a CEO's cognitions, values, and perceptions (Carpenter et al., 2004).

Although individuals may appear to be alike based on visible surface-level characteristics such as gender or race, their opinions, and feelings may differ. This discrepancy cannot be detected with surface-level attributes alone, thus, scholars have called for additional studies to delve deeper into executives' minds in order to obtain more reliable predictors of firm outcomes (Carpenter et al., 2004). Recent studies have begun to consider the influence of deeper-level psychological constructs on firm-level outcomes, including hubris (Hayward & Hambrick, 1997; Tang et al., 2015), narcissism (Chatterjee & Hambrick, 2007; Cragun et al., 2020), modesty (Ridge & Ingram, 2017), and the Big Five personality traits (Harrison et al., 2019; Nadkarni & Herrmann, 2010). We further add to this discussion by exploring a CEO's emotionality as an important factor in firm outcomes.

Emotions

Historically, many theories about decision-making have posited – either implicitly or explicitly – that individuals make decisions by (1) evaluating the possible outcomes of each choice and (2) assessing the probability that these outcomes will occur (Loewenstein et al., 2001). These theories often overlook the role of emotions in the decision-making process, treating them as inconsequential. However, other scholars have suggested that emotions play a critical role in decision-making and that it is doubtful humans would be able to effectively make decisions without them. For example, Damasio (2006) recounts the story of a man who had the ventromedial frontal lobe of his brain removed, leaving him unable to experience emotion. As a result, this man found it almost impossible to make even the simplest of decisions, such as what to eat at a restaurant. This suggests that in the case of risky or stressful decisions, the less intensely an individual experiences emotion the more likely they are to take a cautious approach to decision-making since they will not feel the intensity of the risk – or the stress associated with it – as strongly.

As the existing literature has advanced beyond the question of *whether* emotions impact decision-making, increased focus has been placed on determining *how* and *when* emotions influence choice. Several studies have attempted to understand the impact of specific affective states on decision-making. For example, studies have shown that happiness increases risk aversion while anger increases the propensity to take risks (Lerner & Keltner, 2001). Positive affective states have been shown to speed up decision-making, but also decrease information-seeking (Isen & Means, 1983). In contrast, sadness tends to lead to increased risk-seeking, while anxiety has the opposite effect (Raghunathan & Pham, 1999). While these studies are revealing about how emotions influence decision-making, they may not be particularly applicable to the context of strategic management. This is because emotions are typically considered to be emotional states, rather than traits or dispositions. Emotional states (e.g., road rage) are only experienced for a short period of time, are reactive to external stimuli, and are experienced continuously during their duration (Fridhandler, 1986), whereas traits or dispositions are generally stable throughout one's life, discontinuous, and internally caused (Fridhandler, 1986). For example, the character Eeyore from A. A. Milne's Winnie-the-Pooh has a negative disposition, which means that he tends to experience the world negatively. This tendency arises from within, rather than as a result of an external event. However, it is important to note that his disposition is considered discontinuous since there are times when he experiences positive affect.

While both states and traits are given extensive consideration within the psychology literature, it would be challenging to theoretically or empirically examine emotional states in the context of strategic management (i.e., in relation to the CEO). This is because states tend to be short in duration whereas strategic decisions – and the processes leading to them – may last months or even years. Since CEOs are likely to experience a wide range of emotional states throughout this period, it would be incredibly difficult to determine the exact emotional state they were in when making each substantial decision. For this reason, traits and dispositions are likely to be more practical and accurate predictors of strategic decision-making than states.

Affect Intensity

Loewenstein et al. (2001) proposed that emotions and cognition are intertwined when an individual is evaluating a decision. The cognitive appraisal is based on probabilities and outcome expectations. Although emotions are still impacted by these variables, they are much less sensitive to them than the cognitive process. Instead, as individuals evaluate their decisions, emotions such as stress, anxiety, or fear are induced and are influenced by the vividness of anticipatory emotions and temporal proximity. Although the specific emotions experienced are salient to the decision-making process, the intensity of those emotions is perhaps even more important to take into consideration.

Larsen and Diener (1987, p. 2) define affect intensity as "stable individual differences in the strength with which individuals experience their emotions." Consider how this trait-based attribute would impact the assessment of a decision. Two individuals may feel anxiety when evaluating a decision. However, while one may feel anxiety mildly, the other may experience this emotion so intensely that it becomes debilitating. In this case, the emotions of the latter will have a greater impact on the final decision than the emotions of the former. Hence, the appraisal of a decision reflects the amalgamation of the cognitive process based on probabilities and expectations and the emotional reaction constructed from the intensity of the emotions experienced or anticipated. Since the two processes are influenced by disparate variables, there are times when an individual will knowingly make a suboptimal decision because it simply "feels right" (Loewenstein et al., 2001).

For instance, when a firm fails to reach its aspirational performance levels and operates in a "loss frame," CEOs with high affect intensity become more likely to recognize the consequences of underperformance and will desire to rectify their performance shortfall to a much greater degree since failure to do so will likely result in their dismissal from the firm. Formally, CEOs who experience high affect intensity are likely to engage in risk-taking behaviors at much higher levels when their firms fail to achieve performance aspirations than CEOs with low affect intensity. Therefore, we argue that it is imperative to account for the intensity of the experienced emotions and not just the cognitive evaluation of risk when examining strategic decision-making.

P1. The negative relationship between a firm's performance relative to aspirations and risk-taking behavior will be moderated by CEO affect intensity, such that the relationship becomes stronger as CEO affect intensity increases.

Cognitive Complexity and Its Impact on the Risk-performance Relationship

The degree to which a firm takes calculated risks is important for its ability to sustain operations. For example, firms that proactively seek risk are "more likely to engage in behaviors that lead to process enhancements, highly competitive new products or services, [and] innovative marketing techniques" (Gilley et al., 2002, p. 99). By doing so, they may be able to capitalize on these opportunities and reap the benefits, leading to improved performance (e.g., Dess et al., 1997; Knight et al., 2001; McNamara & Bromiley, 1999). However, engaging in risky behavior may not always result in optimal outcomes. If firms are unable to use the resources gained from risk-taking, they may experience decreased firm performance (see Quigley et al., 2019; Sanders & Hambrick, 2007). Thus, we expect that risk-taking will lead to extreme outcomes about performance, but its directionality will be contingent upon an important CEO characteristic: cognitive complexity.

Cognitive complexity was first introduced within the framework of personal construct theory (Kelly, 1955). Personal construct theory suggests that individuals continually seek to understand, control, and predict the events around them. To do this, individuals create personal constructs or templates to make sense of the world. These constructs are typically based on dichotomous dimensions (e.g., fast or slow, large or small, black or white) and are systematically organized and connected within the mind, allowing individuals to integrate these divergent constructs to accurately predict and understand events around them.

Building upon this work, Bieri (1955) introduced the idea of cognitive complexity, which can be described as one's ability to see the world either in black and white or in shades of gray. Therefore, whereas cognitively simple individuals see an issue from one perspective, cognitively complex individuals will examine the same issue from multiple perspectives and integrate them into a more complex mental model of their surroundings. In other words, cognitive complexity is one's ability to categorize and organize thoughts and the perceptions preceding them (Owens & Wedeking, 2011). Unfortunately, the term cognitive complexity has been used in the literature to describe a variety of constructs, including mental models (Cheng & Chang, 2009), cognitive maps (Calori et al., 1994), and decision models (Hitt & Tyler, 1991). While these other constructs may be similar to cognitive complexity, they are conceptually distinct from the original constructs developed by Kelly (1955) and Bieri (1955).[1]

Cognitive complexity was originally conceptualized as a trait-like characteristic. However, prior research has suggested that state-like qualities, including situational characteristics like accountability (Tetlock, 1983), stress (Guttieri et al., 1995), information overload (Tadmor & Tetlock, 2007), and exposure to different cultures (Conway et al., 2001) can influence an individual's cognitive complexity. As such, scholars now categorize and measure cognitive complexity as both a state (e.g., integrative complexity) and a trait (e.g., conceptual complexity) within the literature (de Vries & Walker, 1987). For the purpose of our chapter, we focus on conceptual complexity rather than integrative complexity, because it focuses on examining the long-term effects of cognitive complexity and not the short-term impact of the environment on a CEO's thinking style.

As noted above, CEOs do not always behave rationally because they are capable of processing only the most relevant and important information when attempting to make optimal decisions (Cyert & March, 1963; Ocasio, 1997). Thus, either there is information that is unavailable to them or the complexity or total quantity of information is so great that the individual is unable to reasonably absorb and process it (i.e., they experience bounded rationality; Cyert & March, 1963). Of course, the business environment is becoming increasingly complex, which only increases the likelihood that bounded rationality will impede the decision-making process (Wry et al., 2013).

Cognitive complexity is likely an important trait for CEOs to possess. Cognitive complexity is positively related to a number of characteristics beneficial to CEOs such as assertiveness (Bruch et al., 1981), openness, creativity (Miron-Spektor et al., 2011), flexibility, and tolerance for ambiguity. It is also associated with positive communication skills (Montuori, 2000) and increased information search (Suedfeld, 2010). As such, we expect that CEOs who are high in cognitive complexity will be able to observe subtle environmental changes and effectively adjust their business strategies accordingly (Larson & Rowland, 1974). Additionally, CEOs who are high in cognitive complexity will be less likely to experience bounded rationality because they have a higher tolerance for ambiguity and can handle a greater amount of information, which should enable them to make more rational decisions. Conversely, those low in cognitive complexity may miss critical information, struggle with ambiguity, reject valid viewpoints, and be more dogmatic in their decision-making (Suedfeld, 2010; Suedfeld & Rank, 1976).

CEOs must differentiate and integrate a wide variety of information (i.e., market conditions, consumer preferences, government policies, etc.) in order to make an optimal decision that will result in the highest payout. Therefore, the quality of the decisions made by a CEO will be influenced by their cognitive complexity, such that CEOs with high cognitive complexity will make better decisions regarding which specific risk-taking actions will be of greatest benefit to the firm. We expect that CEOs with high cognitive complexity will experience positive performance when engaging in risk-taking behaviors, while CEOs low in cognitive complexity will experience negative performance following the same strategy.

P2. The relationship between a firm's risk-taking behavior and its subsequent performance will be moderated by CEO cognitive complexity, such that the firm's performance will be higher when its CEO has higher levels of cognitive complexity.

DISCUSSION AND CONCLUSION

While commonly used theories in the strategic management literature – such as BTF – do not consider how individual differences among executives can serve as a salient boundary condition when examining the relationships between risk-taking and performance, we propose that individual differences are particularly important factors to consider. Specifically, we argue that a CEO's affect intensity can be a pivotal boundary condition through which firms evaluate a gain or loss frame, thereby affecting the degree to which they pursue risk-taking behaviors. We also posit that CEO cognitive complexity is an important moderator that can determine the relationship (e.g., either positive or negative) between risk-taking and subsequent performance. We believe that scholars should give greater attention to these constructs in future studies, as doing so will provide a greater understanding of how executives interpret their environments and make decisions.

When examining the extant literature on decision-making, there is little doubt that executive cognitive style and emotions play an important role in how they make decisions (Kahneman, 2011; Lerner & Keltner, 2001; Loewenstein & Lerner, 2003). However, UE scholars have consistently shown that it can be difficult or impractical to measure these constructs directly using self-report surveys (see Cycyota & Harrison, 2006; White & Borgholthaus, 2022). In recent years, researchers have started to use various unobtrusive methods to obtain data on CEO psychological constructs – measuring them in an indirect manner. Examples include CEO personality (e.g., Chatterjee & Hambrick, 2007; Harrison et al., 2019; Ridge & Ingram, 2017), political affiliation (Gupta et al., 2018, 2021), and temporal (Gamache & McNamara, 2019), or regulatory (Gamache et al., 2020) focus.

Still, it can be challenging to obtain appropriate CEO-related data to draw conclusions about the impact of any given emotional or cognitive construct on decision-making – resulting in many underexplored areas of research. For example, to examine the impact of emotional states on executive decision-making, scholars would need to assess the executive's emotional state at the precise moments when they make important decisions. The length and complexity characteristic of these decisions further complicates the problem because they often have far-reaching consequences and require a longer period of time than the average emotional state (Fridhandler, 1986).

To advance research in this area, we suggest several options for future studies. For example, scholars can use an approach similar to Graf-Vlachy et al. (2020) to measure cognitive complexity. In their study, they developed a novel index based on CEO language patterns during the Q&A portion of a firm's quarterly earnings calls. This method consisted of three unique dictionaries related to three distinct elements of cognitive complexity: differentiation, nuance, and comparison. To operationalize CEO affect intensity, researchers could develop a tool that incorporates elements of the Affect Intensity Measure (AIM), a commonly used 40-item scale within the psychology literature (Larsen & Diener, 1987; Larsen et al., 1986). Such a tool should carefully identify linguistic patterns that distinguish between the frequency of emotional response (e.g., "I often feel happy") and the intensity with which emotion is experienced (e.g., "When I am happy the feeling is one of intense bliss"). Finally, we encourage future research to consider how CEOs' affect intensity can change decision-making when they experience strong negative affect intensity versus strong positive affect intensity.

NOTE

1. It should also be noted that cognitive complexity is not simply another measure of intelligence. Although cognitive complexity has been shown to be related to some measures of intelligence, such as verbal ability and crystallized intelligence, these correlations have been modest at best (Suedfeld & Coren, 1992). Similarly, it would be incorrect to assume that someone is more intelligent because they are more cognitively complex. For example, the late supreme court justice Antonin Scalia was shown to be cognitively simple, yet very intelligent.

REFERENCES

Andrade, E. B., & Ariely, D. (2009). The enduring impact of transient emotions on decision making. *Organizational Behavior and Human Decision Processes*, *109*(1), 1–8.

Andrews, A. O., & Welbourne, T. M. (2000). The people/performance balance in IPO firms: The effect of the Chief Executive Officer's financial orientation. *Entrepreneurship Theory and Practice*, *25*(1), 93–106.

Bieri, J. (1955). Cognitive complexity-simplicity and predictive behavior. *The Journal of Abnormal and Social Psychology*, *51*(2), 263–268.

Boeker, W. (1997). Strategic change: The influence of managerial characteristics and organizational growth. *Academy of Management Journal*, *40*(1), 152–170.

Borgholthaus, C. J. (2021). *Three essays on the consequences of CEO personality* [Doctoral dissertation]. The University of Nebraska-Lincoln.

Borgholthaus, C. J., White, J. V., & Harms, P. D. (2023). CEO dark personality: A critical review, bibliometric analysis, and research agenda. *Personality and Individual Differences*, *201*, 111951.

Bromiley, P., & Rau, D. (2016). Social, behavioral, and cognitive influences on upper echelons during strategy process: A literature review. *Journal of Management*, *42*(1), 174–202.

Bruch, M. A., Heisler, B. D., & Conroy, C. G. (1981). Effects of conceptual complexity on assertive behavior. *Journal of Counseling Psychology*, *28*(5), 377–385.

Busenbark, J. R., Krause, R., Boivie, S., & Graffin, S. D. (2016). Toward a configurational perspective on the CEO: A review and synthesis of the management literature. *Journal of Management, 42*(1), 234–268.

Calori, R., Johnson, G., & Sarnin, P. (1994). CEOs' cognitive maps and the scope of the organization. *Strategic Management Journal, 15*(6), 437–457.

Carpenter, M. A., Geletkanycz, M. A., & Sanders, W. G. (2004). Upper echelons research revisited: Antecedents, elements, and consequences of top management team composition. *Journal of Management, 30*(6), 749–778.

Charlton, S., & Bakan, P. (1989). Cognitive complexity and creativity. *Imagination, Cognition and Personality, 8*(4), 315–322.

Chatterjee, A., & Hambrick, D. (2007). It's all about me: Narcissistic chief executive officers and their effects on company strategy and performance. *Administrative Science Quarterly, 52*(3), 351–386.

Cheng, S. -L., & Chang, H. -C. (2009). Performance implications of cognitive complexity: An empirical study of cognitive strategic groups in semiconductor industry. *Journal of Business Research, 62*(12), 1311–1320.

Conway, L. G., III, Schaller, M., Tweed, R. G., & Hallett, D. (2001). The complexity of thinking across cultures: Interactions between culture and situational context. *Social Cognition, 19*, 228–250.

Cragun, O. R., Olsen, K. J., & Wright, P. M. (2020). Making CEO narcissism research great: A review and meta-analysis of CEO narcissism. *Journal of Management, 46*(6), 908–936.

Crossland, C., & Chen, G. (2013). Executive accountability around the world: Sources of cross-national variation in firm performance–CEO dismissal sensitivity. *Strategic Organization, 11*(1), 78–109.

Cycyota, C. S., & Harrison, D. A. (2006). What (not) to expect when surveying executives: A meta-analysis of top manager response rates and techniques over time. *Organizational Research Methods, 9*(2), 133–160.

Cyert, R. M., & March, J. G. (1963). *A behavioral theory of the firm.* Prentice Hall.

Damasio, A. R. (2006). *Descartes' error: Emotion, reason, and the human brain.* Penguin Publishing Group.

de Vries, B., & Walker, L. J. (1987). Conceptual/integrative complexity and attitudes toward capital punishment. *Personality and Social Psychology Bulletin, 13*(4), 448–457.

Delgado-García, J. B., & De La Fuente-Sabaté, J. M. (2010). How do CEO emotions matter? Impact of CEO affective traits on strategic and performance conformity in the Spanish banking industry. *Strategic Management Journal, 31*(5), 562–574.

Dess, G. G., Lumpkin, G. T., & Covin, J. G. (1997). Entrepreneurial strategy making and firm performance: Tests of contingency and configurational models. *Strategic Management Journal, 18*(9), 677–695.

Fiegenbaum, A. (1990). Prospect theory and the risk-return association: An empirical examination in 85 industries. *Journal of Economic Behavior & Organization, 14*(2), 187–203.

Finkelstein, S., & Hambrick, D. C. (1990). Top-management-team tenure and organizational outcomes: The moderating role of managerial discretion. *Administrative Science Quarterly, 35*(3), 484–503.

Flett, G. L., Blankstein, K. R., & Obertynski, M. (1996). Affect intensity, coping styles, mood regulation expectancies, and depressive symptoms. *Personality and Individual Differences, 20*(2), 221–228.

Fridhandler, B. M. (1986). Conceptual note on state, trait, and the state–trait distinction. *Journal of Personality and Social Psychology, 50*(1), 169–174.

Gamache, D. L., & McNamara, G. (2019). Responding to bad press: How CEO temporal focus influences the sensitivity to negative media coverage of acquisitions. *Academy of Management Journal, 62*(3), 918–943.

Gamache, D. L., Neville, F., Bundy, J., & Short, C. E. (2020). Serving differently: CEO regulatory focus and firm stakeholder strategy. *Strategic Management Journal, 41*(7), 1305–1335.

Gilley, M., Walters, B., & Olson, B. (2002). Top management team risk taking propensities and firm performance: Direct and moderating effects. *Journal of Business Strategies, 19*(2), 95–114.

Graf-Vlachy, L., Bundy, J., & Hambrick, D. C. (2020). Effects of an advancing tenure on CEO cognitive complexity. *Organization Science, 31*(4), 936–959.

Gupta, A., Briscoe, F., & Hambrick, D. C. (2018). Evenhandedness in resource allocation: Its relationship with CEO ideology, organizational discretion, and firm performance. *Academy of Management Journal, 61*(5), 1848–1868.

Gupta, A., Fung, A., & Murphy, C. (2021). Out of character: CEO political ideology, peer influence, and adoption of CSR executive position by Fortune 500 firms. *Strategic Management Journal, 42*(3), 529–557.

Guttieri, K., Wallace, M. D., & Suedfeld, P. (1995). The integrative complexity of American decision makers in the Cuban Missile Crisis. *Journal of Conflict Resolution, 39*(4), 595–621.

Hambrick, D. C., & Mason, P. A. (1984). Upper echelons: The organization as a reflection of its top managers. *Academy of Management Review, 9*(2), 193–206.

Harinck, F., Van Dijk, E., Van Beest, I., & Mersmann, P. (2007). When gains loom larger than losses: Reversed loss aversion for small amounts of money. *Psychological Science, 18*(12), 1099–1105.

Harrison, J. S., Thurgood, G. R., Boivie, S., & Pfarrer, M. D. (2019). Measuring CEO personality: Developing, validating, and testing a linguistic tool. *Strategic Management Journal, 40*(8), 1316–1330.

Hayward, M. L., & Hambrick, D. C. (1997). Explaining the premiums paid for large acquisitions: Evidence of CEO hubris. *Administrative Science Quarterly, 42*(1), 103–127.

Hitt, M. A., & Tyler, B. B. (1991). Strategic decision models: Integrating different perspectives. *Strategic Management Journal, 12*(5), 327–351.

Holmes, R. M., Hitt, M. A., Perrewé, P. L., Palmer, J. C., & Molina-Sieiro, G. (2021). Building cross-disciplinary bridges in leadership: Integrating top executive personality and leadership theory and research. *The Leadership Quarterly, 32*(1), 101490.

Isen, A. M., & Means, B. (1983). The influence of positive affect on decision-making strategy. *Social Cognition, 2*(1), 18–31.

Judge, W. Q., & Speitzfaden, M. (1995). The management of strategic time horizons within biotechnology firms: The impact of cognitive complexity on time horizon diversity. *Journal of Management Inquiry, 4*(2), 179–196.

Kahneman, D. (2011). *Thinking, fast and slow.* Macmillan.

Kahneman, D., & Tversky, A. (1979). Prospect theory: An analysis of decisions under risk. *Econometrica, 47*(2), 263–291.

Kelly, G. A. (1955). *The psychology of personal constructs: Clinical diagnosis and psychotherapy.* Norton.

Knight, D., Durham, C. C., & Locke, E. A. (2001). The relationship of team goals, incentives, and efficacy to strategic risk, tactical implementation, and performance. *Academy of Management Journal, 44*(2), 326–338.

Larsen, R. J., & Diener, E. (1987). Affect intensity as an individual difference characteristic: A review. *Journal of Research in Personality, 21*(1), 1–39.

Larsen, R. J., Diener, E., & Emmons, R. A. (1986). Affect intensity and reactions to daily life events. *Journal of Personality and Social Psychology, 51*(4), 803–814.

Larson, L. L., & Rowland, K. M. (1974). Leadership style and cognitive complexity. *Academy of Management Journal, 17*(1), 37–45.

Lerner, J. S., & Keltner, D. (2001). Fear, anger, and risk. *Journal of Personality and Social Psychology, 81*(1), 146–159.

Liu, D., Fisher, G., & Chen, G. (2018). CEO attributes and firm performance: A sequential mediation process model. *Academy of Management Annals, 12*(2), 789–816.

Loewenstein, G., & Lerner, J. S. (2003). The role of affect in decision making. In R. Davidson, K. Scherer, & H. Goldsmith (Eds.), *Handbook of affective sciences* (pp. 619–642). Oxford University Press.

Loewenstein, G. F., Weber, E. U., Hsee, C. K., & Welch, N. (2001). Risk as feelings. *Psychological Bulletin, 127*(2), 267–286.

Love, E. G., Lim, J., & Bednar, M. K. (2017). The face of the firm: The influence of CEOs on corporate reputation. *Academy of Management Journal, 60*(4), 1462–1481.

Malhotra, S., & Harrison, J. S. (2022). A blessing and a curse: How CEO cognitive complexity influences firm performance under varying industry conditions. *Strategic Management Journal, 43*(13), 2809–2828.

McNamara, G., & Bromiley, P. (1999). Risk and return in organizational decision making. *Academy of Management Journal, 42*(3), 330–339.

Miron-Spektor, E., Gino, F., & Argote, L. (2011). Paradoxical frames and creative sparks: Enhancing individual creativity through conflict and integration. *Organizational Behavior and Human Decision Processes, 116*(2), 229–240.

Montuori, L. (2000). Organizational longevity-integrating systems thinking, learning and conceptual complexity. *Journal of Organizational Change Management, 13*(1), 61–73.

Mount, M. P., & Baer, M. (2022). CEOs' regulatory focus and risk-taking when firms perform below and above the bar. *Journal of Management, 48*(7), 1980–2008.

Mukherjee, S., Sahay, A., Pammi, V., & Srinivasan, N. (2017). Is loss-aversion magnitude-dependent? Measuring prospective affective judgments regarding gains and losses. *Judgment & Decision Making, 12*(1), 81–89.

Nadkarni, S., & Herrmann, P. (2010). CEO personality, strategic flexibility, and firm performance: The case of the Indian business process outsourcing industry. *Academy of Management Journal, 53*(5), 1050–1073.

Ocasio, W. (1997). Towards an attention-based view of the firm. *Strategic Management Journal, 18*(S1), 187–206.

Owens, R. J., & Wedeking, J. P. (2011). Justices and legal clarity: Analyzing the complexity of US Supreme Court opinions. *Law & Society Review, 45*(4), 1027–1061.

Quigley, T. J., & Graffin, S. D. (2017). Reaffirming the CEO effect is significant and much larger than chance: A comment on Fitza (2014). *Strategic Management Journal, 38*(3), 793–801.

Quigley, T. J., & Hambrick, D. C. (2015). Has the "CEO effect" increased in recent decades? A new explanation for the great rise in America's attention to corporate leaders. *Strategic Management Journal, 36*(6), 821–830.

Quigley, T. J., Hambrick, D. C., Misangyi, V. F., & Rizzi, G. A. (2019). CEO selection as risk-taking: A new vantage on the debate about the consequences of insiders versus outsiders. *Strategic Management Journal, 40*(9), 1453–1470.

Raghunathan, R., & Pham, M. T. (1999). All negative moods are not equal: Motivational influences of anxiety and sadness on decision making. *Organizational Behavior and Human Decision Processes, 79*(1), 56–77.

Ridge, J. W., & Ingram, A. (2017). Modesty in the top management team: Investor reaction and performance implications. *Journal of Management, 43*(4), 1283–1306.

Rubin, R. B., & Henzl, S. A. (1984). Cognitive complexity, communication competence, and verbal ability. *Communication Quarterly, 32*(4), 263–270.

Sanders, W. G., & Hambrick, D. C. (2007). Swinging for the fences: The effects of CEO stock options on company risk taking and performance. *Academy of Management Journal, 50*(5), 1055–1078.

Seo, M. -G., & Barrett, L. F. (2007). Being emotional during decision making—good or bad? An empirical investigation. *Academy of Management Journal, 50*(4), 923–940.

Shimizu, K. (2007). Prospect theory, behavioral theory, and the threat-rigidity thesis: Combinative effects on organizational decisions to divest formerly acquired units. *Academy of Management Journal, 50*(6), 1495–1514.

Suedfeld, P. (2010). The cognitive processing of politics and politicians: Archival studies of conceptual and integrative complexity. *Journal of Personality, 78*(6), 1669–1702.

Suedfeld, P., & Coren, S. (1992). Cognitive correlates of conceptual complexity. *Personality and Individual Differences, 13*(11), 1193–1199.

Suedfeld, P., & Rank, A. D. (1976). Revolutionary leaders: Long-term success as a function of changes in conceptual complexity. *Journal of Personality and Social Psychology, 34*(2), 169–178.

Tadmor, C. T., & Tetlock, P. E. (2007). Integrative complexity. In *Encyclopedia of social psychology* (pp. 486–488). Sage.

Tang, H., Liang, Z., Zhou, K., Huang, G. H., Rao, L. L., & Li, S. (2016). Positive and negative affect in loss aversion: Additive or subtractive logic? *Journal of Behavioral Decision Making, 29*(4), 381–391.

Tang, Y., Qian, C., Chen, G., & Shen, R. (2015). How CEO hubris affects corporate social (ir) responsibility. *Strategic Management Journal, 36*(9), 1338–1357.

Tetlock, P. E. (1983). Accountability and the perseverance of first impressions. *Social Psychology Quarterly, 46*(4), 285–292.

Wangrow, D. B., Schepker, D. J., & Barker, V. L., III. (2015). Managerial discretion: An empirical review and focus on future research directions. *Journal of Management, 41*(1), 99–135.

White, J. V., & Borgholthaus, C. J. (2022). Who's in charge here? A bibliometric analysis of upper echelons research. *Journal of Business Research, 139*, 1012–1025.

Wry, T., Cobb, J. A., & Aldrich, H. E. (2013). More than a metaphor: Assessing the historical legacy of resource dependence and its contemporary promise as a theory of environmental complexity. *Academy of Management Annals, 7*(1), 441–488.

SENTIMENT ANALYSIS FOR ORGANIZATIONAL RESEARCH

Chapman J. Lindgren, Wei Wang, Siddharth K. Upadhyay and Vladimer B. Kobayashi

ABSTRACT

Sentiment analysis is a text analysis method that is developed for systematically detecting, identifying, or extracting the emotional intent of words to infer if the text expresses a positive or negative tone. Although this novel method has opened an exciting new avenue for organizational research – mainly due to the abundantly available text data in organizations and the well-developed sentiment analysis techniques, it has also posed a serious challenge to many organizational researchers. This chapter aims to introduce the sentiment analysis method in the text mining area to the organizational research community. In this chapter, the authors first briefly discuss the central role of sentiment in organizational research and then introduce the traditional and modern approaches to sentiment analysis. The authors further delineate research paradigms for text analysis research, advocating the iterative research paradigm (cf., inductive and deductive research paradigms) that is more suitable for text mining research, and also introduce the analytical procedures for sentiment analysis with three stages – discovery, measurement, and inference. More importantly, the authors highlight both the dictionary-based and machine learning (ML) approaches in the measurement stage, with special coverage on deep learning and word embedding techniques as the latest breakthroughs in sentiment and text analyses. Lastly, the authors provide two illustrative examples to demonstrate the applications of sentiment analysis in organizational research. It is the authors' hope that this chapter – by providing these practical guidelines – will help facilitate more applications of this novel method in organizational research in the future.

Keywords: Sentiment analysis; text analysis; text mining; machine learning; text data; structural topic model

Stress and Well-Being at the Strategic Level
Research in Occupational Stress and Well-Being, Volume 21, 95–117
Copyright © 2024 by Emerald Publishing Limited
All rights of reproduction in any form reserved
ISSN: 1479-3555/doi:10.1108/S1479-355520230000021006

SENTIMENT ANALYSIS FOR
ORGANIZATIONAL RESEARCH

[...] All sentiment is right; because sentiment has a reference to nothing beyond itself, and is always real .... Beauty is no quality in things themselves: It exists merely in the mind which contemplates them; and every individual ought to acquiesce in his own sentiment, without pretending to regulate those of others. Hume (1963, p. 230)

INTRODUCTION

Sentiments – general feelings, attitudes, or opinions about something – are ubiquitous among human beings and critical for our social functioning. From classic job attitudes (e.g., job satisfaction, organizational commitment, and job involvement; Newman et al., 2010) to employee engagement (Kahn, 1990), organizational scientists have been long interested in sentiments in organizations. From call centers to healthcare conglomerates, from banks to universities, organization scientists and practitioners are increasingly interested in analyzing sentiment to reveal what people are feeling and why, which is essential to formulating strategies to improve organizational effectiveness.

Rooted in computer science and technology, *sentiment analysis* is a technique for systematically detecting, identifying, or extracting the emotional intent of words to infer if the text expresses a positive or negative tone, which is particularly useful to quickly understand opinions expressed in a text message (Ghazizadeh et al., 2014). Although human readers are often good at detecting such emotionality, computers – with recent advancements in lexicon-dictionary techniques and various ML algorithms – have been found to be able to perform sentiment analyses more efficiently to evaluate the degree of the sentiment in a text (Liu, 2020). At its core, sentiment analysis is a form of text analysis defined as "the field of study that analyzes people's opinions, sentiments, evaluations, appraisals, attitudes, and emotions towards entities such as products, services, organizations, individuals, issues, events, topics, and their attributes" (Liu, 2012, p. 7). As such, sentiment analysis may also refer to opinion mining, which enables revolutionary assessment for multiple stakeholders: what consumers or employees want, approve or disapprove of, and what measures can be taken to improve or sustain a product or policy (Ahman 2018).

In organizational management, sentiment analysis offers an important means to distill text content collected from online sites, internal surveys, focus groups, and more, as this method is capable of revealing critical insights about organizational strengths and areas for improvement and detecting positive and negative feelings toward a policy or decision, such as benefits packages or mergers, leaders or management practices, workplace culture, etc. Unsurprisingly, human resource (HR) professionals have increasingly utilized this method to obtain quantified, actionable insights into employee sentiment and workplace culture. For example, if HR practitioners analyze employee surveys for sentiment tones to reveal that a new policy is intensely disliked, they may decide to roll back the policy or amend particular core principles that are subject to negative sentiment. Indeed, multiple industries have already begun taking advantage of sentiment analysis, and many large corporations have built their own in-house opinion mining tools, including Microsoft, Google, Hewlett-Packard, SAP, and SAS, as the utility and application explode across industries (Liu, 2012). In addition, the healthcare industry has often applied this technique to evaluate customer reviews and obtain deeper insights for driving reputation and profits.

As such, sentiment and text analyses have opened a new avenue for organizational research – thanks to the abundantly available text data in organizations and the well-developed sentiment analysis techniques. Nevertheless, they have also posed a serious challenge to many organizational researchers. Unlike small datasets we used to collect and handle, the nature of the text data is completely different – they are not only voluminous in size, ranging from gigabits to terabits, but also unstructured. Additionally, text data are often collected in an ad-hoc way and may not lend themselves readily available for scientific investigation. That is, there are no straightforward measures or variables to analyze. In addition, organizational researchers with text data often need to leverage advanced computer science techniques and statistical methods to find meaningful information from these largely unstructured datasets. Yet, competence in these techniques and methods requires a certain level of computer programing skills and advanced data science training, and the training of skills and techniques has not been integrated into the standard academic training in the discipline of organizational science.

Mindful of these challenges, this chapter is aimed at introducing the method of sentiment analysis in the text mining area to the organizational research community. We first delineate research paradigms for text analysis research, advocating the iterative research paradigm (cf., inductive and deductive research paradigms) that is more suitable for text mining research. Then, we introduce the analytical procedures for sentiment analysis with three stages – discovery, measurement, and inference. More importantly, we highlight both the dictionary-based approaches and the ML approaches to sentiment analysis, with special coverage on deep learning and word embedding techniques as the latest breakthroughs in sentiment and text analyses. Lastly, we provide an illustrative example to demonstrate a sentiment analysis by applying the iterative research paradigm and the dictionary-based Linguistic Inquiry and Word Count (LIWC; Pennebaker et al., 2015) techniques to study corporate diversity statements.

THE CENTRAL ROLE OF SENTIMENT IN ORGANIZATIONAL RESEARCH

From job attitudes to employee engagement, sentiment plays a central role in organizational research. The enormous body of literature on job attitudes forms a complicated network of cognitive and affective explanations for a wide range of organizational outcomes such as task performance, organizational citizenship behaviors, withdrawal behaviors, etc. (Judge & Kammeyer-Mueller, 2012). Indeed, in organizational behavior scholarship and HR practices, job attitudes are a venerable keystone for understanding an individual, team, or entire organization's emotional expression, both positive and negative.

Similar to job attitudes, employee engagement is also an affective and moti-vational construct that, when cultivated, is related to many desirable organiza-tional outcomes. Several metrics characterize employee engagement, including customer satisfaction, turnover, absenteeism, employee satisfaction, workplace culture, and more. However, the employee engagement construct faces scru-tiny for its conceptual and empirical conceptual overlap with three classic job attitudes (or *A*-factor; Newman et al., 2010) – job satisfaction, organizational commitment, and job involvement. As Newman et al. (2010) noted, "common job attitudes are intercorrelated, and this pattern of correlations reflects a higher-order job attitude concept (or *A*-factor)" (p. 46).

These affective and attitudinal based concepts can be potentially reconciled through the extraction and application of employee sentiment. By understand-ing the underlying affective component of job attitudes, we implicate the value of exploring sentiment in clarifying conceptual and empirical overlap between job attitudes as a powerful predictor of general work-related behavioral criteria.

TRADITIONAL AND MODERN APPROACHES TO SENTIMENT ANALYSIS IN ORGANIZATIONS

Assessing sentiment is a critical task for organizations that want to understand their employee and customers' preferences or reactions. Traditionally, organiza-tions have heavily relied on employee surveys and self-reported data to assess various sentiments, such as employee commitment, engagement, motivation, and satisfaction (Gelbard et al., 2018). For example, the Procter & Gamble Company (2023) formally surveys all employees worldwide on a yearly basis to gauge their employees' attitudes toward different aspects of their job. Such surveys include both forced-choice items and open-ended questions to learn employees' opinions about their jobs and the organization.

Although the traditional survey-based sentiment assessment has been widely used in organizations, it suffers from serious limitations. First, because such employee surveys that are formally conducted by the organization are typically not anonymous, employees' responses can be biased or distorted due to the fear of job security, and their responses are also prone to contextual influences (e.g., the culture of their work environment), undermining the quality and validity of the sentiment measured in the surveys. Second, self-reported surveys and assessments are time-consuming and costly for both organizations and employees. Finally, survey results are not analyzed in real-time, which delays effective reactions by the organizations and makes it difficult to identify patterns (Almars et al., 2017).

Fortunately, with the development and popularization of computer technol-ogy – specifically, text mining and analysis techniques – the computer-based com-putational approach to sentiment analysis is burgeoning. This approach leverages sophisticated statistical modeling and analyzes a large volume of text data that were otherwise inaccessible by traditional methods to extract and identifies the emotional intent of words and statements to determine whether a text expresses a positive or negative tone toward what (or who), and why. While these sentiments may exist privately, they are often identifiable, measurable, and provide a nuanced assessment of why one may experience differing sentiments toward certain objects relative to a colleague (e.g., feeling elation while a colleague experiences dejection after a social event). In addition, this modern method of sentiment analysis offers an iterative process wherein researchers and practitioners can constantly evaluate, and revise policies or procedures as determined by developing sentiments. Thus, it provides a proactive and prospective framework for evaluating job attitudes as they are impacted, whether positively or negatively. More importantly, the statistically rooted and computational sentiment analysis method enables organizations to automatically detect sentiment patterns and examine their relationships with other organizational events in real time. Thus, organizations will be prepared to find and apply characteristic sentiments toward interventions, perform link analyses to detect patterns and associations, and generate predictive models that regress particular sentiments with particular outcomes.

GENERAL RESEARCH PARADIGMS FOR TEXT-BASED SENTIMENT ANALYSES

Unlike traditional quantitative research in organizational science, where a deductive paradigm is typically preferred, text-based sentiment analysis as a novel and advanced research method is versatile for both deductive and inductive research paradigms. In fact, recent social scientists advocate an iterative research paradigm – combining both deductive and inductive paradigms for text analysis research (Grimmer et al., 2022a). In this section, we will discuss the three research paradigms in light of text-based sentiment analysis (see Fig. 1).

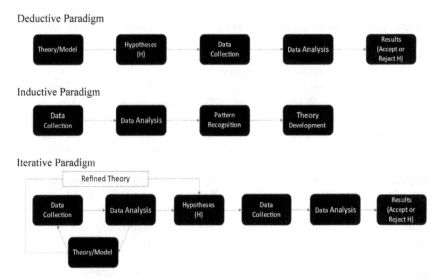

Fig. 1. Research Paradigms for Text Analysis and the Corresponding Procedures.

Deductive Paradigm

The deductive paradigm (aka a top-down or theory-driven approach) starts with existing theories, by which new hypotheses are developed, then data are collected and analyzed to test hypotheses (see the upper panel of Fig. 1). In deductive paradigm research, it is critical to have research hypotheses developed before data collection. The deductive paradigm is so popular in organizational research that the overwhelming majority of articles published in premier organizational journals follow a theory → data collection → data analysis → results approach, painting it as the gold standard of research.

The deductive paradigm has also been applied in text analysis. As an example, Speer (2018) analyzed narrative comments to evaluate employee performance. In HR literature, it has often been theorized that narrative comments may show incremental validity for future performance outcomes such as performance ratings, involuntary turnover, promotions, and pay increases. To test the theory, Speer (2018) utilized text-mining techniques to create a custom dictionary to score performance narratives within a large organization. This was accomplished by analyzing over 15,000 performance ratings from three years of data to derive an algorithm from text comments provided during the performance appraisal. The text analysis results supported the hypothesis that derived narrative scores could explain incremental variance in future performance outcomes and showed that text narratives scores could improve performance measurement.

Inductive Paradigm

Opposite to the deductive paradigm, an inductive paradigm (aka a bottom-up or data-driven approach) involves a set of observations leading to theory formulation. Specifically, this research paradigm discovers new research questions and forms new theories by exploring previously unknown phenomena, which is especially applicable to qualitative research and text analysis. As illustrated in the upper panel of Fig. 1, the inductive approach to research typically starts with data collection (in most cases qualitative or text data), followed by data analysis to identify patterns and develop theories.

Although the majority of the studies in organizational research followed a deductive paradigm, Spector et al. (2014) critiqued overemphasis on theory-driven deductive research. Indeed, when exploring novel data sources, the deductive approach may not always be the best option. Insistence of having a theory/an a priori hypothesis before observing a dataset may lead researchers to form preconceived notions, which may then consequently create a tunnel vision whereby only variables of interest are tested, leaving out other important variables in the equation that could also be explaining the phenomena. This is not to say that deductive reasoning is not a sound approach but to argue that when exploring a completely novel data source like text data, the deductive approach may inevitably prevent researchers from discovering new concepts, variables, or questions that emerge from the data source. In such cases, researchers (e.g., McAbee et al., 2017) advocated that an inductive approach may be more suitable as variables or patterns discovered from the dataset do not have to fit a preconceived theoretical model. Instead, their discovery can lead to the formulation of a theory. In addition, an inductive approach also allows organizational researchers to interpret the results with the closest approximation of their meaning instead of attempting to make them meaningful based on a preconceived theoretical model.

Nevertheless, a few studies in the text analysis literature adopts an inductive paradigm. For example, Pyun and Rha (2021) conducted a text analysis to explore and identify major research trends in the past 10 years of digital supply chain management. Specifically, they conducted a network text analysis to extract patterns from unstructured text data and found "sustainability" as the most influential keyword in the network, thereby identifying the research trends as focused on the implications of the digital supply chain to achieve sustainable management. Such applications can also be extended to OB literature to explore research patterns by text analyzing large textual datasets. For instance, DeChurch et al. (2018) analyzed all the journal articles that included the keyword "team" or "teamwork" in the massive Web of Science database to assess how the research on teams evolved over time across different disciplines (e.g., Applied Psychology, Management, Communication, Health Care, Engineering, etc.).

Iterative Paradigm

It is noteworthy that text analysis can be applied as a means to an end rather than the end itself by combining both inductive and deductive paradigms. That is, the result of the test analysis may reveal constructs or themes from a corpus and provide a base for further studies relating to new variables under observation. Indeed, an iterative paradigm has been advocated to better conduct research with text data (Grimmer et al., 2022a). Like a deductive paradigm, the iterative approach also begins with a research question within a particular data source. However, instead of having a preconceived theory before exploring the data, this approach iteratively explores the data until researchers have enough information to develop a theory. More importantly, after initially studying and analyzing the data, a new set of data should be further collected and analyzed to consequently test the theory deductively. As Grimmer et al. (2022b) argued, this iterative approach could not only avoid the pitfalls that concerned many social scientists by taking a deductive approach – e.g., p-hacking, forking paths, etc., but also reduce the possibility of inaccuracies through biases and subjectivity of researchers when applying inductive methods through iterative refinements.

As illustrated in the lower panel of Fig. 1, there is a theory refinement process in the iterative paradigm, which analyzes the initial data to preliminarily explore the existing theories and develop research hypotheses. Once hypotheses are developed, the paradigm of research allows revisiting the theoretical model in lieu of new data or discoveries from existing data. As such, this approach improves the theories with every iteration and allows for the discovery of new constructs and variables that may have been overlooked in earlier iterations.

A recent study by Wang et al. (2022) has well demonstrated the iterative paradigm. In order to understand how Fortune 1000 companies released public statements to condemn racism and affirm their stance on diversity, equity, and inclusion (DEI). Wang et al. (2022) first collected text data on corporate diversity statements that were publicly released by Fortune 1000 companies. Then they took an iterative research approach and analyzed the text data with the structural topic modeling (STM; Roberts et al., 2014) to identify the latent semantic topics underlying the diversity statements. These semantic topics were quantitatively measured as prevalence – the probability that a semantic topic emerged from a text document. After the inductive research in which text topics were identified and measured, Wang et al. (2022) then took a deductive approach to conduct a second study, in which they further collected additional data on employees' DEI ratings retrieved from www.Glassdoor.com. This deductive study combined with the prevalence of sematic topics discovered from the inductive research to test hypotheses and make inferences. Specifically, they leveraged the identity-blindness and identity-consciousness theoretical frameworks (Leigh & Melwani, 2019) and hypothesized that companies that emphasized identity-conscious (vs identity-blind) topics in their diversity statements were more positively rated by their employees on organizational diversity and inclusion.

RECOMMENDED ANALYTICAL PROCEDURES FOR SENTIMENT ANALYSIS

After clarifying research paradigms for sentiment and text analyses, in this section, we now move to elaborate on the analytical procedures by which a text analysis study should be conducted. Specifically, we follow the iterative paradigm advocated by Grimmer et al. (2022b) and recommend the three stages of Discovery, Measurement, and Inference, highlighting two approaches to measuring sentiment concepts in text analysis – the dictionary-based approach and ML models. We will also introduce the latest developments in deep learning models and word embedding techniques for text analysis.

Stage 1: Discovery

As with any other scientific pursuit, sentiment analysis often starts with problem definition, as this guides the direction and conduct of the analysis. Indubitably, the general task is to identify sentiment from text. However, the point of application should be clear such as applying sentiment to forecast stock prices or detect public sentiment on social issues (e.g., anti-LGBT campaign). As such, the first stage of sentiment analysis deals with developing a research question through discovery. That is, trying to identify what concepts and constructs need to be measured and why the question needs to be answered. By narrowing down the concepts we are interested in, we can simplify the complexity of data sources and focus on the select elements. For example, if we wish to analyze CEOs' retirement statements over the years, we must first identify what aspect of the retirement statements is of research interest. Is it the content of the statement or the sentiment? Or is it semantic topics that could vary by organization? Do you wish to organize the data based on CEO demographics or company characteristics?

These questions are answered in the discovery stage, which can help us manage the documents accordingly.

With the research questions identified, we may perform a thematic analysis and organize all the documents that have similar themes in the CEO statement. We may also distinguish how these clustered groups of statements differ from each other with a summary of data that provides an approximation of thematic similarities or differences. Then, we may organize the documents by sentiment or certain keywords of interest. While not all forms of organization would make sense, researchers can identify a strategy based on previous literature on which organization would be meaningful to analyze. Indeed, there are always some forms of discovery involved in every research process. However, by explicitly going through the process of discovery, researchers are able to explore the text data based on intuition rather than restricting themselves to the dimensions of a preconceived theory.

Once a research problem has been properly conceptualized, the next step is to identify text data sources and conduct text data collection. Some popular sources include customer feedback, user comments, user reviews, and posts that are uploaded to online platforms such as social media websites and interest group forums. Other sources are document repositories (both print and digital), such as periodicals and company reports. Apart from secondary sources, primary text data may include interview transcripts, responses to open-ended survey questions, and speech-to-text transcriptions from audio-visual sources (Sasangohar et al., 2021).

Stage 2: Measurement

Once we have identified research concepts to explore and collected the desired text data sources, we now need to choose a methodology that can measure the concepts or their characteristics. Although the method of measurement varies by the concept of interest, it generally involves assigning numeric values to quantify constructs and variables derived from the text data. Measurement is the main analysis component in sentiment and text analyses.

According to a recent review of 54 research articles in the domain of sentiment analysis, there are two categories of different sentiment analysis: the lexicon-based approach and the ML approach (Medhat et al., 2014). While the former includes the dictionary- and corpus-based methods, the latter consists of supervised and unsupervised statistical learning models as well as various deep learning techniques. Below we will briefly introduce the dictionary-based approach and elaborate on the ML and deep learning approaches, which have become increasingly popular in the text analysis field yet are still new to many organizational researchers.

Dictionary-based Approaches to Sentiment Analysis

The dictionary-based approach counts the frequency of occurrences of a selected group of words (i.e., a lexicon dictionary) within a document and calculates its percentage as a means to quantify the prevalence of the dictionary in the document.

The most common technique underneath this approach is Language Inquiry and Word Count (LIWC; Pennebaker et al., 2015), which has developed and integrated dozens of dictionaries, including the positive emotions dictionary (e.g., "love," "nice," "sweet," etc.) and the negative emotions dictionary (e.g., "hurt," "ugly," "nasty," etc.). Because of its ease to use, LIWC has been widely adopted for psychological and organizational research (e.g., Wang et al., 2016). More recently, the LIWC dictionary approach has also been applied to analyze job applicants' cover letters and resumes to predict application outcomes (Brandt & Herzberg, 2020).

Although the dictionary-based approach is simple to apply and useful in many cases, it, unfortunately, suffers from a number of limitations. One limitation is the need to maintain and constantly update a lexicon wherein each word has corresponding sentiment ratings or scores, often on several dimensions. Another limitation is that other word features or sentence-level characteristics that may signify a sentiment are ignored. On the other hand, the ML approach is capable of addressing these limitations by combining sentiment-lexicon-based features with other word features such as the word's part of speech tag and lexical features. The features are then used as input to classifiers such as Random Forest, Support Vector Machines, Naïve Bayes, and Maximum Entropy models, among others. Furthermore, ML are inductive approaches that automatically learn (or extract) the underlying patterns in data and map these patterns to sentiments.

Typical ML Approaches to Sentiment Analysis
ML is an advanced statistical method and has been increasingly utilized in sentiment and text analyses. For example, Sang and Stanton (2020) wished to automate a moderation tool to identify hate speech posted online. To create a measure of hate speech, they trained a ML model by using text data collected from 18,187 posts from the online platform Reddit; they further extracted the semantic content from the titles of the posts using word embedding. Word embedding identifies the patterns of co-occurrence among words and places them in a multidimensional space whereby the words that are closer in this space share more meaning, such as "dog" with "bark" (see a detailed introduction in the next section). A 50-position vector was then assigned to each word using a pre-trained model, and then using Latent Dirichlet Allocation, the topic models identifying the post's "emotions" were created as a hate speech criterion based on the emotions of the individual posting the statements.

After research problems are formulated and text data sources are identified and collected, sentiment analysis using ML typically proceeds in the following manner: (1) text data pre-processing and transformation, (2) training ML models, (3) model testing and validation, and (4) model deployment and updating.

Text Pre-Processing and Transformation.   Text data may contain elements that are irrelevant for sentiment detection and hence must be removed to reduce complexity and noise. Various text pre-processing procedures may be applied, such as tokenization, stop word removal, case folding (converting text to lowercase or uppercase), stemming and lemmatization, and sometimes punctuation or number deletion. After the pre-processing, text transformation is performed, this step transforms the text into a mathematical structure that serves as input to the ML technique. Usually, a unit of analysis is determined, such as a sentence, paragraph, or even the whole document. Each text unit is transformed into a vector by applying the vector space model, where the elements are the frequencies of the words appearing in the text. The size of the vector corresponds to the size of the vocabulary, which is the set of all terms in the text data collection. The vectors are then combined into what is termed the Document-by-term matrix, wherein each row is the vector representation of each text unit. Another alternative vector-based transformation is the one-hot encoding technique. In this representation, each word is represented by a vector, the elements of which are zero except for the component that corresponds to the word, which is set equal to 1. If the unit of analysis is not the word, then the input is a matrix which is just the row-wise concatenation of the vector representation of each word comprising the text unit. The one-hot encoding is commonly used in deep learning methods, which shall be discussed in a separate section. Further transformations may be applied to the resulting transformed text, such as computing the tf-idf scores of each word or applying several weighting schemes. The purpose of this is to either filter out some terms to reduce the matrix dimensionality or to assign different weights to the words to highlight their importance in the analysis.

As mentioned, the Document-by-term matrix or the matrix from the one-hot encoding serves as input to the ML technique. However, prior to running any ML technique, a subset of the collection must be annotated. A group of labelers is employed to identify the sentiment of each text unit or to score it according to its sentiment polarity, perhaps, on several dimensions. Because identifying sentiment is somewhat subjective, to ensure the reliability of labels, each text unit should be annotated by two or more labelers and then examined for consistency. When there are inconsistencies, the labelers must reach a consensus to resolve the discrepancies and assign the most appropriate sentiment score. The consensus can also be reached through automated strategies such as applying the majority rule. The annotated data are further broken down into training, test, and validation datasets. The training dataset will be used to estimate the parameters of the ML techniques, and performance measures will be computed using the test data. The validation set is set aside and is not part of the model-building process, as it is only used to assess the final performance of the model. There are standard procedures for splitting the dataset, such as splitting them according to proportions example, using a 70-20-10 split. That is, 70% of the text units are assigned to the training dataset, 20% are for the test, and the remaining is assigned to the validation test. Another is to use cross-validation procedures or bootstrapping on the combined train and test datasets.

Training ML Models.   Ordinarily, multiple ML models are run and compared. For the ML technique, the researcher has a wealth of ML models to choose from:

The Random Forest Mmodels. The random forest models are an ensemble model that combines several decision trees. Each decision tree is generated using a subset of the features (in this case, the words in the vocabulary) and bagging (sampling text units with replacement).

Gradient Boosted Trees. Gradient boosted trees are another ensemble-based technique that is also based on decision trees. In contrast to random forest, gradient boosted trees is a model that is built iteratively wherein the latest iteration of the model is better than the previous one. Both tree ensemble learning algorithms have been shown to reduce model bias and variance. Random forest classifier has been used for sentiment classification in the Indonesian language, such as detecting sentiments about the anti-LGBT campaign from tweets (Fitri et al., 2019) and identifying sentiments from reviews (Fauzi, 2018). Other applications include extracting opinions from customer reviews in an online shopping platform (Karthika et al., 2019) and product recommendations (Khanvilkar & Vora, 2018).

Support Vector Machine. The third technique is the support vector machine which is a large margin classifier suitable for data with high dimensionality and nonlinearity that is typical of text data. Support vector machines have been applied to forecast stock prices by analyzing the sentiments of investors (Ren et al., 2018). Moreover, support vector machine is the basis of a model that was developed to detect sentiments from student reviews of teaching performance (Esparza et al., 2018).

Naïve Bayes Model. Fourth is the naïve Bayes model, which is a probabilistic model that assumes conditionally independent predictors. The naïve Bayes classifier has been shown to perform well on other text analysis applications. The technique of naïve Bayes has been used to analyze the sentiments of Indonesians toward COVID-19 vaccines (Pristiyono et al., 2021). Also, naïve Bayes was used to identify political sentiments (Elghazaly et al., 2016).

Maximum Entropy Model. Fifth is the maximum entropy model, which is also a probabilistic classifier but, in contrast to naïve Bayes, does not assume that predictors are conditionally independent; instead, it learns the distribution. Maximum entropy was used to extract social sentiments embedded in user-contributed comments to improve business profitability (Rao et al., 2016).

Model Testing and Validation.   In practice, research often runs multiple ML models and then evaluates the model performance by calculating performance measures such as accuracy, *F*-score, or area under the curve. After the best performance is determined, it is further subjected to validity analysis. Determining the validity of the model is the same as asking, "are we measuring the thing that we are trying to measure?" in this case, the sentiments embedded in the text. For determining validity, we may compare the sentiments generated by the model to the sentiments identified by domain experts, and this would establish face validity. It is also possible to establish predictive validity, such as using the sentiments to predict a certain outcome (e.g., stock price) and compare these predictions to predictions obtained using another data source.

Model Deployment and Updating.   Once validity has been established, the model may now be deployed to its intended application or subjected to further investigation, such as confirming a theory or maybe generating a new theory. Since circumstances may change, it is important to occasionally update the model to ensure that the model does not give erroneous sentiment predictions. For example, language use may vary, and new terms must be incorporated into the model.

There are other considerations during model building that we did not elaborate on in our discussion here, such as how to address the lack of training data (since in some applications, building training data can be laborious, time-consuming, and costly), how to perform the term weighting, and how to deal with nuances in language use such as irony and sarcasm. For the first two, we refer the readers to numerous references tackling these concerns, and for the third, this can be partly addressed by performing natural language processing and increasing the size of the training text data. Also, deep learning models have been developed for sarcasm analysis. Nevertheless, the steps outlined in the preceding paragraphs are enough to provide an overview of how sentiment analysis can be conducted using ML techniques.

Deep Learning Models and Word Embedding Techniques
Deep learning models are based on neural networks. Moreover, since texts are sequential in nature, it is possible to use sequence-based techniques such as conditional random fields (Xia et al., 2020). One may try different ML models and subsequently compare their performances. It is also possible to just combine the models to give an overall prediction.

One group of techniques that are popular nowadays is based on deep learning, which is essentially *artificial neural network models*. Although there have been previous studies that used neural networks in sentiment analysis, these studies were limited by the amount of training data and the size and architecture of the neural network. The computational inspiration of deep learning and neural network, in general, is the human brain. Although it is evident that the human brain is more complex than what can be represented in an artificial neural network.

In a nutshell, deep learning consists of several layers consisting of numerous nonlinear processing units called neurons. These neurons take care of feature extraction and transformation and are effective in dealing with nonlinearity in the data. The first layer is the input layer which receives the text data (in vector format). From the input layer, the data are fed to the succeeding layers and the data undergo several transformations. Each layer can be construed as extracting a specific pattern in the data. Finally, the last layer outputs the prediction, in our case, the sentiment of the text.

There are several deep learning architectures; each is designed to handle a specific type of data. The convolution neural network architecture is suitable for image data, although there were attempts to use it on text data as well. Another is the recurrent neural network which has been developed to specifically handle sequence data such as text. Examples of recurrent neural networks are bidirectional recurrent neural networks, deep bidirectional neural networks, and long-term short memory networks. The deep learning networks have been successfully applied to several natural language processing tasks, such as automatic question–answering systems, machine translation, and document generation. Many recurrent neural network architectures cannot handle long-term dependencies. Hence, a technique called the attention mechanism has been proposed. The mechanism is embedded in existing RNN architectures to improve their performances.

Not all deep learning techniques are developed for prediction tasks. Other techniques are used for data transformation and dimensionality reduction. The most popular in this group are Autoencoders, which are like principal component analysis or latent semantic analysis. One technique that is useful for word representation is word embedding. This technique transforms each word into a vector representation, but instead of just one or zero elements, vector values can be continuous, and the size of the vector is significantly smaller than the size of the vocabulary. Hence, these word embeddings can be used as input data for a sentiment detection model. The progenitor of word embedding techniques is the Word2Vec model, a computationally efficient neural network that learns word embeddings from textual sources. The embeddings are either learned using the skip-gram model or the bag of words model.

The same steps are followed for sentiment analysis as enumerated in the preceding section, even when using Deep learning techniques. Deep learning has become a de facto method for complex tasks that involve natural language. In fact, numerous studies have proposed deep learning as the technique for sentiment analysis, specifically on multilingual sentiment analysis and related tasks such as opinion mining, aspect level sentiment prediction, sarcasm analysis, emotion analysis, and multimodal data sentiment analysis.

Stage 3: Inference

Based on the concepts discovered in Stage 1 and the variables measured and modeled in Stage 2, we may now make predictions about future events or relationships of other variables. This is the inference stage in text analysis. For instance, after analyzing CEOs' retirement statements and establishing a quantitative relationship between concepts or variables developed from the text data (e.g., semantic topics, positive or negative sentiment, etc.) and organizational outcomes (e.g., employee engagement, stock price, etc.) based on the collected data, we may predict similar outcomes for a new organization. As such, the goal of inference is to predict outcomes from new data, making inferences and validating theories.

ILLUSTRATIVE EXAMPLES

To illustrate the applications of sentiment analysis in organizational research, we provide two examples with different approaches and real data sources. The first example was a traditional approach based on millions of employee attitudinal ratings toward various aspects of their job and organizations. The second example was text data-based, applying the LIWC dictionary approach to corporate diversity statements and examining if the positive or negative sentiment tones measured from the statements impacted employees' ratings on organizations' diversity and inclusion.

Study 1

The first study focused on the traditional survey approach to sentiment analysis. Specifically, we turned to Glassdoor.com to retrieve millions of employee attitudinal ratings on 10 aspects of the Fortune 1,000 companies. Glassdoor.com is one of the most popular jobs posting websites and "the most dominant company reviews website by far" (Winkler & Fuller, 2019). The website is completely free to use, allowing current and former employees to anonymously review their companies. As the massive number of reviews provides valuable insights for potential job seekers, the website attracts about 60 million users per month.

At the time of writing, Glassdoor allowed current and former employees to rate companies on 10 dimensions, including seven dimensions rated on a 1–5 star rating scale (i.e., overall rating, diversity, and inclusion, culture, and values, work/life balance, senior management, compensation and benefits, career opportunities) and three other dimensions on a dichotomous thumbs-up or thumbs-down scale (i.e., recommendation to a friend, approval of CEO, and positive business outlook). As the labels for the rating dimensions are self-explanatory, no detailed definitions of these terms were provided in the rating system. As the ratings reflected employees' subjective opinions, they provided valuable information regarding employees' sentiments about these organizations.

With such sentiment data at hand, we were able to examine a research question related to whether a company publicly released a diversity statement was associated with more favorable sentiments rated by the employees. Indeed, organizational theories suggest that diversity statements can generate positive perceptions by clarifying support for and inclusion of minoritized employees. According to social identity theory, people can gain esteem from the social groups they belong to and identify with (Tajfel & Turner, 1986), including being a member of an organization (Ashforth & Mael, 1989). From this perspective, a company showing support for injustice would make employees feel more assured that their company cares about them and their community. Therefore, public speaking on these topics would have strong implications for DEI within that company and help cultivate the positive benefits that can emerge when companies value their employees' identities. Thus, we may hypothesize:

H1. Companies that released a diversity statement are associated with more favorable sentiments rated by their employees than companies that did not release a statement.

We conducted a series of *t*-tests to compare the sentiment ratings over the 10 dimensions between companies that released vs did not release a diversity statement. As presented in Table 1, the results revealed that the sentiments toward the companies that released a diversity statement were more favorable across the 10 dimensions ($p < 0.0001$), supporting *H1*. In addition, the effect size indicated by Cohen's *d* showed that the sentiment rating differed most on the *diversity & inclusion* dimension ($d = 0.532$; medium size), which made great sense as the two groups were categorized by whether or not the companies released a diversity statement, followed by the effect on the *culture and values* ($d = 0.491$; medium size) and *overall rating* ($d = 0.420$; medium size) dimension. The effect size for the other sentiment rating dimensions ranged from 0.253 (*compensation & benefit*, and *positive business outlook*) and 0.383 (*career opportunity*). We further visualized the sentiment distributions and differences among the two groups of companies in Fig. 2.

Table 1. Comparative Results of Employee Sentiment Ratings Over 10 Dimensions on Glassdoor.com Between Companies Releasing Versus Not Releasing Statements.

Rating Dimension	Companies That Released Statements		Companies That Did Not Release Statements		*t*	*p*	Cohen's *d*
	M	*SD*	*M*	*SD*			
Diversity and inclusion	3.903	0.433	3.644	0.536	8.268	0.000	0.532
Overall rating	3.771	0.352	3.611	0.408	6.529	0.000	0.420
Culture and values	3.692	0.448	3.457	0.505	7.623	0.000	0.491
Work/life balance	3.564	0.407	3.412	0.448	5.492	0.000	0.354
Senior management	3.343	0.402	3.194	0.466	5.281	0.000	0.340
Compensation and benefits	3.692	0.403	3.585	0.445	3.919	0.000	0.253
Career opportunities	3.467	0.386	3.314	0.412	5.938	0.000	0.383
Recommend to a friend	0.710	0.127	0.658	0.144	5.882	0.000	0.379
Approval of CEO	0.827	0.142	0.772	0.170	5.442	0.000	0.350
Positive business outlook	0.601	0.153	0.560	0.167	3.922	0.000	0.253

Notes: $N_{\text{Released Statements}} = 458$ and $N_{\text{No Statements Released}} = 489$.

Study 2

In the second example, we followed the principles of text-mining research to demonstrate the process of text-based sentiment analysis. Specifically, leveraging on corporate diversity statements, we applied the LIWC dictionary and text topic model methods to examine if the positive or negative sentiment tones measured from the statements impacted employees' ratings on organizations' diversity and inclusion.

Stage 1: Developing Concepts and Identifying Research Questions
In this illustrative example, our goal is to better understand the impact of the sentiment tones conveyed in diversity statements that corporations publicly released to condemn racism, especially in the context of a large-scale social mega-threat of racism. As such, we first need to conceptualize and measure emotional tones expressed in those diversity statements and identify research questions. In this case, we decided to conceptualize sentiment tones by counting words with positive or negative emotions built in the LIWC dictionaries. After conceptualizing the concept, we then ask research questions on its consequences. For example, we attempt to understand how such sentiments impacted employees' reactions to organizations' diversity and inclusion policies.

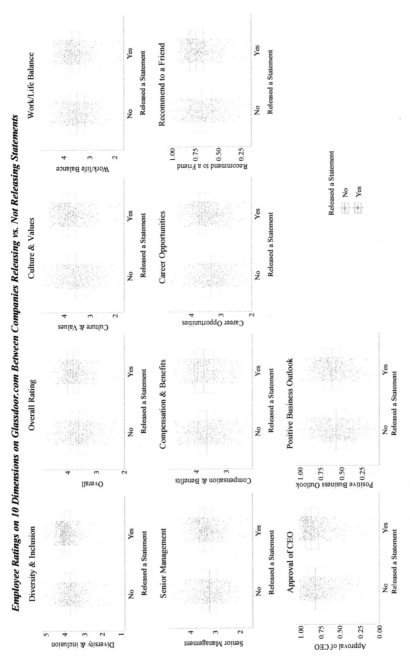

Fig. 2. Employee Ratings on 10 Dimensions on Glassdoor.com Between Companies Releasing Versus Not Releasing Statements.

Table 2. Descriptive Statistics and Correlations.

Variable	M	SD	1	2	3	4	5	6
1. Topic 1 (general DEI terms)	0.36	0.31	1.00					
2. Topic 2 (supporting Black community)	0.25	0.30	−0.52**	1.00				
3. Topic 3 (acknowledging Black community)	0.21	0.25	−0.24**	−0.39**	1.00			
4. Topic 4 (committing to diversifying workforce)	0.11	0.19	−0.33**	−0.04	−0.25**	1.00		
5. Topic 5 (miscellaneous words)	0.05	0.13	−0.17**	−0.17**	−0.04	−0.04	1.00	
6. Topic 6 (titles and companies)	0.02	0.10	−0.09†	−0.11*	−0.08†	−0.06	−0.06	1.00
7. Diversity and inclusion	3.90	0.43	−0.09†	0.06	0.08†	0.01	−0.01	−0.12**
8. Overall rating	3.77	0.36	−0.16**	0.07	0.16**	0.01	0.00	−0.13**
9. Culture and values	3.69	0.45	−0.15**	0.06	0.16**	0.03	0.01	−0.17**
10. Work–life balance	3.56	0.41	−0.08†	0.02	0.13**	0.02	−0.03	−0.15**
11. Senior management	3.34	0.40	−0.12**	0.08†	0.12*	−0.01	−0.03	−0.12*
12. Compensation and benefits	3.69	0.40	−0.06	0.03	0.09*	−0.06	0.02	−0.04
13. Career opportunities	3.47	0.39	−0.06	0.06	0.11*	−0.04	−0.02	−0.16**
14. Recommend to a friend	0.71	0.13	−0.12*	0.03	0.16**	0.01	0.01	−0.15**
15. Approval of CEO	0.83	0.14	−0.04	0.05	0.06	0.00	−0.03	−0.14**
16. Positive business outlook	0.60	0.15	−0.11*	0.08†	0.08†	0.00	−0.02	−0.08†
17. Positive emotions	4.51	3.03	0.26**	−0.03	−0.14**	−0.09†	−0.10*	−0.09†
18. Negative emotions	2.02	1.80	0.10*	−0.19**	0.31**	−0.23**	−0.03	−0.06

Note: $N = 469$.
† $p < 0.1$, * $p < 0.05$, and ** $p < 0.01$.

After a research question is identified, we then decide on text data sources and conduct text data collection. In this step, we turned to the list of Fortune 1,000 companies retrieved from https://fortune.com and manually collected diversity statements that were publicly released by these companies. We searched for such statements from all different web sources, including the company's official website, Twitter, Facebook, or LinkedIn page, or statement released to a news outlet – using the search terms such as "racial equity," "diversity," "inclusion," "open letter," "newsroom," "news press," "press release" and other keywords. Eventually, we were able to collect diversity statements for 511 companies on the Fortune 1,000 list.

Stage 2: Measuring Sentiment Tones
In order to measure sentiment tones in the text data, we needed to prepare the text data for transformation. As part of the pre-processing preparation, stop words such as "a," "the" etc., and punctuations were removed. Full words were also converted to stem forms, like "diverse," "diversity," "diversified," "diversification," to "divers," etc. In addition, low-frequency words and documents with less than 10 words were also removed. This process led to a final sample of 469 documents.

In this example, we took the dictionary-based approach to measure sentiment tones by using the Language Inquiry and Word Count (LIWC; Pennebaker et al., 2015) technique. LIWC is a widely used lexical dictionary for various text analysis

7	8	9	10	11	12	13	14	15	16	17
1.00										
0.66**	1.00									
0.73**	0.91**	1.00								
0.58**	0.75**	0.81**	1.00							
0.67**	0.91**	0.91**	0.74**	1.00						
0.43**	0.71**	0.61**	0.52**	0.62**	1.00					
0.60**	0.83**	0.78**	0.57**	0.85**	0.63**	1.00				
0.62**	0.90**	0.88**	0.73**	0.86**	0.64**	0.81**	1.00			
0.48**	0.73**	0.69**	0.58**	0.73**	0.50**	0.66**	0.76**	1.00		
0.52**	0.78**	0.73**	0.54**	0.78**	0.56**	0.76**	0.79**	0.73**	1.00	
−0.09†	−0.15**	−0.14**	−0.12*	−0.17**	−0.11*	−0.14**	−0.14**	−0.12**	−0.11*	1.00
0.05	0.05	0.07	0.05	0.08†	0.05	0.06	0.08†	0.02	0.05	−0.10*

methods, especially in psychological and organizational research (e.g., Wang et al., 2016). This method calculated the percentage of the positive or negative words that appeared in a statement based on the positive and negative emotional words built-in dictionaries. Specifically, the built-in positive emotions dictionary contained 620 words such as "love," "nice," "sweet," etc., and the negative emotions dictionary contained 744 words such as "hurt," "ugly," "nasty," etc. Thus, the percentages of positive and negative emotion words in a diversity statement measured the positive and negative sentiment tones, respectively. The LIWC analysis revealed that, on average, more positive emotion words (4.51%) were used in the corporate diversity statements than negative emotion words (2.02%).

In addition, we utilized the structural topic modeling method (STM; Roberts et al., 2014; see Wang et al., 2022 for an example), an unsupervised ML model, to extract latent topics as covariates in examining the predictive validity of the LIWC based sentiment scores.

Stage 3: Collecting New Data and Testing Hypothesis
After we conceptualized and measured the sentiment variables, we proceeded to answer a research question: How did sentiments expressed in the diversity statements were associated with employees' favorability ratings on the ten dimensions? To answer this question, we followed a deductive research paradigm and further collected data on employees' ratings from www.glassdoor.com. See Study 1 for a brief introduction to the 10 ratings.

Table 3. The Effect of Topic Prevalence Covered a Statement in Predicting Employee Ratings on 10 Dimensions on Glassdoor.com After Controlling for LIWC Positive and Negative Emotion Words.

Variable	D&I		Overall		Culture		Work/Life		Management	
	B	*SE*	*B*	*SE*	*B*	*SE*	*B*	*SE*	*B*	*SE*
Constant	3.39***	0.20	3.34***	0.16	2.99***	0.20	2.97***	0.18	2.92***	0.18
Topic 1	0.48*	0.21	0.39*	0.17	0.62**	0.21	0.60**	0.20	0.43*	0.19
Topic 2	0.61**	0.21	0.55***	0.17	0.82***	0.21	0.67***	0.19	0.59**	0.19
Topic 3	0.64**	0.21	0.68***	0.17	0.97***	0.21	0.80***	0.20	0.62**	0.20
Topic 4	0.56*	0.22	0.48***	0.18	0.80***	0.22	0.68**	0.21	0.45*	0.20
Topic 5	0.46†	0.25	0.44*	0.20	0.69**	0.25	0.50*	0.23	0.35	0.23
Posemo	−0.01	0.01	−0.01*	0.01	−0.02*	0.01	−0.01*	0.01	−0.02***	0.01
Negemo	0.01	0.01	0.00	0.01	0.01	0.01	0.00	0.01	0.01	0.01
R^2	0.035*		0.076**		0.082**		0.054**		0.068**	

D&I, diversity and inclusion; Overall, overall rating; Culture, culture and values; Work/Life, work/life balance; Management, senior management; Compensation, compensation and benefits; Career, career opportunities; Recommend, recommend to a friend; CEO, approval of CEO; Outlook, positive business outlook; Posemo, positive emotion words by LIWC; and Negemo, negative emotion words by LIWC.
†$p < 0.1$, *$p < 0.05$, **$p < 0.01$, and ***$p < 0.001$.

Before we collected this additional data on employees' online ratings, we delved into the previous literature to develop research hypotheses. According to Bernat et al. (2001), positive (vs negative) emotion words improved recipients' favorable (vs unfavorable) evaluations and attitudes. Thus, we proposed the following hypothesis:

H2. Positive (vs negative) sentiment tone expressed in the diversity statement released by a company will be significantly related to employees' favorable (vs unfavorable) ratings of the company's diversity and inclusion.

We first conducted descriptive statistics and ran a correlation among the three variables: positive sentiment, negative sentiment, and employees' diversity ratings. As shown in Table 2, the positive sentiment derived from the diversity statement by the LIWC method was positively related to latent Topic 1 ($r = 0.26$, $p < 0.01$), yet negatively related to Topic 3 ($r = -0.14$, $p < 0.01$), overall job satisfaction ($r = -0.15$, $p < 0.01$), satisfaction with cultural and values ($r = -0.14$, $p < 0.01$), work/life balance ($r = -0.12$, $p < 0.05$), senior management ($r = -0.17$, $p < 0.01$), compensation and benefits ($r = -0.11$, $p < 0.05$), career opportunity ($r = -0.14$, $p < 0.01$), recommend to a friend ($r = -0.14$, $p < 0.01$), approval of CEO ($r = -0.12$, $p < 0.01$), and positive business outlook ($r = -0.11$, $p < 0.01$). In contrast, the negative sentiment was positively related to Topic 3 ($r = 0.31$, $p < 0.01$), yet negatively related to Topic 2 ($r = -0.19$, $p < 0.01$) and Topic 4 ($r = -0.23$, $p < 0.01$). And the positive and negative sentiment scores were negatively correlated ($r = -0.10$, $p < 0.01$).

We further ran a regression model to predict online ratings with both sentiment tones, after controlling for text topics. As shown in Table 3, the positive sentiment scores were statistically predictive of overall job satisfaction

Compensation		Career		Recommend		CEO		Outlook	
B	SE	B	SE	B	SE	B	SE	B	SE
3.54	0.19	2.89***	0.17	0.53***	0.06	0.64***	0.07	0.48***	0.07
0.16	0.20	0.63***	0.18	0.17**	0.06	0.21**	0.07	0.10	0.07
0.24	0.19	0.71***	0.18	0.21***	0.06	0.23***	0.07	0.16*	0.07
0.29	0.20	0.76***	0.19	0.26***	0.06	0.23***	0.07	0.16*	0.08
0.06	0.21	0.55**	0.20	0.20**	0.06	0.20**	0.07	0.13	0.08
0.23	0.23	0.54*	0.22	0.19**	0.07	0.16†	0.08	0.10	0.09
−0.01*	0.01	−0.02**	0.01	0.00	0.00	−0.01**	0.00	0.00	0.00
0.00	0.01	0.00	0.01	0.00	0.00	0.00	0.00	0.00	0.00
0.026†		0.063**		0.071**		0.042**		0.036*	

($b = -0.01$, $p < 0.05$), satisfaction with culture and value ($b = -0.02$, $p < 0.05$), work/life balance ($b = -0.01$, $p < 0.05$), management ($b = -0.02$, $p < 0.01$), compensation ($b = -0.01$, $p < 0.05$), career ($b = -0.02$, $p < 0.01$), and CEO approval ($b = -0.01$, $p < 0.05$). However, the negative sentiment scores did not show a significant effect on these ratings.

CONCLUSION

Sentiment analysis, as a novel method for text analysis, has become increasingly popular in organizational research. Because of its capabilities of systematically detecting, identifying, or extracting the emotional intent of words to infer positive or negative tone, this method opens an exciting new avenue for organizational research, mainly due to the abundantly available text data in organizations and the well-developed sentiment analysis techniques. Yet, this new method has inevitably posed a serious challenge to many organizational researchers. This chapter introduced the research paradigms for text analysis research, advocating the iterative research paradigm (cf., inductive and deductive research paradigms) that is more suitable for text mining research. In addition, this chapter further elaborated on the analytical procedures for sentiment analysis with three stages – discovery, measurement, and inference, and highlighted both the dictionary-based approaches and the ML approaches in the measurement stage. To help better facilitate the application of sentiment analysis in organizational research, we also provide two illustrative examples to demonstrate a sentiment analysis by applying the traditional survey method and the iterative research paradigm, and the dictionary-based LIWC techniques to study corporate diversity statements.

We hope these practical guidelines will help facilitate more applications of this promising method in organizational research in the future.

Conflict of Interest Statement

The authors have no known conflict of interest to disclose.

REFERENCES

Ahman, M. (2018). Sentiment analysis using SVM: A systematic literature review. *International Journal of Advanced Computer Science and Applications, 9*(2), 182–188.

Almars, A., Li, X., Zhao, X., Ibrahim, I. A., Yuan, W., & Li, B. (2017, November 5–6). Structured sentiment analysis. In *Proceedings of the 13th international conference on Advanced data mining and applications, ADMA 2017, Singapore* (Vol. 13, pp. 695–707). Springer International Publishing.

Ashforth, B. E., & Mael, F. (1989). Social identity theory and the organization. *Academy of Management Review, 14*(1), 20–39. https://doi.org/10.5465/amr.1989.4278999

Bernat, E., Bunce, S., & Shevrin, H. (2001). Event-related brain potentials differentiate positive and negative mood adjectives during both supraliminal and subliminal visual processing. *International Journal of Psychophysiology, 42*(1), 11–34. https://doi.org/10.1016/S0167-8760

Brandt, P. M., & Herzberg, P. Y. (2020). Is a cover letter still needed? Using LIWC to predict application success. *International Journal of Selection and Assessment, 28*(4), 417–429.

DeChurch, L. A., Wang, W., Harris, A. M., & Contractor, N. S. (2018, July). *Mapping the modern science of teams* [Paper presentation]. 13th Interdisciplinary Network for Group Research (INGRoup) annual meeting, Washington, DC.

Elghazaly, T., Mahmoud, A., & Hefny, H. A. (2016, March). Political sentiment analysis using twitter data. In D. E. Boubiche, F. Hidoussi, L. Guezouoli, A. Bounceur & H. T. Cruz (Eds.), *Proceedings of the international conference on internet of things and cloud computing* (pp. 1–5). Association for Computing Machinery.

Esparza, G. G., et al. (2018). A Sentiment Analysis Model to Analyze Students Reviews of Teacher Performance Using Support Vector Machines. Distributed Computing and Artificial Intelligence, 14th International Conference. Cham: Springer International Publishing.

Fauzi, M. A. (2018). Random forest approach to sentiment analysis in Indonesian. *Indonesian Journal of Electrical Engineering and Computer Science, 12*(1), 46–50.

Fitri, V. A., Andreswari, R., & Hasibuan, M. A. (2019). Sentiment analysis of social media Twitter with case of Anti-LGBT campaign in Indonesia using Naïve Bayes, decision tree, and random forest algorithm. *Procedia Computer Science, 161*, 765–772.

Gelbard, R., Ramon-Gonen, R., Carmeli, A., Bittmann, R. M., & Talyansky, R. (2018). Sentiment analysis in organizational work: Towards an ontology of people analytics. *Expert Systems, 35*(5), Article e12289. https://doi.org/10.1111/exsy.12289

Ghazizadeh, M., McDonald, A. D., & Lee, J. D. (2014). Text mining to decipher free-response consumer complaints. *Human Factors: The Journal of the Human Factors and Ergonomics Society, 56*(6), 1189–1203. https://doi.org/10.1177/0018720813519473

Grimmer, J., Roberts, M. E., & Stewart, B. M. (2022a). *Text as data: A new framework for machine learning and the social sciences.* Princeton University Press.

Grimmer, J. R., Margaret E., & Stewart, B. M. (2022b). Introduction. In R. Michael Alvarez (Ed.), *Text as data: A new framework for machine learning and the social sciences* (p. 360). Princeton University Press.

Hume, D. (1963). *Essays: Moral political and literary.* Oxford University Press.

Kahn, W.A. (1990). Psychological conditions of personal engagement and disengagement at work. *Academy of Management Journal, 33*, 692–724.

Karthika, P. M., Murugeswari, R., & Manoranjithem, R. (2019). Sentiment Analysis of Social Media Network Using Random Forest Algorithm. 2019 IEEE International Conference on Intelligent Techniques in Control, Optimization and Signal Processing (INCOS).

Khanvilkar, G. (2019). Product recommendation using sentiment analysis of reviews: A random forest approach. *International Journal of Engineering and Advanced Technology, 8*(2S2), 146–152.

Judge, T. A., & Kammeyer-Mueller, J. D. (2012). Job attitudes. *Annual Review of Psychology, 63*, 341–367. https://doi.org/10.1146/annurev-psych-120710-100511

Leigh, A., & Melwani, S. (2019). BlackEmployeesMatter: Megathreats, identity fusion, and enacting positive deviance in organizations. *Academy of Management Review, 44*(3), 564–591. https://doi.org/10.5465/amr.2017.0127

Liu, B. (2012). *Sentiment analysis and opinion mining*. Morgan & Claypool Publishers.

Liu, B. (2020). *Sentiment analysis: Mining opinions, sentiments, and emotions*. Cambridge University Press.

McAbee, S. T., Landis, R. S., & Burke, M. I. (2017). Inductive reasoning: The promise of big data. *Human Resource Management Review, 27*(2), 277–290.

Medhat, W., Hassan, A., & Korashy, H. (2014). Sentiment analysis algorithms and applications: A survey. *Ain Shams Engineering Journal, 5*(4), 1093–1113. https://doi.org/10.1016/j.asej.2014.04.011

Newman, D. A., Joseph, D. L., & Hulin, C. L. (2010). Job attitudes and employee engagement: Considering the attitude "A-factor". In *Handbook of employee engagement*. Edward Elgar Publishing.

Pennebaker, J. W., Boyd, R. L., Jordan, K., & Blackburn, K. (2015). *The development and psychometric properties of LIWC2015*. Austin, TX: University of Texas at Austin.

Pristiyono, Ritonga, M., Ihsan, M. A. A., Anjar, A., & Rambe, F. H. (2021). Sentiment analysis of COVID-19 vaccine in Indonesia using Naïve Bayes algorithm. *IOP Conference Series: Materials Science and Engineering, 1088*(1), 012045. https://doi.org/10.1088/1757-899X/1088/1/012045

Procter & Gamble Company. (2023, January 8). *Employees*. https://us.pg.com/ethics-and-corporate-responsibility/employees/

Pyun, J., & Rha, J. S. (2021). Review of research on digital supply chain management using network text analysis. *Sustainability, 13*(17), 9929.

Rao, Y., Xie, H., Li, J., Jin, F., Wang, F. L., & Li, Q. (2016). Social emotion classification of short text via topic-level maximum entropy model. *Information & Management, 53*(8), 978–986.

Ren, R., Wu, D. D., & Liu, T. (2018). Forecasting stock market movement direction using sentiment analysis and support vector machine. *IEEE Systems Journal, 13*(1), 760–770.

Roberts, M. E., Stewart, B. M., & Tingley, D. (2014). stm: R package for structural topic models. *Journal of Statistical Software, 10*(2), 1–40. https://doi.org/10.18637/jss.v000.i00

Sasangohar, F., Dhala, A., Zheng, F., Ahmadi, N., Kash, B., & Masud, F. (2021). Use of telecritical care for family visitation to ICU during the COVID-19 pandemic: An interview study and sentiment analysis. *BMJ Quality & Safety, 30*(9), 715–721.

Sang, Y., & Stanton, J. (2020, July). Analyzing hate speech with Incel-Hunters' critiques. In *International conference on social media and society* (pp. 5–13). London: Toronto Metropolitan University & University of the Arts.

Spector, P. E., Rogelberg, S. G., Ryan, A. M., Schmitt, N., & Zedeck, S. (2014). Moving the pendulum back to the middle: Reflections on and introduction to the inductive research. *Journal of Business and Psychology, 29*(4), 499–502.

Speer, A. B. (2018). Quantifying with words: An investigation of the validity of narrative-derived performance scores. *Personnel Psychology, 71*(3), 299–333.

Tajfel, H., & Turner, J. C. (1986). The social identity theory of intergroup behavior. In S. Worchel & W. G. Austing (Eds.), *Psychology of intergroup relations* (2nd ed., pp. 7–24). Nelson-Hall.

Wang, W., Dinh, J. V., Jones, K. S., Upadhyay, S., & Yang, J. (2022). Corporate diversity statements and employees' online DEI ratings: An unsupervised machine-learning text-mining analysis. *Journal of Business and Psychology, 38*, 45–61.

Wang, W., Hernandez, I., Newman, D. A., He, J., & Bian, J. (2016). Twitter analysis: Studying US weekly trends in work stress and emotion. *Applied Psychology, 65*(2), 355–378. https://doi.org/10.1111/apps.12065

Winkler, R., & Fuller, A. (2019, January 22). How companies secretly boost their Glassdoor ratings. *Wall Street Journal*. https://www.wsj.com/articles/companies-manipulate-glassdoor-by-inflating-rankings-and-pressuring-employees-11548171977

Xia, H., Yang, Y., Pan, X., Zhang, Z., & An, W. (2020). Sentiment analysis for online reviews using conditional random fields and support vector machines. *Electronic Commerce Research, 20*(2), 343–360.

LEADER ENERGY DRIVING PERSONAL AND FIRM-LEVEL WELLNESS: LESSONS FROM 20 YEARS OF THE LEADERSHIP PULSE*

Theresa M. Welbourne

ABSTRACT

In 2023, the Leadership Pulse project will have been running for two decades. Since the inception of the program, we have engaged thousands of leaders around the world to quickly learn from them via short pulse surveys conducted multiple times per year. This chapter is the first overall discussion of what we learned during the last 20 years about leader energy, energy flow, predictors of energy, and outcomes of energy, which have been focused on individual and firm-level performance. Over the years, we learned that leaders are not immune to personal energy challenges; in fact, we find that their energy is continually tested by extreme demands within and outside their organizations. Also, we learned that there are solutions for helping leaders manage their energy better, and these do not have to be expensive, outsourced programs. In this chapter, we review key findings from the data and hope to help leaders continue learning to help themselves, their employees, customers, and the organizations they work in overall. I also will review three different interventions that we found to help leaders and employees work and stay at their best and enhance overall organizational goals and outcomes.

Keywords: Leadership; energy; employee energy; wellness; measurement; pulse surveys; employee surveys; leadership energy; strategy

---

* Leadership Pulse® is a registered trademark of eePulse, Inc.

Stress and Well-Being at the Strategic Level
Research in Occupational Stress and Well-Being, Volume 21, 119–136
Copyright © 2024 by Emerald Publishing Limited
All rights of reproduction in any form reserved
ISSN: 1479-3555/doi:10.1108/S1479-355520230000021007

INTRODUCTION

The average person puts only 25% of his energy and ability into his work. The world takes off its hat to those who put in more than 50% of their capacity and stands on its head for those few and far between souls who devote 100%. Andrew Carnegie (1835–1919)

The world has changed since Mr Carnegie made this comment. Today we applaud people who are energized about their work, and simultaneously, we have learned to be concerned about work–life balance and the short- and long-term well-being and health of leaders and the people they lead (Gragnano et al., 2020; Parkes & Langford, 2008). Because leaders set the tone of what is expected of employees, it is important to understand how leaders are spending their time and how they are expending their energy at work and outside of work. This is because leader wellness is related to their decision making, how they interact and influence others, and ultimately how leaders impact their organization's ability to achieve overall strategic goals and objectives.

The Leadership Pulse is a partnership between eePulse, Inc., and the Center for Effective Organizations, Marshall School of Business, University of Southern California designed to measure and trend leadership confidence and energy. Over the past 20 years of research and across 49 separate studies, a great deal has been learned about both energy, leadership, and firm performance.

The Leadership Pulse sample has evolved and changed over time. The initial sample consisted of alumni from the executive education program at the University of Michigan, and over time added people who attended university or professional association programs, conferences, and webinars. Responses for each of the studies or pulses have ranged from a high of about 1,300 to a low of 140. Each individual respondent receives his/her personal report after the pulse survey is closed. They have access to their own online report that shows their scores, including trend data, compared to the summary benchmarking data from the survey. They also can see their data versus results based on other demographics (e.g., industry, size of company, job type, etc.). Many of the surveys provide participants with workbooks and tools to use with their data; this provides enhanced learning and ways to communicate the results and issues with team members. Individual participation is at no cost. The surveys are sent out to the base population via email and today also launched on social media sites (e.g., LinkedIn and Twitter) so that individuals can opt into the program. We have a wide range of companies, leadership levels, and areas, locations and demographics participating in this initiative.

Overall Insights From 20 Years of the Leadership Pulse Research

Before going into detail on some of the key topic areas that we studied over time, below are some of the key overall findings from the project:

(1) Across several studies, we continue to find that 90% or more of leaders are reporting energy levels below where they are at their best. This means they are less productive and less well than they should be. If we can discover why this is the

case and help leaders change habits and behaviors, those leaders can be more productive and better able to deliver on the firm's strategic goals. Stacking work syndrome is often a major contributor to suboptimal leader functioning. More precisely, it isn't that leaders have too much work to do, rather the challenge is that they are not sure which stack of work to focus on first to produce the best results. Leaders and the people who work for them need ongoing help to focus their energy on the right projects (direction). Leaders have been reporting that it is the continuous stacking of more projects without taking away older ones that are causing them to deplete energy levels. Also, each stack is associated with a person, and in an effort to not disappoint, they spread themselves thin by doing a little on each stack and then not taking enough work to completion. Meeting goals and finishing projects help leaders re-energize. The constant lack of direction or focus depletes energy and has negative effects on the organization's overall ability to meet bigger goals and objectives.

(2) Energy, and particularly, leader energy, is contagious. The level of and variance of leader energy over time affects employees on their teams. A high variance in energy is worse than consistent low or high energy. Employees are often unsettled by inconsistency in what to expect from their leaders.

(3) Leaders are rarely aware of what their typical energy level is; they need time to assess and learn from their own trends. Although they frequently assume that they are aware of what energizes and de-energizes them, they are frequently surprised by what the data tells them.

(4) During COVID-19, as people started to work from home, we set up a daily pulse experiment. This revealed a common daily pattern that led to new additional research, and this work and results are discussed in the later section of this manuscript focused on interventions.

(5) Economic downturns frequently impact director-level leaders the most. These individuals often do not have the same kind of insights that the more senior people have concerning the strategic plan of the organization (knowledge about business plans, customers, etc.), but they are nonetheless getting a barrage of questions from employees and have a lot of responsibility to deliver in less predictable circumstances.

(6) The CEO and other C-core executives often have results different from the rest of the leadership team; however, the CEO scores are not always higher than others. For example, one of the most surprising results of the Leadership Pulse studies has been that C-suite leaders reporting less confidence in their business strategies and in their own leadership teams.

(7) Response rates have gone down over time. When the Leadership Pulse study started, the concept was novel and there were high levels of participation, but the normalization of this technology has meant that it now must compete with several other programs for the attention of already busy individuals.

(8) Reflective learning works at all levels when the process is simple and easy to use. Employees must manage their own energy; managers can help, but the employee is in charge. Thus, leaders do well when they engage employees in this same learning.

RESEARCH TOPICS

From its conception in 2003, the Leadership Pulse assessed leadership confidence and added assessments of energy in 2004. The first survey asked five different questions associated with confidence in leaders. Using a scale of not at all confident (1) to very confident (5), we asked respondents to rate their confidence in the following items:

- Your organization's leadership team overall.
- The economic climate of your organization.
- That your organization has the right people and skills.
- Your organization's ability to execute on its vision.
- Your organization's ability to change as needed.

A few years later, an additional question asking people to rate their confidence in their own personal management skills was added. Fig. 1 shows trends in the overall leadership confidence scale scores over time. The overall score (using a 1–5 scale) ranged from a high of 3.91 when we started the project to a low of 3.52 in 2023. However, all in all, the mean score for the scale has not varied tremendously over the years.

The early studies from 2003 were used to assess the reliability and validity of confidence and growth measures. The questions have not changed over time other than adding confidence in personal leadership to the overall scale.[1] In addition to demographic variables, later versions also asked about job levels, functional areas where they work, and organizational questions including the name of the company (optional), ticker symbol if a public company, industry, annual revenue in the last year, number of employees in the last year, rate of change (0-to-100-point scale), and country. Also added was a question on financial performance, asking them to rate their company's overall performance compared to others that are like them (in the same industry, size, and age). These data revealed a strong and positive relationship between the self-report financial performance data and public financial records.

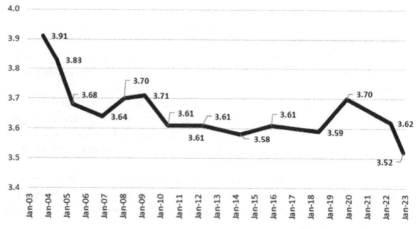

Fig. 1.   Leadership Confidence Trend Data From 2003 to the End of the Year 2022.

In the very first survey in 2003, the highest scoring item was confidence in their leadership team (3.97), and the lowest was confidence in their ability to change (3.71). All of the growth questions were relatively high (4.07 the lowest and 4.68 the highest, out of a maximum of 5.0).

THE ENERGY CONSTRUCT DEFINED

One of the key constructs introduced and then used ongoing in the Leadership Pulse is human energy, the measurement of which is grounded in the literature concerning employee motivation (see Ambrose & Lulik, 1999; Landy & Becker, 1987). Specifically, the Leadership Pulse was concerned with energy exerted at work (vs on other non-work activities) and borrowed from the research on employee energy in sports physiology (Welbourne et al., 2005, p. 56), where this body of work

> specifically describes and assesses human energy directed at optimization of performance (in both its physical and mental aspects). In reviewing this literature, it was concluded that one key difference between sports physiology and the management motivation theories is that within the sports literature, more motivation or more human energy is not always better. In fact, the sports literature would suggest that athletes or anyone attempting to maximize bodily energy should find the level of exertion that is best for that individual. In other words, energy is something that should be optimized not maximized.

This body of work is also consistent with the concept of flow (Csikszentmihalyi, 1991), which leads to energy being in the "zone" for optimal performance. Being at an energy level that is best for an individual, per these theories, leads to optimal output and wellness.

The sports physiology concept of energy also fits with definitions from the field of physics, where energy is defined as the ability to do work (Welbourne, 2014). This body of research lays out the fact that there are two types of energy: (1) potential or stored energy; and (2) kinetic or moving energy. In order to be at an ideal energy level, where work can be done, potential energy must be converted to moving energy. Thus, these two concepts of an optimal level of energy (where someone is at his/her best) and current working energy (which is the energy level being converted into work), were consistent with the sports physiology and physics definitions of energy.

In order to create measures of energy, we merged these two concepts of energy (from physics and sports physiology) by assessing not only how much energy one has, but also the optimal or ideal energy level for getting work done. The goal was not just helping leaders learn to get work done but to do it in a way that does not lead to burnout or other negative outcomes. Like athletes, they needed to be trained to optimize rather than maximize.

Athletes have ideal or target heart rates; they are not told by their coaches to maximize but work out in a way that keeps them "in their target heart rate zone." The idea is to work at a rate that is ideal for your body type so that you do not exhaust yourself and to assure you have enough air to continue breathing, burning calories, and stretching muscles (Gilbert & Jamison, 1994; Hargrove, 1995;

Leifer, 1988; Perry & Jamison, 1997). This type of recommendation shows up in overall health-related Surgeon General Reports as well as in today's searches for new wearable devices to help optimize exercise (e.g., Duking et al., 2017).

The energy research done through the Leadership Pulse as well as in other settings suggests these same guidelines should be used when talking about human energy at work. Find the work level of exertion that is optimal, then measure where you are today and learn to close the gap so that you are working in a range that is best for you. When engaging in sports, no one wants to be harmed; the same idea applies to work. Get the work done but do it in a way that keeps every employee and leader healthy and well.

Energy and Related Constructs

There are a number of constructs that often accompany discussions of energy at work. Employee engagement has become part of most organizations' annual employee survey strategies and made its way to academic research. In some cases, energy is seen as part of the engagement, and some researchers talk about different types of energy (Loehr & Schwartz, 2003). The challenge in understanding the research on the topic of employee engagement is that the idea grew from the practitioner world and then was brought into academics; therefore, there is no pure theory of engagement, and definitions differ significantly.

According to Macey and Schneider (2008, p. 3),

> The notion of employee engagement is a relatively new one, one that has been heavily marketed by human resource (HR) consulting firms that offer advice on how it can be created and leveraged. Academic researchers are now slowly joining the fray, and both parties are saddled with competing and inconsistent interpretations of the meaning of the construct.

A number of psychological models have been added to the discussion (Csikszentmihalyi, 1991Saks, 2006), and in addition to engagement, the topic of vitality has been added to the mix (Ryan & Deci, 2008; Ryan & Frederick, 1997).

In our research, we have found that the three-item employee energy measure correlates with engagement, but the evidence also suggests that these two were different constructs (Welbourne, 2014). For example, energy (and the gap between optimal and working energy) predicted numerous performance indicators, whereas measures of engagement did not predict those same measures.[2] Engagement data did predict a number of different variables, many of that were collected in the same surveys (e.g., employee satisfaction, intent to turnover, pay satisfaction metrics, and more). The differential predictors suggest that although these two key metrics are related, they are uniquely different in their ability to predict future outcomes.

The study of energy and engagement continues to evolve and has become quite substantial (e.g., Kular et al., 2008; Macey et al., 2009). As noted in a fairly recent literature review,

> employee engagement is an important issue in management theory and practice. However, there are still major differences in the concept, theory, influencing factors and outcomes of employee engagement, and there is still no authoritative standard. (Sun & Bunchapattanasakda, 2019, p. 63)

Two other relatively newer terms are being used, thriving and vitality (Porath et al., 2012). In an article published by Spreitzer and Porath (2012), they note that "thriving employees are highly energized, but they know how to avoid burnout." This concept describes the way energy is measured in the Leadership Pulse study; thriving seems to be similar to what our research measures as being "in the zone." Energy is not too high, but at a level where an employee is at his/her best or optimized. Vitality is an outcome of ideal energy levels; people are happy, enjoying life, and positive (Bruch & Vogel, 2011).

MEASURING EMPLOYEE ENERGY

As noted earlier, the measure of employee energy grew out of a very large (over 150 questions) study on the drivers of firm-level growth (e.g., stock price growth, earnings growth, growth in employees, and survival) and transitioned to three questions asked weekly. The first pilot study was with a company going through an initial public offering (IPO) where weekly assessments were collected before, during, and after the IPO (Welbourne & Felton, 1997). This allowed more refined analyses and understanding of the predictors of individual employee performance, changes in performance, and the percentage of stocks sold when employees were able to purchase shares, sales, and bonuses.

The three questions asked participants to rate their energy on a 0–10 scale. Using the optimization concept, the measurement process starts by asking respondents to rate their working energy and optimal energy, and then a gap score is calculated. The measurement works with 0 being no energy, then moving to low and medium energy (5–6), and 7–9 high and very high energy. But at those higher levels 9–10, individuals are so overwhelmed that their energy is being depleted. Thus, rating yourself a 10 may not lead to a good outcome. The gap is calculated by taking working energy (where you are today) minus optimal energy (where you are at your best). The resulting score can be positive or negative. For example, if I report I am at a 6, and my ideal is 7, my score is –1. If I am at a 6, and my ideal is 4, then I am +2 (over my ideal level). This gap, along with the standard deviation over time (variance from week to week) predicts outcomes. See www.whatsmyenergy.com to see the measure and reports. The graphic used in the assessment of energy is shown in Fig. 2.

The energy measurement graphic has a radar icon on it that allows respondents to move around the donut graph. Participants see this graphic two times, and first score their working energy (today) and their optimal energy on a second page (where they are at their best). As they move the radar around the donut picture, descriptors of what each number represents pop up on the screen.

Another key measurement aspect of energy is the body of calibration work we developed. According to this work, energy is a function of pace, efficiency, and job satisfaction with pace having a linear relationship with energy, but efficiency and job satisfaction being curvilinear or more related to the gap between working and optimal energy. Figs. 3 and 4 provide an example from one of the Leadership Pulse studies. In Fig. 4, the relationship between the energy gap and

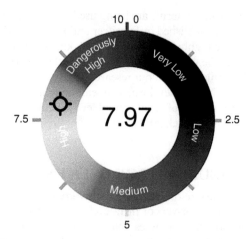

Fig. 2. Energy Pulse® Online Measurement Graphic. This is an interactive measurement tool that allows the user to move the radar (black ring near the 7.5 scores in this figure) and choose which energy level he/she is at. As they move around the donut, descriptors of the various numbers pop up. Once an answer is chosen, the survey taker hits enter, and the score is recorded. The donut is used for two questions: (1) what your energy is today (working energy), then it pops up again and the user answers a second question and (2) at what energy level are you at your best (optimal energy). Lastly, a third open-ended question is used, and participants record what's affecting their energy; this is put into a journal that they can review.

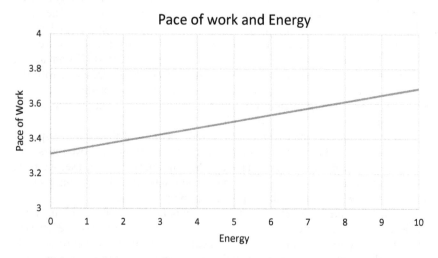

Fig. 3. Pace Versus Energy Results. This analysis is run on a regular basis to calibrate energy. To date, the data show that as the pace of work goes up, energy goes up. Calibration is also run with efficiency and job satisfaction.

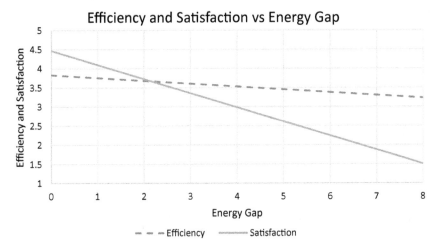

Fig. 4. Energy Gap Versus Satisfaction and Efficiency. This analysis, which is part of the calibration exercise, shows that as energy goes up, efficiency goes down, and satisfaction goes down. This supports the optimization versus maximization concept behind the sports physiology approach to measuring energy. This calibration exercise has been done in various surveys in the Leadership Pulse and with companies using these metrics. To date, the results have been the same. Note that in this analysis, the gap between working energy (where one is today) and optimal energy (where at best) is used; the results are similar when using the overall mean of energy.

the two outcomes is plotted (the gap is calculated by taking today's energy minus optimal energy; the number can be negative or positive, and we use the absolute value for the purpose of creating the graphic). The data show that as the gap closes, individuals are more efficient and satisfied at work.

SPECIFIC LEARNING FROM SUBSETS OF THE LEADERSHIP PULSE DATA

Fig. 5 shows the trend for mean energy from 2003 to early 2023. The last few years, from 2019 to 2023, have presented systemic shifts in how business is done, and with that, big challenges, and changes for leaders. In this section, I will present findings from pulse data during this time and second, via an experiment we ran doing daily pulsing with leaders during the summers of 2020, 2021, and 2022.

First, from the beginning of COVID-19 until April 2022, we see that leader energy declined (see Fig. 5). The mean scores change from 6.46 to 6.32 between 2019 and 2020, and then 5.69 in 2022. In April 2022, as companies were recovering from the pandemic and coming back to the office (in some cases), we asked questions focused on leadership confidence. For the overall scale, there was not much change from the prior year; however, a review of the individual confidence

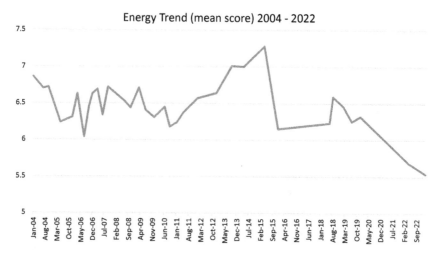

Fig. 5. Energy Trend Data (Average Energy for Each Pulse Survey; 0–10 Scale).

questions showed a decrease in confidence in both the overall leadership team and in the individual's confidence in their own personal leadership and management skills. It is not unusual to have confidence in leaders decline during times of high change and stress, but we rarely find confidence in "me" going down. The confidence questions range from 1 to 5 with 1 being not at all confident and 5 being very confident. Confidence in the leadership team went down (from 3.93 to 3.70) while confidence in "your own personal leadership and management skills" went down from 4.08 to 3.85.

In a study from 2010 that examined confidence and firm performance (using self-reported firm performance data, confirmed by comparing with financial data in the subset of publicly traded firms), we found that when the economy declined higher performing firms had a pattern of data showing that the senior leaders had more confidence in their teams than in themselves personally. Fig. 6 shows the confidence data from 2 years. Note that in this sample (about 700 executives, 40% C-level; 60% directors up to C-level), the only item that improved from year 1 to year 2 is economic climate; everything else declined, including confidence in their own leadership skills. In addition, Fig. 7 shows the data cut by firm performance (assessed high or low for ease in displaying the data). Only in the lower performing firms is confidence in "me" higher than confidence in the leadership team (even though, recall, these people are part of the leadership team).

A similar pattern emerges with the data from the COVID-19 years. For example, data from 2022 show that in very high performing firms (see Fig. 8), confidence in the leadership team is 4.09 compared to confidence in personal leadership skills of 3.89 (team higher than individual). But in the low and very low performing firms, the opposite pattern exists; confidence in the leadership team is 3.62, and confidence in personal leadership skills is 3.85 (personal

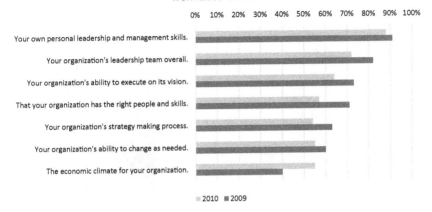

Fig. 6. Change Percent Confident in Leadership Confidence Items From 2009 to 2010.

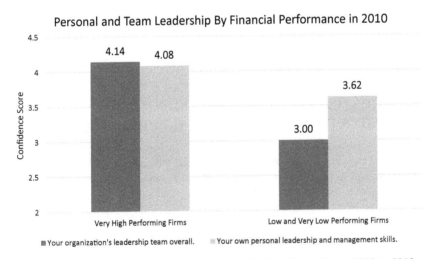

Fig. 7. Change in Personal and Team Leadership Confidence From 2009 to 2010. Differences in confidence from very high to very low financial performance are statistically significant at the 0.05 level.

higher than a team). External pressures from the economy affect how leaders work with their employees, and we have seen over the years that leaders are more likely to give credit to their whole teams when dramatic events they are living through shine a light on the fact that to get the needed work quickly done it really does take a team.

Personal and Team Leadership By Financial Performance in 2022

Fig. 8. Change in Personal and Team Leadership From 2020 to 2022. Changes in leadership team from very high to very low performance (4.09 vs 3.62) are statistically significant at the 0.05 level; differences for personal leadership are not significantly different (3.89 vs 3.85); however, the trend is in the same direction as in the 2010 data where only in high performing firms is confidence in the confidence in the team higher than confidence in me.

THREE INTERVENTIONS TO MOVE FORWARD ON LEADER WELLNESS AND FIRM-LEVEL WELLNESS

Three interventions have been used to help leaders move beyond stacking work syndrome and feelings of being overwhelmed with the massive amounts of unknown and change they are experiencing. Of course, the first step in these interventions is ongoing measurement; it is hard to reflect, discuss, and change factors that are not out in the open.

Reflective Learning

The first intervention is personal, and it is focused on helping individual leaders. It's also fairly simple, but it does take time. There is a long tradition of helping individuals move forward with new habits via reflective learning. From the perspective of our project, we use data to help leaders track their own energy levels and focus on what's affecting them positively and negatively and then also learn how they are affecting the people around them. This is not a complex process. There are four steps:

Data: Collect data to provide a source of reflective learning. In our case, they engage in the Leadership Pulse, and they receive personal reports back that show their responses versus benchmark data. They also keep a journal and can view their comments on various dates. This is all an automated process for the participants, and it is something that any organization can do to help employees get through challenging times.

Dialogue: Leaders reflect on their own results and then engage in dialogue with others; this may be their coaches, their employees, family, or peers. Dialogue is an important piece of their learning.

Action: Leaders put a plan together to change their habits and actions. I use a model that plots actions based on two criteria: (1) I own the action, or I can influence someone who owns the action; and (2) the action is short-term or long-term. We work with leaders to help them focus on actions in the "I own" and "short-term" buckets.

Results: By focusing on actions that lead to short-term results, leaders are motivated to continue to change habits. This is particularly important when leaders have data (cycle start over again), showing that their actions had measurable results. The advantage of starting with data and ending with data (results) is that you can share learning with others, and this is a particularly helpful habit for leaders to engage in doing. Openness begets trust, and as we saw in the earlier comments about confidence and energy, this type of sharing of results also can positively affect confidence, which then affects energy that is extremely important for all employee wellness, productivity, health, and leaders' ability to achieve more positive organizational outcomes.

Ambassadors Engage in Action Taking

The Leadership Pulse project and the pulse surveys have been running for over 20 years, but early on it was apparent that the thought of getting frequent data from employees was not a priority agenda item for many leaders. Their first thought was typically "oh – another way to ding me with some secret and different performance measurement process." Leaders did not want more complaints; there are many who do not think employee surveys of any sort are good for their careers.

In order to change this paradigm, the ambassador program was developed. This initiative utilizes a reflective learning exercise, but the reflections are handed over to employees. Leaders are asked to assign a group of employees to be ambassadors and help with the habit-breaking work. Using data, the ambassadors ask their peers to reflect on what they said in their own surveys (employees have copies of their own results and personal journals so they can go in and find these data). Instead of refining complaints, they work on suggestions and idea development with their peer ambassadors taking the lead in managing the dialogue.

The resulting action recommendations are provided to leaders. Leaders get help; employees engage in reflective learning; and this turn has been leading to very positive outcomes.

The 20 years of Leadership Pulse data and learning have led to some important findings, more than I can cover in this chapter. However, I would say one important outcome has been to help leaders think about habits versus big and hard to understand concepts. Habits can be changed, and in general, leaders resonate with that assumption because they see examples in their daily lives of helping children change habits.

Leaders often are taught such highly complex ideas that they ignore them. The beauty of the Leadership Pulse project has been providing simple and easy-to-use data as a guide to leaders who want to learn from their own reflections and from their peers. Perhaps our biggest insights on leader wellness came from an experiment we ran during the first summer of COVID-19 and then in the years after.

Learning While Disrupted: Daily Energy Pulse Experiment

Before COVID-19, the most frequent data collection that I engaged in doing was weekly. Although consideration was given to daily assessments, the potential tradeoff of overwhelming employees was thought to be too high. However, things changed during the pandemic, and many people were suffering from fear and loneliness. In response, we decided to run the Daily Energy Pulse experiment during the summers of 2020 and 2021 and then for groups of leaders in several organizations at other times from 2020 to 2022. We had about 100 people participate in the experiment, and with some, we also met with them to discuss the data and how it was changing from week to week. Overall, what we found is summarized below:

- Over time energy improved, the energy gap decreased, and the variance in energy scores over time was lower.
- We taught participants how to use reflective learning techniques focused on their energy trend data and personal journals. We instructed them to reflect on what was negatively and positively affecting their energy, and as a result, they found ways to take control of many of the factors affecting them and make changes. Their actions focused on changing habits led to less variance and more time "in their zone."
- By studying the comments (from the journal work) and running group sessions with participants, we found that the reflection process led participants to work through a specific pattern. What people wrote about and what they changed from week 1 to the end of the project represented a pattern that reminded me of the long-studied Maslow's needs hierarchy. In the first few weeks participants focused on and wrote about things like food, time of meals, what they ate, how much they drank, and exercise – did they go for a walk, work out, etc.? In week 3 or 4, they went beyond this and became more focused on what I would call wellness – learning new habits to help them cope with stress, including meditation, participating in regular exercise programs through new apps, etc. Then after this phase, we started to see comments and changes focused on family, friends, and social relationships. Along with this social phase, they moved to the topic of work – how they did their job, when they were most effective, how long they could sit at a computer before they needed a break, people who energized or de-energized them, work they liked to do and not do.

Participants tended to move from the inner circle areas of Fig. 9 as the focus of their habit changed to the outer ring, but different from the Maslow model, they easily went back and forth between the various groupings of activity over time.

Fig. 9.   Emergent Themes from the Daily Energy Pulse.

Their movement from ring to ring after the initial progression from inner to outer ring appeared to be based on what goals they set for themselves and their sense of accomplishment over time.

As we learned from them, we started bucketing interventions to help participants target their actions. Fig. 10 is an example of various intervention targets they can focus on in any ring. The concept helped encourage dialogue about habits that could be changed in order to drive personal wellness. For each ring from the inner circle to the outer, we had them focus their activities on targeted relations at work, at home, in their social network, and with other connections. This simple model seemed to help the participants take easy actions to take to help them improve their energy.

In our era, at least in the United States where this study was conducted, wellness appears to have taken hold as an established need that individuals can personally control. Ample resources, be it via classes, employers, or apps are available to help individuals create their own new habits and environment where wellness is an achievable goal. Caring about personal health and taking time to improve oneself is seen as a good use of time, and most know that doing a bit more today for personal well-being translates to longer-term positive health results.

The other learning from the daily energy pulse experiment was that after wellness goals are discussed, we found participants moved to the next levels in their ring hierarchy. They started to talk about friends and family or social needs. Additionally, participants found that they were very energized by helping others in their social circles improve their energy. This gets back to the idea that energy

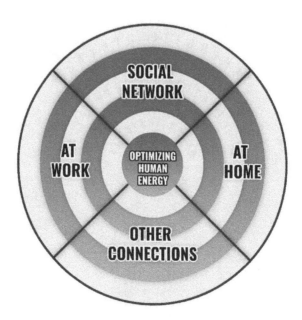

Fig. 10.   Target of Intervention Activities.

is catchy, but what we did not observe as much earlier was that the actions to help others improve their energy appear to be having a very positive impact on the person teaching and modeling positive energy habits.

CONCLUSION

Energy is something that employees and leaders understand. Leaders will tell you they can "feel" the energy in an office or a plant. People who are by nature energized and positive know that they are sharing their energy with others. As much as people may think they understand energy, it does not mean they know how to measure it or manage it. The challenge for leaders is being intentional and making sure they help themselves and their employees, and this takes some rigor and often changing habits. However, when successful, our research has documented positive outcomes at the overall firm level.

   One additional concept that comes out of this body of work is recovery. We know by experience that every organization will be hit with negative experiences; well-loved leaders leave, companies engage in mergers or acquisitions, large customers leave and maybe layoffs result. In all these situations, our data show big declines in employee and leader energy. Lower scores, in these situations, are less important than the time it takes to recover. Thus, understanding how these big events impact employee energy and confidence is critical for developing strategic recovery plans that pull the employee population out of the negative spiral that usually happens after these types of events. And the people who start a recovery initiative are the leaders.

Leader wellness, self-awareness, and the ability to energize others are all key to the type of decision making that leads to long-term firm health and performance. The Leadership Pulse, and the new daily energy experiment, provide evidence that some regular processes of collecting meaningful data, engaging in dialogue and reflective learning, taking action to change habits, and again measuring results can lead to positive changes.

NOTES

1. The current version of the Leadership Pulse uses only three items.
2. The outcome data we studied included sales per salesperson, patient satisfaction in hospital settings, customer service ratings in call centers, performance appraisal scores, unwanted turnover, and number of suggestions made in companies that use these programs.

REFERENCES

Ambrose, M. L., & Kulik, C. T. (1999). Old friends, new faces: Motivation research in the 1990s. *Yearly Review of Management of the Journal of Management, 25*, 231–292.

Bruch, H., & Vogel, B. (2011, July 20). *Fully charged*. Harvard Business Review Press. https://www.conference-board.org/blog/postdetail.cfm?post=873

Csikszentmihalyi, M. (1991). *Flow: The psychology of optimal experience*. HarperCollins.

Duking, P., Holmbert, H.-C., & Sperlich, B. (2017). Instant biofeedback provided by wearable sensor technology can help to optimize energy and prevent injury and overuse. *Frontiers in Psychology, 8*, 167. https://doi.org/10.3389/fphys.2017.00167

Gilbert, B., & Jamison, S. (1994). *Winning ugly: Mental warfare in tennis – Lessons from a master*. Simon & Schuster.

Gragnano, A., Simbula, S., & Miglioretti, M. (2020). Work–life balance: Weighing the importance of work–family and work–health balance. *International Journal of Environmental Research and Public Health, 17*(907), 1–20.

Hargrove, R. (1995). *Masterful coaching: Extraordinary results by impacting people and the way they think and work together*. Jossey-Bass.

Kular, S., Gatenby, M., Rees, C. Soane, E., & Truss, K. (2008, October). *Employee engagement: A literature review* [Working paper series, No 19]. Kingston University. https://eprints.kingston.ac.uk/id/eprint/4192/1/19wempen.pdf

Landy, F. J., & Becker, W. S. (1987). Motivation theory reconsidered. *Research in Organizational Behavior, 9*, 1–38.

Leifer, E. M. (1988). Trails of involvement: Evidence for local games. *Sociological Forum, 3*(4), 499–524.

Loehr, J., & Schwartz, T. (2003). *The power of full engagement*. The Free Press.

Macey, W. H., & Schneider, B. (2008). The meaning of employee engagement. *Industrial and Organizational Psychology, 1*, 3–30.

Macey, W. H., Schneider, B., Barbera, K. M., & Young, S. A. (2009). *Employee engagement: Tools for analytics, practice and competitive advantage*. Wiley-Blackwell.

Parkes, L. P., & Langford, P. H. (2008). Work–life balance or work–life alignment? A test of the importance of work–life balance for employee engagement and intention to stay in organizations. *Journal of Management and Organization, 14*, 267–284.

Perry, J. M., & Jamison, S. (1997). *In the zone: Achieving optimal performance in business—As in sports*. Contemporary Press.

Porath, C., Spreitzer, G., & Garnett, F. G. (2012). Thriving at work: Toward its measurement, construct validation, and theoretical refinement. *Journal of Organization Behavior, 33*(2), 250–275.

Ryan, R. M., & Deci, E. L. (2008). From ego depletion to vitality: Theory and findings concerning the facilitation of energy available to self. *Social and Personality Compass*, *2*(2), 702–717.

Ryan, R. M., & Frederick, C. (1997). On energy, personality, and health: Subjective vitality as a dynamic reflection of well-being. *Journal of Personality*, *65*(3), 529–565.

Saks, A. M. (2006). Antecedents and consequences of employee engagement. *Journal of Management Psychology*, *21*(7), 600–619.

Spreitzer, G., & Porath, C. (2012, January–February). Creating sustainable performance. *Harvard Business Review*, *90*(1–2), 152.

Sun, L., & Bunchapattanasakda, C. (2019). Employee engagement: A literature review. *International Journal of Human Resource Studies*, *9*(1), 63–80.

Welbourne, T. M. (2014). Two numbers for growth, innovation, and high performance: Working and optimal employee energy. *Organization Dynamics*, *43*, 180–188.

Welbourne, T. M., Andrews, S. B., & Andrews, A. O. (2005). Back to basics: Learning about employee energy and motivation from running on my treadmill. *Human Resource Management*, *44*(1), 55–66.

Welbourne, T. M., & Felton, R.W. (1997). *Improving technology-based change processes: A case study on Indus International*. Cornell University Library. https://ecommons.cornell.edu/handle/1813/77027.

INDEX

Printed in the USA
CPSIA information can be obtained
at www.ICGtesting.com
JSHW050005170524
63287JS00004B/48

9 781837 973590